INTERNATIONAL CENTRE FOR MECHANICAL SCIENCES

COURSES AND LECTURES - No. 219

INFORMATION THEORY
NEW TRENDS AND OPEN PROBLEMS

EDITED BY
G. LONGO
UNIVERSITY OF TRIESTE

SPRINGER-VERLAG WIEN GMBH

Originally published by Springer Verlag Wien-New York in 1975

ISBN 978-3-211-81378-2 **ISBN 978-3-7091-2730-8 (eBook)**
DOI 10.1007/978-3-7091-2730-8

CONTENTS

PREFACE

The birth of Information Theory is placed officially in 1948, when Claude E. Shannon published his first epoch-making paper on this subject. In spite of the enormous importance and far-reaching consequences of this contribution, which turned Information Theory into a science, one should be aware of the constant presence, at least in Western philosophy, of a line of thought for which form, structure, relation and the like were more basic than matter, energy or substance. This line of thought, which goes back to the Pythagoreans, was mostly succumbing in front of the bold partisans of matter and energy, especially when matter and energy proved to be exploitable for improving man's standard of life (besides having other less desirable but equally conspicuous uses).

Quite recently, however, form and structure began to prevail and this influence – not only in philosophy or science, but also in technology and even in everyday life – is now increasingly felt. It is no more on things that we concentrate, but rather on the way they are related. Once you realize that it is information that triggers actions and energy, and that information is contained in the differences between objects and not in the objects themselves, you also become aware that the actual objects used for communicating, i.e. for conveying information, are unimportant. Only differences (i.e. relations) matter. This is actually the starting point of any theory of information.

It is perhaps recognizing this feature of information that gives rise to many attempts (epistemologically unjustified) to apply methods and results of Information Theory, as founded by Shannon, to problems that have little or nothing to do with communication engineering. It would be sad if we had to admit that such attempts are originated by the mere presence of the word *information,* without any analysis of its meaning: Shannon Information Theory applies only in those contexts where its precise assumptions hold, i.e.

never in reality.

This obviously does not imply that an attempt to create a more general Theory of information should not be pursued. On the contrary, it *should*. The existing theory is actually too restrictive. The first steps towards a more general theory are likely to be imprecise and loose, and they will probably irritate many people familiar with the neat and clear-cut nature of what they call a theory. But this is by no means a reason for dismissing the search: a certain distortion is unavoidable, as we know, and this is true also in theory-making. It is after all likely that what we think today of the features of a theory will not be true in the future. No physicist of the 19th century would have accepted an indeterminacy principle, nor would a mathematician have ever thought of the possibility of a theorem like Gödel's.

When I organized the 1975 CISM Summer School on Information Theory, my aim was to offer the audience a survey of the newest directions in the two classical areas of Information Theory, namely Shannon Theory and Coding, and to point out this somewhat relativistic character, i.e. that they are the consequence of a choice and that this choice precludes either different or more general developments. The essays of Part One, I believe, clearly show the possibility of building other, more comprehensive or simply alternative theories, in which what has deliberately been excluded by Shannon in his construction is included again. The concept of information, in its presystematic aspects, is here in the middle of a vast territory, and the underlying central question is: How does an information source (typically: Nature) generate information? and, also: What are the features of the information generated by a source which are relevant to a user?

The contributions of Part Two specialize to classical Information Theory, and offer a thorough survey of two of its most rapidly evolving branches, i.e. Rate-Distortion Theory and Multi-User Communication Theory. Apart from their intrinsic beauty and interest,these two subjects are of great potential value for applications, e.g. in information processing, data compression and in all cases where an information network has to be dealt with (typically a network of computers).

Likewise, Part Three deals with another well-established area of research pushed forward by the promises contained in Shannon's coding theorem. Although the "golden fruit" of these promises has not been grasped yet – and there is also some doubt as to whether it will ever be – people working in this area seem satisfied with what is being done, which is actually beautiful and practically relevant. It is interesting to remark that, while exploiting existing mathematical tools, Algebraic Coding Theory in turn is having a useful feedback on some areas of discrete mathematics. The information theoretical motivations are here rather diluted and far away, but there is little doubt that a survey of what is going on in Information Theory research today should include something on algebraic coding theory.

In the audience's opinion, the Summer School from which this book came out had a good success. The merit of this goes to the lecturers on one side and to the attendants on the other side, since the communication process is always bidirectional. I therefore thank all the participants, especially those who were so kind as to give a seminar and those who organized the panel discussions and made them interesting and lively.

Finally, I wish to thank the staff of the International Centre for Mechanical Sciences, whose help, assistance and courtesy were essential ingredients for the success of the Summer School.

Giuseppe Longo

Udine, September 1975

Part One

FOUNDATIONS

LECTURE NOTES ON CONCEPTS AND MEASURES OF INFORMATION

HANS W. GOTTINGER
UNIVERSITY OF BIELEFELD
P.O.B. 8640
F.R. OF GERMANY

INTRODUCTION.

In recent years a considerable amount of work has been done on concepts and measures of information within and beyond the fields of engineering and mathematics.

In these notes an attempt is made to trace the main sources and motivations of various approaches to conceptualize and measure information. The development so far showed that information may explain different things in different contexts, hence it will not make sense to apply a general measure of information to practical situations in which information obtains different meanings.

We will start by exhibiting the structure of the Shannon-Wiener theory of information, then, in Section 2, we turn to approaches that give axiomatizations of entropy and information measures without using probability measures. Recently, also A.N. Kolmogorov [1,2] has shown that the basic information-theoretic concepts can be formulated without recourse to probability theory. In Section 3 we outline a specific approach of Domotor in which qualitative information and entropy structures are considered and qualitative conditions are found that permit representation by suitable information or entropy measures. Clearly, this construction finds its roots in problems of model or measurement theory. In Section 4 we essentially expose our own ideas (Gottinger [3,4])on qualitative information in which information is considered to be a 'primitive concept', separate from probability, e.g. a binary relation in an algebra of informative propositions. This approach suggests a rigorous axiomatic treatment of semantic information. Also we discuss some epistemological aspects of qualitative information, in connection with a general theory of inductive inference. In Section 5,6,7 we are concerned with 'information provided by experiments' as used in statistical decision theory. The concept originated in works of D. Blackwell [5], Blackwell and Girshick [6] and is now extensively used in the statistical decision literature as well as in the related literature in economics.

The intention of this review is to familiarize information theorists with other concepts and measures of information which do not arise from the traditional Shannon theory and are motivated from considerations to handle the many-sided concept of information beyond the engineering-technical viewpoint. It is believed that information theory itself may benefit from these considerations and may even substantially increase its potentialities toward application not restricted to engineering science.

1. THE STRUCTURE OF INFORMATION THEORY.

Shannon's Problem. The abstract problem of information theory established by C.E. Shannon [7] and in a somewhat different form by N. Wiener [8] is this: Given a probability space $(S,\mathcal{S},P)$, where S denotes the space of elementary events (basic space), $\mathcal{S}$ a σ-algebra of subsets of S and P a probability measure on $\mathcal{S}$, how much information do we receive about a (randomly selected) point $s\in S$ by being informed that s is in some subset A of S.

It is relatively easy to see that the answer depends on the dimension or measure of A, given in terms of the probability measure P attached to A. Hence an information measure is a real-valued set function on $\mathcal{S}$ defined by

$$F\,[P(A)] = IoP(A) = I_P(A) \text{ for any } A\in\mathcal{S},$$

where F denotes some appropriate monotonic transformation. Conceptually, information adopts here the nature of a surprise value or unexpectedness. In this context, note, that I_P is a measurable mapping from $\mathcal{S}$ onto $[0,\infty]$ composed of the measurable mappings $P:\mathcal{S}\to[0,1]$ and $I:[0,1]\to[0,+\infty]$, with a commutative property. Hence we have the following commutative diagram:

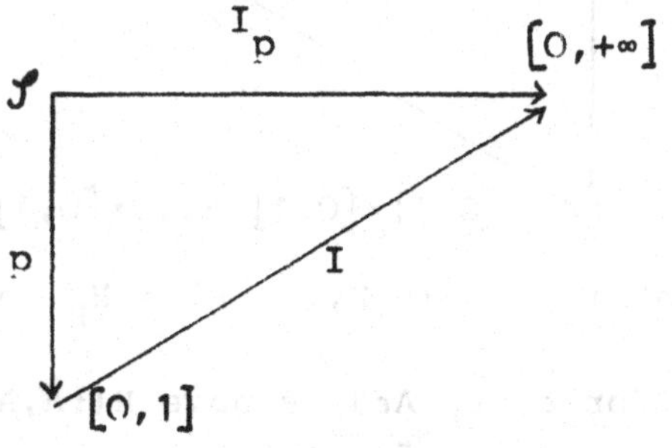

$IoP = I_P$ with I being continuous. It is also natural to assume that I_P is nonnegative and continuous.

Moreover, for any two probabilistically independent events $A,B\in\mathcal{T}$, write $A \perp\!\!\!\perp B \Longleftrightarrow AB \times S \sim A \times B$, we have $A \perp\!\!\!\perp B$ $I_p(A\cap B) = I_p(A) + I_p(B)$.

Now it has been shown by Shannon that I_p satisfies the additive representation if it can be represented by $I_p(A) = -\, c \log_2 P(A)$, where c is any positive real constant (sometimes called Boltzmann's constant in analogy to thermodynamics).

More generally, let $\pi = \{A_i\}_{i=1}^{n}$ be an n-fold uniform partition into finitely many equiprobable events, sometimes referred to as an experiment. Then the natural question arises what would be the average amount of information, called the entropy H_p with respect to a given partition π. This is computed as

$$(*) \quad H_p(\pi) = \sum_{A\in\pi} P(A) \cdot I_p(A), \text{ and } I_p(A) = -\log_2 P(A),$$

if we choose c, by convention, as unit of measurement.

Let Π be the set of all possible partitions of S.
The diagram

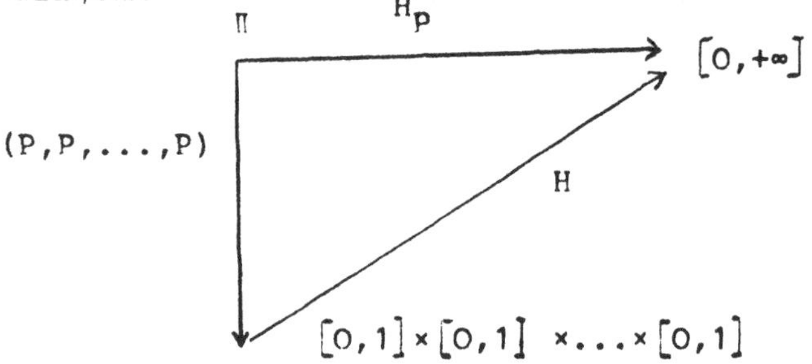

commutes, that is $H \circ (P,P,\ldots,P) = H_p$, and H is continuous.

Furthermore, for every $A\in\Pi$ we have $H(\{A,\bar{A}\}) = 1$ if $P(A) = P(\bar{A})$, and $H([B|A\cap B, \bar{A}\cap B]\Pi) = H(\Pi) + P(B) \cdot H(\{A,\bar{A}\})$ if $A \perp\!\!\!\perp B$, where $A,B\in\mathcal{T}$ and $[B|A\cap B, \bar{A}\cap B]\Pi$ is the conditional experiment resulting of replacing B in the partition Π by two disjoint events $A \cap B$, $\bar{A} \cap B$. It has been shown by D.K.Fadeev [9], using P. Erdös' [10] number-theoretic lemma on additive arithmetic functions that the only function H_p satisfying the above conditions is of the form (*).

The entropy may be interpreted in various ways, either as an average measure of uncertainty removed or as an average measure of information conveyed. Which interpretation one prefers over the other is irrelevant - as will be clear in the sequel. Thus we see that there is a complete correspondence between uncertainty and information. The definition of information is here naturally tied up to probability, only the existence of the latter enables the measurement of the former.

If we say, roughly, that we have gained information when we know something now that we didn't know before, then it actually means that our uncertainty expressed in terms of probability at one instance of time has been removed at a later instance of time - according to whether the event has occurred or has not occurred. Introducing the notion of a random experiment in a statistical context we may talk about uncertainty before an experiment is carried out, at a moment where we have not yet observed anything, and we may talk about information after having performed the experiment. Sometimes Shannon's measure of information has been termed probabilistic information or selective information (Mackay [11]). There are several approaches (see Rényi [12], and Kolmogorov [2]) how to establish the measure H_p, either on pragmatic grounds arising from coding theory or, in an axiomatic way or by starting with the notion of an invariant from ergodic theory. Surprisingly, H_p may even result from gambling theory (Kelly [13]). Shannon's original axioms for the entropy measure have been replaced several times subsequently by weaker conditions (see D.K.Fadeev [9],

A.I. Khinchin [14], H. Tveberg [15], D.G. Kendall[16] and many others). The weakest set of axioms known so far seems to be that given by P.M. Lee[17]. Mathematically, the representation of information involves a study of particular classes of functional equations.

As A.N. Kolmogorov [1] remarked the probabilistic approach seems appropriate for describing and predicting the transmission of (uniform) mass information over (physically bounded) communication channels $C|H$ as illustrated by the following scheme:

$X_1, X_2, \ldots, X_n$ ——encoding——→ [channel] ——decoding——→

where $X_1, X_2, \ldots, X_n$ is a well-defined sequence of random variables (information source). Such kinds of problems are of fundamental importance in the engineering and physical sciences where probability measures can roughly be identified experimentally as limiting frequencies for a sufficiently long (precisely infinite) sequence of trials forming a collective in the sense of von Mises. But what sense does it make to talk about the entropy of receiving messages from a certain novel of Tolstoi, or about the experiments getting married once, twice or even three times?

In other words, can we talk about entropy in the sense of Shannon's theory if we do not have a well-established random sequence forming our information source, if events are not repeatable? Philosophers and linguists consider as a basic flaw of Shannon's measure the fact that the probability measure defined is obviously confined to a frequency interpretation. Hence, to the same extent as probability concepts gave rise to extensive discussions up to recent time probabilistic information theory is affected by these discussions concerning the adequate application of the underlying probability concept (see H.W. Gottinger [18]).

The motivation for Carnap and Bar-Hillel [19] is somewhat different from the theory of transmission of uniform mass information, e.g. the question is how can we evaluate the information provided by a sentence structure which defies representation in a random sequence. In the context of semantic information the concept of an 'ideal receiver' as one with a perfect memory plays a much similar role as that of an ideal 'rational person' assumed in the theory of logical probability due to Carnap.

As a matter of fact it turns out that semantic information theory in the sense of Carnap and Bar-Hillel leads to similar properties as Shannon's entropy measure, however, relative frequences are replaced by logical probabilities (degree of confirmation). If h represents a hypothesis, e evidence, thus c(h,e) the degree of confirmation of a hypothesis h given the evidence e, then by characterizing h as message and e as knowledge the information received from h given e is the greater the more improbable we consider h given e. This again lends itself to the interpretation of information as a surprise value, i.e. information provided by a logical true sentence is zero, and that of a logically false sentence infinity.

The question then naturally comes up as to which extent one can base a theory of prediction on a theory of information that uses a rather restrictive probability concept for real-life situations. This concept only applies to carefully prepared situations of well shuffled decks of playing cards, controlled casts of dice and in random sampling.

The problem to achieve rational predictions or making inferences from data has plagued numerous philosophers since D. Hume (see H.Jeffreys [20]), and this has been reconsidered more recently. It has given rise to a logical theory of probability predominantely based on inductive inference. However, this theory incorporated evidence as conditional probability statements, but it did not show the links between information processing (in the human mind) and probability evaluation. Information only comes in by repeatedly revising conditional probability statements as, for instance, propagated by the Bayesian approach in statistical decision theory. But treatment of information processing is essential for any theory of prediction, and it is genuine for any kind of human judgment. Of course, we cannot dispense with probabilities in a general theory of prediction, for if we can, any such theory would be either completely deterministic or arbitrary. In this I do not share the pessimism of P.J. van Heerden [21], based on the assertion 'that a number expressing the probabilities of the different possible outcomes in real life does not exist' (p.21).

In fact, what we might do is to build a theory of probability on the basis of a completely separate theory of information by generating 'qualitative information', and giving conditions under which numerical probabilities can be established. This procedure would entail a satisfactory theory of prediction.

Some approaches in this direction, including the author's, will be discussed in the next two sections.

Of course, probabilistic information theory, as it stands now, will continue to play a major role in those circumstances in which it makes sense to talk about information in a random sequence which is perfectly legitimate under conditions stated by Kolmogorov [1].

However, its value for general applications beyond those anticipated by Shannon appears to be rather limited.

2. INFORMATION WITHOUT PROBABILITY.

In recent years some information theorists were not completely satisfied with probabilistic information theory. The motivation for their dissatisfaction was, of course, different from that of statisticians and philosophers. Although the axiomatics of information theory was considerably refined and weakened, the natural question was raised whether one could develop an information theory without involving the concept of probability (distributions), at least in the basic axiomatic structure. The contribution by R.S. Ingarden and K. Urbanik [22], Ingarden [23,24] answered this question affirmatively. It was the first step to challenge the hitherto accepted view-point that information theory is a branch of probability theory which is also reflected in the organization of textbooks on probability theory (see Rényi [25]). Interestingly enough, the basic motivation evolved from certain experimental situations in physics where it appeared to be meaningful in some situations to talk about information regarding the state of a system (e.g. the entropy of some macroscopic system) although its probability distribution is not known.

Formally, Ingarden and Urbanik achieve to define H (the entropy) directly on a pseudo-metric space of finite Boolean rings (of events) satisfying convenient properties of monotonicity and continuity. A. Rényi [26] claimed that these results can be achieved by using Shannon's measure in terms of a uniquely defined conditional probability measure which follows from the Ingarden-Urbanik technique so that defining information without probability inevitably leads to introducing probability at a later stage. Rényi's straight-forward conclusion is that the information cannot be separated from probability. However, this misses the real point. First of all, as stated before, in some experimental situations it makes more sense to start with some basic knowledge, experience, evidence of the experimenter on the state or movement of a system (physical, biological or any system which is subject to experimental control) rather than specifying probabilities in terms of which information should be defined. Second, in a more general context of human decision making or drawing inferences from observations it is often the case that information processing precedes probability evaluations in betting on the future and making predictions on uncertain events. Most reasonable persons would deny that situations of this kind are comparable or even identical with random experiments - as probabilistic information theory does suggest.

Significant work has also been done by J. Kampé de Fériet and B. Forte (see Kampé de Fériet [27] for a summary and exposition of his results) on constructing information measures without using probabilities. Information is defined as a σ-additive, nonnegative measure (invariant with respect to translations) on a monotone class of events $\mathcal{J}$, retaining its customary nature of 'surprise value' as in probabilistic information theory. The system basically rests on three assumptions:

(1) $I: \mathcal{J} \to \bar{R}^*$, where $\bar{R}^*$ is the extended real line $[0,\infty]$.
The second is a monotonicity assumption in the form:

(2) $[(A,B) \in \mathcal{J} \times \mathcal{J},\ B \subset A] \Rightarrow I(A) \leq I(B),\ A,B \in \mathcal{J}$.

Hence, given the zero element o and the unit element S in $\mathcal{J}$, we have naturally for any $A \in \mathcal{J}$

$$0 \leq I(S) = \inf_{A \in \mathcal{J}} I(A) \leq \sup_{A \in \mathcal{J}} I(A) = I(o) \leq \infty.$$

(2) already suggests the nature of information as a 'surprise

value', in particular $I(S) = I(o) = +\infty$, so that information derived from the sure event is zero, the information derived from the impossible event, provided it happens to occur ('surprise'), is infinite.

An additional assumption imposes the condition of monotone continuity, i.e. for a <u>countable sequence</u> of events $\{A_n, n = 1,2,\ldots\}$ we have either

$$(3)\quad A_n \subset A_{n+1} \Rightarrow A = \bigcup_1^\infty A_n \in \mathcal{J} \text{ or}$$

$$A_{n+1} \subset A_n \Rightarrow A = \bigcap_1^\infty A_n \in \mathcal{J}$$

which implies, for information defined, as in (1) and (2):

$$[A_n \in \mathcal{J}, A_n \uparrow A] \Rightarrow I(A_n) \downarrow I(A)$$

$[A_n \in \mathcal{J}, A_n \downarrow A] \Rightarrow I(A_n) \uparrow I(A)$, known as monotone sequential continuity.

In particular, we have a similar property (as in probabilistic information theory), i.e. for probabilistically independent pairs of events $A_n \in \mathcal{J}, n = 1,2,\ldots$:

$$I(\bigcap_1^\infty A_n) = \sum_1^\infty I(A_n).$$

An immediate consequence of assumption (2) is that information is of Inf-type, e.g. $I(A \cup B) \leq \text{Inf}[I(A), I(B)]\, A,B \in \mathcal{J}$ so that $I(A \cup B) = F[I(A), I(B)]$ where F is a suitable monotone function. This motivates the introduction of a <u>partial operation</u> T of composition $I(A)TI(B) = F[I(A), I(B)]$ which is familiar from the theory of partially ordered algebras and its representation by functional equations. Since $\mathcal{J}$ can be completed to a σ-algebra we have $I[\bigcup_1^\infty A_n] = \mathop{T}_1^\infty I(A_n), A_n \in \mathcal{J}, \bigcap_1^\infty A_n = o$, hence T is σ-composable. T then satisfies well-known algebraic properties for defining an abelian semigroup (see Fuchs [28], Chap. 10). It is not difficult to show the connection between information measure and the underlying algebraic structure.

Let T be defined here in terms of the union $\cup$, and define a dual operation T* in terms of intersection $\cap$. The presentation of partial operations in terms of the more familiar operations $\cup$ and $\cap$ proves to be convenient in case of forming ordered groups generated by T. We require that the existence of T implies a unique T*, and (T*)* = T, by definition.

The following properties hold for any $A,B\in\mathcal{Y}$, T defined, and provided ATB or AT*B exist in $\mathcal{Y}$.

P.1: $A\in\mathcal{Y}\Longrightarrow$ [AT*A = A&ATA = A] for all $A\in\mathcal{Y}$.

P.2: ATB = BTA, and dually for T* for all $A,B\in\mathcal{Y}$. (commutativity)

P.3: (ATB)TC = AT(BTC), for all $A,B,C\in\mathcal{Y}$, and dually for T*. (associativity)

P.4: ATB $\Longrightarrow$ AT*(ATB) = AT(AT*B) and dually for T* (distributivity)

Define AT*B $\Longleftrightarrow$ A $\leq\cdot$ B and '$\leq\cdot$' means 'not more probable than' a relation of qualitative probability.

Then it is relatively easy to see that the properties P.1 - P.4 will make $\mathcal{Y}$ a lattice-ordered algebra which is also distributive, and hence a Boolean algebra endowed with a binary relation $\leq\cdot$.

Note that it presents no great difficulties to invoke continuity properties for T* so that $\mathcal{Y}$ becomes a topological Boolean algebra (in the order topology). Since T is defined in terms of $\cup$ it is then easy to verify that monotone continuity is equivalent to continuity of the partial operation T and any information measure defined is σ-additive on $\mathcal{J}$.

It is therefore interesting to note here that the introduction of a partial operation suggests certain assumptions about the qualitative ordering in a partially ordered algebra so that information measures are compatible with this ordering. In terms of this construction it would then appeal to be most natural to present information measures as Boolean homomorphisms on $\mathcal{J}$ (see Sikorski [29]).

Finally, we remark that due to the nature of information as a 'surprise value' the compatible information measure is order-reversing (antitone) w.r.t. qualitative probability rather than order-preserving (isotone).

The dual properties of T and T* can be shown in the representation of '$\precsim$' in $\mathcal{J}$ by (information) measures. Since T is commutative it follows that $I(A)TI(B) = I(ATB) = T(I(A),I(B))$, let $I(A)TI(B) \Longleftrightarrow I(A) \geq I(B)$. As defined $AT^*B \Longleftrightarrow A \precsim B \Longleftrightarrow A \subseteq B$ in this case yielding $AT^*B = A$, and conditions for T* are reformulations of axioms for a partial order $\precsim$. Then $I(ATB) = I(A)TI(B) \Longleftrightarrow I(A) \leq I(B) \Longleftrightarrow AT^*B$, by strict compatibility with $A \precsim B$.

3. QUALITATIVE INFORMATION AND INFORMATIVE INFERENCE.

Only in very recent time, motivated by related developments in (subjective) probability and measurement theory (see H.W. Gottinger [30]) one has shown some interest to introduce qualitative information as a primitive notion and to show whether and under which conditions we have $A \leq: B \Longleftrightarrow I(A) \leq I(B)$, for all $A,B \in \mathcal{J}$ where the binary relation '$\leq:$' stands for 'not more informative than'. Such a problem is genuine to measurement theory.

We should emphasize here that the problem of compatibility between a qualitative information structure $\langle S, \mathcal{S}, \leq : \rangle$ and a quantitative structure $\langle S, \mathcal{S}, I \rangle$ is important in view of various applications. In behavioral as well as in natural sciences we find ample experimental evidence that there is often no direct way in constructing information (or probability) measures but only indirectly via a qualitative ordering of events, propositions, statements, etc., according to qualitative information (or qualitative probability). It also comes closer to the procedure of how individuals or groups actually evaluate information. Hence it is natural to interpret qualitative information in a subjective sense.

An elaborate axiomatic system of qualitative information (consisting of 15 qualitative axioms) has been proposed recently by Z. Domotor [31]). Postulating an infinite Boolean algebra of events $\mathcal{S}$ he establishes his qualitative information structure by endowing $\mathcal{S}$ with an algebraic independence relation '$\perp\!\!\!\perp$' and the familiar order relation $\leq$:.

Hence, we may introduce a binary relation $\leq$: on the Boolean algebra of events $\mathcal{S}$ (rather than on the set of partitions as in case of entropy) with the intended interpretation:

$A \leq : B$ means that event A does not convey more information than event B. Then one is interested in necessary and sufficient conditions to have $A \leq : B \Longleftrightarrow I_p(A) \leq I_p(B)$ for all $A, B \in \mathcal{S}$.

The results will lead to information measures in the standard information-theoretic sense. It has been the first attempt so far to derive information-theoretic notions, without recourse to probability theory at the primitive, qualitative level although the link to probability theory becomes obvious at the level of representation by information measures.

By restricting to finite structures the results will be somewhat weaker, e.g. non-unique representations are possible and we will examplify this situation next in view of defining qualitative entropy structures.

For deriving qualitative entropy structures the well-known fact is used (see O.Ore [32]) that any finite structure $\langle S, \mathcal{S}, \leq: \rangle$ gives rise to a finite partition - the set of possible partitions is called a class of experiments - so that for any two partitions $\pi_1, \pi_2 \varepsilon \Pi$ (one of which is finer or coarser than the other) a qualitative ordering of partitions can be represented by the entropy measure, e.g.

$$\pi_1 \leq: \pi_2 \Longleftrightarrow H_p(\pi_1) \leq H_p(\pi_2).$$

Then $\pi_1 \leq: \pi_2$ means that experiment π_1 does not have more entropy than the experiment π_2.

One could consider '$\leq:$' as a linear ordering, e.g. being reflexive, transitive, antisymmetric and connected but these order properties are obviously insufficient to guarantee the existence of a function H_p.

Along the lines of Z.Domotor we develop qualitative entropy in an algebra of experiments.

First of all, we need some technicalities regarding partitions or experiments. Given two partitions π_1, $\pi_2 \varepsilon \Pi$ we say that π_1 is a finer than $\pi_2 (\pi_1 \subseteq \pi_2)$ if for all $A \varepsilon \pi_1$ there exists at least one $B \varepsilon \pi_2$ such that $A \subseteq B$.

Example

$\{\emptyset,\bar{A},A\bar{B},AB\bar{C},ABC\} \subseteq\cdot \{\emptyset,\bar{A},A\bar{B},AB\} \subseteq\cdot \{\emptyset,\bar{A},A\}$.

Dually, we can define a coarser than relation.

One can introduce some lattice operations in the set of partitions.

We observe that if π_1 and π_2 are partitions of the basic space S then also $\pi_1 \cdot \pi_2$ and $\pi_1 + \pi_2$ are partitions in Π and the binary operations '.' and '+' determine the inf (g.l.b.) and sup (l.u.b.) respectively, hence satisfy the definition af a lattice.

Define $\pi_1 \cdot \pi_2 \equiv \{A \cap B : A \in \pi_1 \ \& \ B \in \pi_2\}$, or, in general, $\prod_{i=1}^{n} \pi_1 \equiv \{ \bigcap_{i=1}^{n} A_i : A_i \in \pi_i$ for all $i\}$. Then $\pi_1 \cdot \pi_2$ is the greatest experiment finer than both π_1 and π_2 such that

(i) $\pi_1 \cdot \pi_2 \subseteq\cdot \pi_1$ and $\pi_1 \cdot \pi_2 \subseteq\cdot \pi_2$,

(ii) $\pi \subseteq\cdot \pi_1$ and $\pi \subseteq\cdot \pi_2 \Longrightarrow \pi \subseteq\cdot \pi_1 \cdot \pi_2$.

Dually,define the sum of experiments by

$$\pi_1 + \pi_2 \equiv \{A \cup B : A \in \pi_1 \& B \in \pi_2\},$$

or generally

$$\sum_{i=1}^{n} \pi_i \equiv \{ \bigcup_{i=1}^{n} A_i : \text{all } A_i \text{ are overlapping events in } \pi_1 \cup \pi_2 \cup \ldots \cup \pi_n\}.$$

$\pi_1 + \pi_2$ is the smallest experiment coarser than both π_1 and π_2, i.e.

(iii) $\pi_1 \subseteq\cdot \pi_1+\pi_2$ and $\pi_2 \subseteq\cdot \pi_1+\pi_2$

(iv) $\pi_1 \subseteq\cdot \pi$ and $\pi_2 \subseteq \pi \Longrightarrow \pi_1+\pi_2 \subseteq\cdot \pi$.

Finally one defines the partitions $o = \{\emptyset, S\}$ as the <u>maximal experiment</u>, and the partition $U = \{\{s\} : s\in S\} \cup \{\emptyset\}$ is called the minimal experiment. We have $U \subseteq\cdot \pi \subseteq\cdot o$ for any $\pi\in\Pi$. The following operations are obvious:

$$\pi \cdot o = \pi \quad \text{and} \quad \pi + o = o$$
$$\pi \cdot U = U \quad \text{and} \quad \pi + U = \pi.$$

In order to extend the lattice structure, induced by these operations, to a full algebraic structure we need to introduce a relation of independence on experiments. Such an independence relation is certainly natural in a probabilistic context, but it is essentially an algebraic property, and applies directly to qualitative (probability or information) structures (see S. Maeda [33]).

Let $(S,\Pi, \subseteq\cdot)$ be the lattice of experiments, then $\pi_1,\pi_2\in\Pi$ are said to be independent, $\pi_1 \perp\!\!\!\perp \pi_2$, if $AB\times S \simeq A\times B$, where $\simeq$ means isomorphic to.

Then $\perp\!\!\!\perp$ satisfies the following properties for all $\pi,\pi_1,\pi_2 \in\Pi$:

(1) $o \perp\!\!\!\perp \pi$,

(2) $\pi \perp\!\!\!\perp \pi \Longrightarrow \pi = o$

(3) $\pi_1 \perp\!\!\!\perp \pi_2 \Longleftrightarrow \pi_2 \perp\!\!\!\perp \pi_1$,

(4) $\pi_1 \perp\!\!\!\perp \pi_2$ & $\pi_2 \subseteq\cdot \pi_3 \Longrightarrow \pi_1 \perp\!\!\!\perp \pi_3$

(5) $\pi_1 \perp\!\!\!\perp \pi_2$ & $\pi_2 \perp\!\!\!\perp \pi_3 \Longrightarrow (\pi_1 \cdot \pi_2 \perp\!\!\!\perp \pi_3 \Longleftrightarrow \pi_1 \perp\!\!\!\perp \pi_2 \cdot \pi_3)$,

(6) $\pi_1 \amalg \pi$ & $\pi_2 \amalg \pi \Longrightarrow \pi_1 \cdot \pi_2 \amalg \pi$, if $A \cup B = S$, $A \in \pi_1$, $B \in \pi_2$.

(7) $\pi_1 \amalg \pi_2 \cdot \pi_3$ & $\pi_1 \cdot \pi_2 \amalg \pi_3 \Longrightarrow (\pi_1 \amalg \pi_2 \Longleftrightarrow \pi_2 \amalg \pi_3)$,

(8) $\pi \amalg \pi_1$ & $\pi \amalg \pi_2 \Longrightarrow (\pi \cdot \pi_1 = \pi \cdot \pi_2 \Longleftrightarrow \pi_1 = \pi_2)$,

(9) $\pi_1 \amalg \pi_2$ & $\pi_1 \subseteq \pi_2 \Longrightarrow \pi_2 = o$

Furthermore, by applying the independence relation to Π, we get the set-theoretic operation of complementation out of it, e.g. we then have for any $A \in \pi$:

$\bar{A} = \{B : A \cup B = S \;\&\; A \amalg B$ for all $A, B \in \pi\}$. Extending this to partitions define

$\bar{\pi} = \prod_{\pi \cdot U = U} \{U\}$ with $\pi_1 \wedge \pi_2 = (\bar{\pi}_1 \cdot \bar{\pi}_2)^-$, $\pi \amalg U$, $\wedge$ being a 'meet-operation', in Π. Then we get a Boolean algebra for a collection of all elements of Π for which complements do exist in this way. Therefore, in general, the introduction of $\amalg$ into Π only induces a Boolean algebra $\mathcal{B}$ **firmly embedded in Π.**

Then one finds conditions under which an entropy function (quasi-entropy) exists on the entire Π.

The main characteristics of a finite qualitative quasi-entropy structure can be collected in the following properties.

Let $(S, \Pi, \leq:, \amalg)$ be a qualitative (quasi-)entropy structure, and $A, B, C \in \mathcal{Y}$ be elements of any partition π in Π.

(1) $\pi_1 \subseteq \pi_2 \Longrightarrow \pi_2 \leq: \pi_1$,

(2) $\pi_1 \leq: \pi_2$ and $\pi_2 \leq: \pi_3 \Longrightarrow \pi_1 \leq: \pi_3$

$\pi_1 \leq: \pi_2$ or $\pi_2 \leq: \pi_1$

$\pi_1 <: \pi_2 \Longleftarrow \pi_1 \leq: \pi_2$ and not $\pi_2 \leq: \pi_1$

$\pi_1 \ddot{=} \pi_2 \Longleftarrow \pi_1 \leq: \pi_2$ and $\pi_2 \leq: \pi_1$, $\ddot{=}$ is an

equivalence relation,

(3) $o \leq: \pi$ for any $\pi \in \Pi$ and $o <: \pi$ if $\pi \ddot{=} E$, where $E = \{A, \bar{A}\}$ denotes Bernoulli experiments.

(4) $o \leq: \{A, \bar{A}\} \leq: \{A, \bar{A}B, \bar{A}\bar{B}\} \leq: \{A, \bar{A}B, \bar{A}\bar{B}C, \bar{A}\bar{B}\bar{C}\}$

$\leq: \ldots \leq: U \Longleftarrow U \subseteq \ldots \subseteq \{A, \bar{A}B, \bar{A}\bar{B}\} \subseteq \ldots \subseteq o.$

(5) $\pi_1 \leq: \pi_2 \Longleftrightarrow \pi_1 \cdot \pi \leq: \pi_2 \cdot \pi$, if $\pi \perp\!\!\!\perp \pi_1, \pi_2$,

(6) $\pi_1 \leq: U_1$ and $\pi_2 \leq: U_2 \Longrightarrow \pi_1 \cdot \pi_2 \leq: U_1 \cdot U_2$

if $\pi_1 \perp\!\!\!\perp \pi_2$ and $U_1 \perp\!\!\!\perp U_2$.

(7) $\pi_1 \ddot{=} \pi_2$ and $\pi_2 \cdot \pi_3 \leq: \pi_4 \Longrightarrow \pi_1 \cdot \pi_3 \leq \pi_4$

if $\pi_3 \perp\!\!\!\perp \pi_1, \pi_2$.

(8) <u>If for all</u> $U_o, U_1, \ldots, U_n, \pi_o, \pi_1, \ldots, \pi_n$

<u>in</u> Π <u>it is true that</u>

$\pi_i \leq: U_i$ <u>for all</u> $i, 0 \leq i < n$ <u>and</u> $\prod_{i \leq n} \bar{\pi}_i \ddot{=} \overline{\prod}_{i \leq n} \bar{U}_i$, $\pi_i \perp\!\!\!\perp_{i \leq n}$ & $U_i \perp\!\!\!\perp_{i \leq n}$.

<u>Then</u> $\pi_n :\geq U_n$.

Condition (8) is a kind of consistency condition for the representation of a qualitative structure and it is due to D. Scott [34]. This condition essentially forces Π to be a Boolean algebra in the relevant elements being complemented.

Having stated some properties in a qualitative entropy structure one is led to represent this structure by a compatible entropy function. The situation is analogous to the problem of representing qualitative probability by compatible probability measures.

Suppose $(S,\Pi,\lesssim:,\perp\!\!\!\perp)$ exists. Then there is a (quasi) entropy function $H:\Pi\to Re$, representing the structure such that for all $\pi_1,\pi_2\in\Pi$:

(i) $\pi_1 \lesssim: \pi_2 \Longleftrightarrow H(\pi_1)\leq H(\pi_2)$,

(ii) $\pi_1 \perp\!\!\!\perp \pi_2 \Longrightarrow H(\pi_1\cdot\pi_2) = H(\pi_1)+H(\pi_2)$,

(iii) $\pi_1 \subseteq \pi_2 \Longrightarrow H(\pi_2)\leq H(\pi_1)$,

(iv) $H(o) = 0, H(\bar{o}) = \infty$,

(v) $H(\pi) = 1$, if $\pi \ddot{=} E$ and E denotes all equiprobable experiments in Π.

Conditions (i) - (v) are appropriate adjustments of similar conditions used for representation theorems of qualitative probability, hence basically the same proof techniques can be used for proving the theorem (see D. Scott [34], H.W. Gottinger [30]). Condition (ii) constitutes the most important property of entropy, e.g. additivity. Domotor [31] provides a sufficiency proof of the theorem that is in the spirit of Scott's result, it involves an interesting technique.

Let us sketch the technique by translating everything into a geometric picture.
We associate to every partition π a vector of partitions $\hat{\pi}$, all of these are to be considered linearly independent and $\hat{\pi} \varepsilon V(\hat{\Pi})$ where $\hat{\Pi}$ is the basis of the n-dimensional vector space $V(\hat{\Pi})$ depending on the number of linear independent $\hat{\pi}$'s. Then make Π a finite subset of $V(\hat{\Pi})$ and extend the ordering to $V(\hat{\Pi})$. Scott's result on representation of ordered, finite-dimensional real vector spaces by linear functionals immediately applies and hence we can find a linear functional $\psi : V(\hat{\Pi}) \to R_e$ and a compatible functional $V: \Pi \to Re$ satisfying properties (i) - (v) such that $\psi(\{A,\bar{A}\}) > o$ and the quasi-entropy function is normalized by

$$H(\pi) = \psi(\pi) / \psi(\{A,\bar{A}\}).$$

If we want to establish a connection between the Shannon-Wiener entropy and entropy derived from qualitative entropy structures it would be necessary then to investigate the interrelationship between qualitative probability and qualitative information. The reason is seen in that the entropy function decomposes itself into representations of probability and information. The result obtained so far is rather weak since the prefix 'quasi' should indicate that the entropy representation is not unique. It is an open problem to find unique entropy functions derived from qualitative structures. It is rather obvious that the answer to this problem depends on imposing further structural conditions on the relations '$\perp\!\!\!\perp$' and '$\leq:$' as well as on the interaction between both. There also have to be interconnecting conditions between qualitative entropy and qualitative probability structures. However, the axiomatic setup for this is awfully complicated and we will not dwell upon this question here. Some hints in this direction have been provided by Domotor.

The results can be extended to conditional entropy in which the underlying qualitative structure will be a difference structure. No further technical difficulties are encountered.

4. QUALITATIVE SEMANTIC INFORMATION AND INFORMATIVENESS.

It has been observed by Shannon [7] that the 'semantic aspects of communication are irrelevant to the engineering problem'. As noted earlier, a semantic theory of information along Shannon's line has been provided by Carnap and Bar-Hillel[19]. Unfortunately, the latter theory does not cover aspects that are important in semantic information-processing, e.g. those related to informativeness, information-content of statements, propositions, sentences, etc. Surprisingly, not much work has been done on this over the last two decades.

R. Wells [35] made a step into the right direction and developed a semantical theory of informativeness based on qualitative comparison of propositions, sentences according to information-content. One may again point out that the nature of 'unexpectedness' covers only one aspect of information, another aspect would be to order sentences according to informativeness provided they are logically true. For example, 'the Pythagorean theorem is more informative than the proposition 7 + 5 = 12'. We will pursue the latter aspect in a modified form, substituting logical truth of a sentence by 'occurrence of an event'.

In what follows we will outline one approach (Gottinger[3,4]) toward semantic information which is quite different in spirit and method from the original Carnap-Bar-Hillel approach.

It is basically assumed that information is prior to probability, and hence is more fundamental than probability justifying a separate treatment.

This approach is built upon the following fundamentals:

(1) We deal analytically with 'information' as we deal with events as elements of an abstract algebraic structure, similarly as events are treated as 'undefined terms' in a Kolmogorov-Halmos probability algebra.

(2) We confine the notion of information to information pertaining to events (to occur or not occur) since we are interested in making predictions on future events.

(3) Qualitative information is introduced as a binary relation in an information structure and is meant as 'not more informative than' w.r.t. occurrence of the respective event.

(4) A qualitative (subjective) information structure generates a qualitative (subjective) probability structure by a Boolean homomorphism. This is to make precise the idea that a person will evaluate 'qualitative probability' only via qualitative information.

(5) The theory proposed here is entirely based on a theory of inductive inference.

(6) The ultimate goal is to measure probability in terms of information and not vice versa as suggested by standard information theory.

Note that our approach will exhibit an information measure which is nonnegative and bounded on the unit interval, and therefore is quite different from the definition of information as a surprise value. Consider quantitative information as a nonnegative normed measure on a Boolean algebra of propositions (the information structure) to be ordered according to information content. Assume the value one at the unit element and generate via a Boolean homomorphism a probability measure on a Boolean algebra of events.

Definition 1: The triple $(S,\mathcal{T},\lesssim)$ is called a qualitative (subjective) probability structure (QPS) if

(1) $\lesssim$ is a partial order (p.o.) on $\mathcal{T}$.

If for $A,B,C \in \mathcal{T}$, $A \perp\!\!\!\perp B, B \perp\!\!\!\perp C$ then

(2) $A \lesssim B \Longleftrightarrow A \cup C \lesssim B \cup C$.

(3) $O \lesssim A$, $A \in \mathcal{T}$ and $\exists$ O, $O < S$, O being the nullevent and S the universal event.

Now we assume that '$\lesssim$' is a derived concept and that the basic concept will be a relation '$\precsim$' (qualitative information) defined in a family of information sets or information structure T_o generating an algebra of events. In order to consider a qualitative (subjective) information structure (QIS) we need the following

Definition 2: $(E,T_o,\precsim)$ is called a QIS if

(1) $\precsim$ is a particular order relation in T_o to be specified.

(2) If $\underline{A},\underline{B},\underline{C}$ in T_o, $\underline{A} \perp\!\!\!\perp \underline{B}, \underline{B} \perp\!\!\!\perp \underline{C}$ then

$\underline{A} \precsim \underline{B} \Longleftrightarrow \underline{A} \cup \underline{C} \precsim \underline{B} \cup \underline{C}$

(3) For any fixed $X \in \mathcal{T}$, $\underline{O}_X \precsim \underline{A}$ for all $\underline{A} \in T_o$,
for any fixed $Y \in \mathcal{T}$, $\underline{O}_X < E_Y$,

where $E = \bigcup(\underline{A},\underline{B},\underline{C},\ldots)$, and $\underline{O}_X$ means neg-information with respect to some event $X \in \mathcal{T}$, E_Y means universal information with respect to some $Y \in \mathcal{T}$.

We say a QIS H-generates ($\xrightarrow{H}$) a QPS, $T_o \ni \underline{A} \xrightarrow{H} H(\underline{A})$ if there exists a Boolean homomorphism H that is order and structure-preserving with respect to the operations $\wedge$, $\vee$, $-$ (finite meet, join and complementation).

Suppose we want to have

$\underline{A} \precsim \underline{B} \Longrightarrow \underline{A} \subseteq \underline{B}$ and $\underline{A} \precsim \underline{B} \Longrightarrow H(\underline{A})\_H(\underline{B})$,

so that qualitative information may be put in terms of inclusion.

However, here we face the difficulty that $\underline{A}, \underline{B}$ may contain different semantic information, and the inclusion relation may not hold. One way out of this involves the construction of a <u>standardized</u> structure T, order-isomorphic to T_o. We need the following

<u>Definition</u> 3:

(1) $H : \Omega_X \rightarrow X \doteq o$ (neg-information generates a quasi-null event)

(2) $H : E_Y \rightarrow Y \doteq S$ (universal information generates a quasi-sure event).

The relation $\doteq$ indicates qualitative equiprobability

Then $(S, \mathcal{S}, \precsim)$ is considered to be a qualitative probability structure which does not permit, in its representation, strictly positive measures. By this process one is able to derive a qualitative standardized information structure (QSIS) $(I, T, \precsim)$ order-isomorphic to a QIS with L being the zero and I the unit element such that $L \precsim I \Longrightarrow L \subseteq I$. This type of ordering corresponds to ordering of attributes according to Boole's First Law resulting in a Boolean interval algebra, and in which L, I constitute lower and upper bounds, respectively.

In the next steps we are going to show that imposing on T

some weak order conditions will make T a lattice-ordered algebra being equivalent to some kind of Boolean algebra.

One interesting formal aspect of this approach reveals an exposition of binary relations that play an important role in the study of topological structures, called <u>topogeneous structures</u> according to A. Császar [36].

Let $(I,T,\lesssim)$ be a QSIS. Then $\lesssim$ satisfies the properties of a semi-topogeneous order (STO) if

(1) $L \lesssim L$, $I \lesssim I$ for $L, I \in T$, hence $\lesssim$ is reflexive,

(2) $\alpha \lesssim \beta \Longrightarrow \alpha \subseteq \beta$, $\alpha, \beta \in T$

(3) $\alpha \subseteq \alpha' \lesssim \beta' \subseteq \beta \Longrightarrow \alpha \lesssim \beta$, $\alpha', \beta' \in T$

(4) Furthermore, $\lesssim$ is supposed to be symmetric, i.e. there exists a complementary order $\lesssim^-$ with $(\lesssim^-)^- = \lesssim$ such that (1) - (3) can be reformulated in terms of $\lesssim^-$, for example $\alpha \lesssim^- \beta \Longrightarrow I - \beta \lesssim I - \alpha$.

Conditions (1) and (2) are rather weak, (3) is a kind of transitivity, (4) has far-reaching structural consequences. Finally, it is shown in Gottinger [3] that a STO in $(I,T,\lesssim)$ can naturally be extended to a <u>topogeneous</u> order (TO) provided the following condition is satisfied:

(5) $\alpha_i \lesssim \beta_j \Longrightarrow \left[\bigwedge_{i=1}^{n} \alpha_i \lesssim \bigwedge_{j=1}^{m} \beta_j \;\&\; \bigvee_{i=1}^{n} \alpha_i \lesssim \bigvee_{j=1}^{m} \beta_j\right]$, i.e. the ordering is preserved under lattice operations.

The main result can be obtained after several intermediate steps (see Gottinger [3,4]).

<u>Let $\lesssim$ be a STO generated by a semi-topogeneous structure</u> T. <u>For $\lesssim$ to be a symmetric TO it is necessary and sufficient that</u> T <u>is a Boolean algebra.</u>

Rough sketch of proof. $\Longleftarrow$ is obvious since every Boolean algebra implies a symmetric TO via its partial order. $\Longrightarrow$ 1. Complementarity. It is known that to every STO$\precsim$ generated by T there is associated a complementary order $\precsim^-$ generated by $T^- \ni I-\tau\,(\tau\varepsilon T)$. Let $\alpha\precsim^-\beta, \alpha'\precsim^-\beta'$, for a symmetric TO$\precsim$ each of the following statements is true:

$$(1) \quad [\alpha\precsim^-\beta \;\&\; \alpha'\precsim\beta'] \Longrightarrow \alpha \wedge \alpha'\precsim\beta\wedge\beta'$$

$$(2) \quad |\alpha\precsim\beta \;\&\; \alpha'\precsim\beta'| \Longrightarrow \alpha \vee \alpha'\precsim\beta\vee\beta'$$

if T is a lattice. T has a L and I element and therefore via finite join and meet operations T is relatively complemented and hence complemented.

2. Distributivity. It can also be shown that T is distributive since because of symmetry and (1) we have:

$$(3) \quad I - (\beta\vee\beta') = (I-\beta)\wedge(I-\beta') \precsim (I-\alpha)\wedge(I-\alpha') = I-(\alpha\vee\alpha')$$

and therefore $\alpha\vee\alpha'\precsim\beta\vee\beta'$ which coincides with the conclusion in (2).
Applying de Morgan's Law we have

$I-(\alpha\vee\alpha') = (I\wedge\alpha^-)\wedge(I\wedge\alpha'^-) = \alpha^-\wedge\alpha'^-$,
likewise for $I-(\beta\vee\beta')$. Consequently, $\beta^-\wedge\beta'^-\precsim\alpha^-\wedge\alpha'^-$ and there exists $\precsim^-$ such that we get

$$I-(\alpha^-\wedge\alpha'^-)=I\wedge(\alpha\vee\alpha')=(I\wedge\alpha)\vee(I\wedge\alpha') = \alpha\vee\alpha',$$

analogously for β, hence $\alpha\vee\alpha'\precsim\beta\vee\beta'$.
Similarly, (2) implies (1), namely again by applying de Morgan's Law

$$(4) \quad I-(\beta\wedge\beta')=I\wedge(\beta^-\wedge\beta'^-) = (I-\beta)\vee(I-\beta')\precsim(I-\alpha)\vee(I-\alpha') = I-(\alpha\wedge\alpha').$$

All remaining properties can easily be derived, by analogy, hence T is a complemented, distributive lattice, i.e. a Boolean algebra.

On the basis of this and similar results it is possible to obtain representation theorems in order to construct finitely additive information measures strictly compatible with the OIS. Standard measure-theoretic results by Horn and Tarski [37], Kelley [38] and D. Kappos [39] can be used in this regard.

Then every measure space (I,T,μ) that exists by the representation will induce a probability space via a Boolean homomorphism F. By the analogy of measures and Boolean homomorphisms one can construct a mesure $F\,o\mu = P$ whose properties are shown in the diagram below:

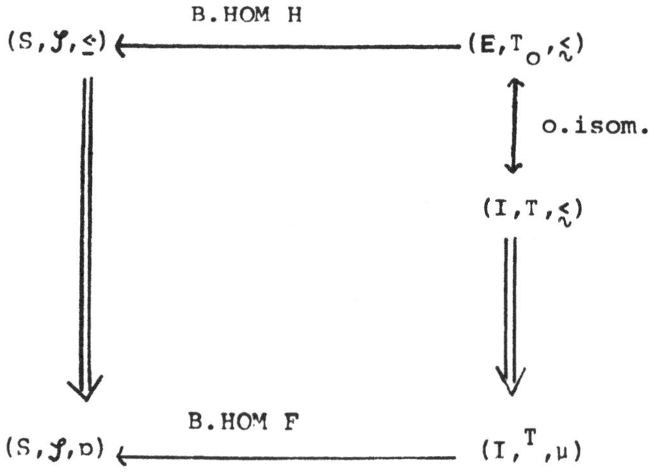

5. INFORMATION IN STATISTICAL DECISION THEORY.

The structure of a statistical game can be outlined as follows. The statistician plays a game against nature, at his disposal is a class A of possible actions which he can take (or decisions he can make) in view of the unknown state of nature (nature's pure strategy) $s \epsilon S$. (By a quick change of notation we now consider S as the set of states of nature.)

He may decide to take an action without experimentation (e.g. without 'spying' on nature's strategies) and for doing this may incur a numerical loss $L(s,a)$. The possibility of performing experiments does exists, thus reducing the loss by gaining at least partial information about s. Therefore the concept of information in this context is naturally tied up with payoff-relevance, any bits of information that do not reduce the loss are considered irrelevant.

What prevents the statistician of getting full knowledge of s is the cost of experiments. This cost may assume specific functional forms, but, in general, is considered to be proportional to the number of experiments. Technical definitions are needed in order to look at the general structure of a statistical game. Let Z be the space of outcomes of an experiment, then a function p is defined on $Z \times S$ such that for a fixed $s \epsilon S$ p_s is a probability distribution. The triple $\mathcal{Z} = (Z,S,p)$ is sometimes referred to as the sample space, in general, one does not distinguish between $\mathcal{Z}$ and Z and both may refer to sample spaces. For every subset $A \subset Z$, the probability of the event A is given by

$$P_s(A) = \sum_{z \epsilon A} p_s(z),$$

and P satisfies all properties of a probability measure. A function $d \epsilon D$, defined on Z mapping $Z \xrightarrow{\text{into}} A$ is called a decision function such that d(z) = a.

A risk function is represented by expected loss, i.e. a function R on S×D:

$$R(s,d) = \sum_{z \in Z} L(s,d(z))p_s(z) = E[L(s,d(z))].$$

Now a mixed or randomized strategy for nature is the same as a prior probability distribtuion (for the statistician) on the set of states of nature S, denoted by $\mu \in \mathcal{M}$.
The problem of collecting information in a statistical game may be generally posed as follows: Does there exist a partition of Z such that every possible risk attainable with a complete knowledge of $z \in Z$ is also attainable with only the information that z belongs to a set of this partition? Such partitions, if they exist, are as informative as the entire sample space. They are given by the principle of sufficiency.

We are concerned with information provided by an experiment. An experiment X is completely described by a random variable associated with the sample space (Z,S,p) giving rise to a set of conditional probability distributions for every possible parameter (state of nature) $s \in S$. X might be of fixed sample size or of a sequential type where the experimenter may collect observations finitely many times. To set up the problem assume you (the experimenter, the statistician or generally the decision-maker) are confronted with an uncertain situation where you wish to know about the true value of a parameter (state of nature) $s \in S$. Of course you can make some wild guesses, but you can only gain knowledge about the true state by experimentation. Let μ be some prior probability distribution of the true state s which indicates the amount of uncertainty or ignorance on your part. (Adopt a Bayesian viewpoint that such μ always exists and is non-null.)

Then the information provided by X may be verbally expressed as the difference between the amount of uncertainty you attach to the prior distribution and that amount of your expected uncertainty of the posterior distribution (after having performed X), i.e. it reflects the residual value of your uncertainty (reduced).

More technically, let $\mathcal{M}$ be the set of prior probability distributions over S (i.e. the space of randomized strategies for nature), define u as a nonnegative, real-valued measurable function on $\mathcal{M}$ which for obvious reasons should be concave, i.e. decreasing with increasing observations. Then $u(\mu)$ represents the amount of your uncertainty (before experimentation) when your distribution over S is μ. In some cases the uncertainty function u is just equivalent to a risk function in a statistical decision problem, in other cases it can be directly assigned. Under specific circumstances it can be identified with the entropy function or can assume some other form that is compatible with its properties of nonnegativity and concavity. Now performing X and observing values of X you may specify a posterior distribution $\phi(X)$, then your measure of information I is determined by

$$I(X,\mu,u) = u(\mu) - E\,[u(\phi(X))\,|\,\mu]$$

where $\phi(X)$ is usually obtained by an appropriate application of the well-known Bayes' theorem to get the posterior distribution (see Blackwell & Girshick [6],Chap.3, de Groot [40,41]).

It is usually assumed for reasons of non-triviality that most experiments provide information and that any experiment being more informative than another is also preferable to the other. Therefore, for any given uncertainty function, I is nonnegative, and also for reasons of convenience, continuous.

As we clearly recognize this measure of information provided by an experiment relative to the specification of u and μ naturally evolves from a model of statistical decision. Usually the determination of the uncertainty function hinges upon the loss structure in a statistical game, this becomes clear when we describe comparisons of experiments according to informativeness.

6. COMPARISON OF INFORMATION.

In the relevant literature of statistical decision theory comparison of experiments are sometimes confined to those which can be represented by Markov matrices (in this context as information matrices). This is very natural in terms of viewing it in the context of a statistical game. Assume the experiment E produces N distinct value $e_1,\ldots,e_N$ (signals, observations) and let be $S = (s_1,\ldots,s_n)$. Then the experiment E can be represented by an n×N Markov matrix $\underline{P} = (p_{ij})$ associated to the sample space (Z,S,p) such that $p_{ij} = \underline{P}_{s_i}(\{s:E(z) = e_j\}), p_{ij} \geq 0$ and $\sum_j p_{ij} = 1$ for each i.

Henceforward, for reasons of simplicity, we adopt an earlier definition of D.Blackwell [5] in terms of defining experiments as random variables. Incidentally, Blackwell's definition is one of the first better known definitions of 'comparative informativeness' in the context of statistical decision theory. Every experiment E associated to a sample space generates a risk function. Then, according to Blackwell, an experiment E is more informative than another experiment E' (the set of experiments being partially ordered) if the risk obtained from E is at least obtainable also from E'. $E > E' \Longleftrightarrow R(E) \leq R(E')$. In other words, the numerical risk for E' is at least as large as that of E. If the distribution over S is known then comparative informativeness hinges upon the loss structure of the decision problem. This immediately gives rise to an economic view on the evaluation of information. There were further generalizations and improvements of Blackwell's results in recent years, in particular, in connection with the foundations of statistical inference ('informative inference') (see A. Birnbaum [42]); these results give the main motivations for economic studies on the subject (see C.B.McGuire [43] and Gottinger [44]). This view has been originated and consistently pursued by J. Marschak*). His 'value of information' $V(\eta)$ (attached to experiment η) w.r.t. any probability distribution μ over S (his space of events uncontrollable to the decision maker) and his benefit function $b : S\times A \to Re$ is just the converse value of Blackwell's risk R(E) this is due to the fact that economists prefer to talk about benefit or utility, whereas statisticians are more pessimistic and talk about losses. Note, again, that the risk function is completely specified by a probability distribution over S and a loss function on $S\times A$.

One can easily see the strong agreement between information provided by an experiment and the value of information by considering an experiment as a Markov matrix. In this case null-information corresponds to identical rows in the Markov matrix, i.e. any observations made through an experiment is independent of any state of nature.

Accordingly, the risk function obtained by the less informative experiment is larger in value than the risk function obtained by the more informative experiment. It is obvious that the dual statement holds if we deal with an economist's benefit function instead of a statistician's loss function.

---

*) See next Section

We have learned of different, but interelated characterizations of an experiment, either as a partition of Z, as a random variable and in particular as a Markov matrix. Comparative informativeness in terms of partitions of Z given by the principle of sufficiency has also been studied by Blackwell & Girschick [6] (Chap.8).

Let X and Y be two experiments whose values are in the sample spaces, denoted by Z_X and Z_Y, respectively.

Then experiment Y is sufficient for experiment X if there exists a nonnegative function h on the product space $Z_X \times Z_Y$ satisfying the following relations

(i) $f_X(x|s) = \int_{Z_Y} h(x,y) f_Y(y|s) d\mu(y)$ for $s \in S$ and $x \in Z_X$,

(ii) $\int_{Z_X} h(x,y) d\mu(x) = 1$ for $y \in Z_Y$

(iii) $0 < \int_{Z_Y} h(x,y) d\mu(y) < \infty$ for $x \in Z_Y$.

h is a stochastic transformation from Y to X. For each fixed value $y \in Z_Y$ the function $h(\cdot,y)$ is a generalized probability density function on Z_X. Since this function does not involve the parameter s, a point $x \in Z_X$ could be generated according to the generalized probability density function by means of an auxiliary randomization.

Thus, Y is sufficient for X, if regardless to the value of the parameter s, an observation on Y and an auxiliary randomization make it possible to generate a random variable which has the same distribution as X. The integrability condition on h in (iii) is introduced for technical convenience only.

If Y is sufficient for X then the statistician is strongly advised not to perform the experiment X when Y is available. In fact, one can prove that the sufficient experiment Y must be at least as informative as the experiment X.

<u>Suppose that experiment</u> Y <u>is sufficient for the experiment</u> X. <u>Then, for any uncertainty function</u> u <u>and any posterior distribution</u> ϕ

$$E[u(\phi(X))] \geq E[u(\phi(Y))]$$

The proof of this result is straight-forward and can be found in M. de Groot[45].

7. ECONOMIZING INFORMATION.

Despite strong trends in economics and related behavioral science in recent years to use basic results of information theory for their purpose some serious doubts have been expressed concerning the usefulness of H_p for application in economics and for decision-making in general.*) Among others, J. Marschak[47] argues that Shannon's entropy does not tell us anything about the benefit of transmitting information since it assumes equal penalty for all communication errors. What he instead has in mind is a concept of behavioral information processing in an economic system, in particular as

*) R.A. Howard[46] has put it this way: '...If losing all your assets in the stock market and having whale steak for supper, then the information associated with the occurrence of either event is the same. Attempts to apply Shannon's information theory to problems beyond communications have, in large, come to grief. The failure of these attempts could have been predicted because no theory that involves just the probabilities of outcomes without considering their consequences could possibly be adequate in describing the importance of uncertainty to a decision maker.'

related to an economic theory of teams (Marschak and Radner[48]). From an economic viewpoint information may be regarded as a particular kind of commodity which will be traded at a certain price yielding benefits for consumers and causing costs for producers. Hence, the economic theory of information (still in its infancy) is an appropriate modification of the approach used in statistical decision theory. To put it in other terms, here we are interested in the economic aspect of usefulness of information (based on some kind of utility or loss function) rather than in the (original) engineering viewpoint of transmitting and controlling information flows through a large (noisy or noiseless) communication channel. As a digression more recently some information theorists tried to remedy the flaw or restrictiveness of 'equal penalty of all communication errors' by weighing entropy in terms of utility. For any partition π of Z they attach to every $A\epsilon\pi$ a utility such that the entropy is given by $H(\pi) = \sum_{A\epsilon\pi} U(A)\cdot P(A)\cdot I_p(A)$ (see Belis & Guiasu [49] and for a further elaboration Guiasu[50]). U(A) satisfies well-known properties of expected utility, i.e. it is for a given preference pattern on π, unique up to positive linear transformations. It is clear that this proposed measure makes sense if the amount of information to be transmitted through a channel exceeds its upper (physical) bound so that a subjective evaluation procedure (via a utility function) reduces irrelevant information. In this approach there is no obvious relationship between the utility of the message and the information derived from the message, and therefore both should be measured separately. Let p_1 be the message 'you will receive five dollars', and let p_2 be 'you will receive five dollars and you will be shot'. Clearly, p_2 is at least as informative as p_1 but p_2 is hardly as desirable as p_1. One could even attach utility to the sources so that the encoder could select only those sources which are

useful to the encoder (see Longo [51]). The approach has been generalized by introducing explicitly a cost function, that is really a tradeoff function being dependent on the length of code words associated to the message (letter) and on the utility of the message. Clearly, the cost is increasing in the first variable but decreasing in the second. The tradeoff function is uniquely fixed as soon as the utility and the cost of coding are determined.
Assessment of the tradeoff and utility function is treated separately. An optimization principle is involved by minimizing the expected tradeoff so determined.

Let us now sketch the basic ingredients of Marschak's approach as discussed in detail in Marschak [47], (see also Marschak [52,53,54]). Information processing is defined as $P = \langle X,Y,\eta,\kappa,\tau \rangle$, where X is a set of inputs, Y is a set of outputs, η a transformation from X to Y, κ is a cost function on X, and τ a time-delay function on X. If you consider, as Marschak does, information as an economic good there is sufficient motivation for looking at the economic system as a mechanism (machine); producing and processing information over time which involves costs and delays. In this respect, information processing is indistinguishable from the processing of physical commodities in, say, a transportation network. (A convenient theoretical framework for studying such processes would be the well-established algebraic theory of sequential machines, and Marschak's approach motivates a study of these machines for economic information processing, please see in this regard Gottinger [55].)

On the other hand, Marschak's approach is firmly embedded in the general statistical decision model. We might then conceive η as a stochastic transformation from the random set X (the space of events, non-controllable to the decision-maker) to the random set Y (the space of available and feasible decision acts), $\eta : X \rightarrow Y$ then establishes a strategy (action). Up to now we have described the particular case of a one-link processing chain, more generally, we may conceive a (time) sequence of information processing $P^1, \ldots, P^N$ such that for every $n = 1, \ldots, N$ we write $P^n = \langle X^n, X^{n-1}, \eta^n, \ldots \rangle$ and $\eta^1 : X^1 \rightarrow X^2, \ldots, \eta^{n-1} : X^{N-1} \rightarrow X^N$ describe experiments with nature, for example. Hence $X^2, \ldots, X^N$ may be referred to as sets of observations or data, whereas $\eta^n : X^N \rightarrow X^{N+1}$ forms a strategy of the decision-maker. A chain of information processing is an information system à la Marschak. Some extensions of this viewpoint with respect to particular organizational forms (such as multi-person control systems, extensive games and dynamic teams) have been recently given by the author [56].

ACKNOWLEDGEMENT:

I am deeply indebted to Professor G. Longo (Trieste) for encouragement and to Mrs. Goergel (IMW-Bielefeld) for superb typing of the manuscript.

REFERENCES

1. Kolmogorov,A.N., 'Three Approaches to the Definition of the Concept "Quantity of Information"', Problemy Peredaci Informacii 1, 1965, 3 (in Russian)

2. Kolmogorov, A.N., 'Logical Basis for Information Theory and Probability Theory', IEEE Trans. Information Theory IT-14,1967,662

3. Gottinger, H.W., 'Qualitative Information and Comparative Informativeness', Kybernetik 13,1973,81

4. Gottinger, H.W., 'Konstruktion subjektiver Wahrscheinlichkeiten', Math. Operationsforschung u.Statist. 5, 1974,50

5. Blackwell, D., 'Comparison of Experiments', Proc.2nd Berkeley Symp.Math. Statist. and Probability, 1953,93

6. Blackwell, D., Girshick,M.A., Theory of Games and Statistical Decisions, Wiley:New York 1954

7. Shannon, C.E., Weaver, W., The Mathematical Theory of Communication, Illinois Uni.Press:Urbana, Ill. 1949

8. Wiener, N., Cybernetics, M.I.T. Press:Cambridge(Mass.) 1948

9. Fadeev, D.K., 'On the Concept of the Entropy for a Finite Probability Model', Uspehi Mat. Nauk 11, 1958,227 (in Russian)

10. Erdös, P., 'On the Distribution Function of Additive Functions', Ann. of Math. 47, 1946, 1

11. MacKay, D.M., Information, Mechanism and Meaning,M.I.T. Press: Cambridge, 1969

12. Rényi, A., 'On Measures of Entropy and Information', Proc. 4th Berkeley Symp.Math. Statist. and Probability, 1961, 547

13. Kelly, J.L., 'A new Interpretation of Information Rate', Bell System Technical Jour. 35,1956,917

14. Khinchin, A.I., Mathematical Foundations of Information Theory, Dover Publ.:New York 1957

15. Tveberg, H., 'A New Derivation of the Information Function', Math. Scand. 6, 1958,297

16. Kendall, D.G., 'Functional Equations in Information Theory', Zeitschr. Wahrscheinlichkeitstheorie 2, 1964,225

17. Lee, P.M., 'On the Axioms of Information Theory', Ann. Math. Statist. 35,1964,415

18. Gottinger, H.W., 'Review of Concepts and Theories of Probability', Scientia (Rivista di Scienza), 109,1974,83

19. Bar-Hillel, Y. and Carnap R., 'An Outline of a Theory of Semantic Information', Tech.Rep.No.247, Research Lab. of Electronics, M.I.T. 1952, in Language and Information, Bar-Hillel,Y. ed.,Addison-Wesley, Reading, Mass. 1964,221

20. Jeffreys, H.,Theory of Probability, 3rd ed., Clarendon Press: Oxford 1961

21. Heerden van, P.J., 'The Foundation of Empirical Knowledge', Uitgeverij Wistik, Wassenaar, Holland 1968

22. Ingarden,R.S. and Urbanik,K., 'Information without Probability', Colloq.Math. 9, 1962, 131

23. Ingarden, R.S., 'A Simplified Axiomatic Definition of Information', Bull.Acad.Sci. Polonaise, Ser. math.,astr. et phys., 11, 1963, 209

24. Ingarden, R.S., 'Simplified Axioms for Information without Probability', Prace Matematyczne 9, 1965,273

25. Rényi, A., Wahrscheinlichkeitsrechnung (mit einem Anhang über Informationstheorie), VEB Deutscher Verlag der Wissenschaften: Berlin 1962

26. Rényi, A., 'On the Foundations of Information Theory', Bull. International Statistical Institute 33, 1965

27. Kampé de Fériet, J., 'Mesure de l'information fournie par un évènement', Les Probabilités sur les Structures Algébriques, Paris: Symp. CNRS, 1970, 191

28. Fuchs, L., Partially Ordered Algebraic Systems, Pergamon: London 1963

29. Sikorski, R., Boolean Algebras, (2nd ed.), Springer, Göttingen-Berlin 1964

30. Gottinger, H.W., 'Konstruktion subjektiver Wahrscheinlichkeiten', Math. Operationsforschung u.Statist.5, 1974, 509

31. Domotor, Z., 'Probabilistic Relational Structures and Applications', Tech. Report 144, Inst. Math. Studies Social Sciences, Stanford University, 1969

32. Ore, O., 'Theory of Equivalence Relations', Duke Mathematical Jour, 9, 1942, 573

33. Maeda, S., 'A Lattice-Theoretic Treatment of Stochastic Independence', Jour.Sci.Hiroshima Univ. 27, 1963,Ser.A-1,1

34. Scott, D., 'Measurement Structures and Linear Inequalities', Jour. Math. Psychology 1, 1964, 233

35. Wells, R., 'A Measure of Subjective Information', Proc. Symp.Appl. Math.(Amer. Math. Soc.) 12, 1961, 237

36. Császar, A., Foundations of General Topology, Pergamon, London 1963

37. Horn, A. and Tarski, A.,'Measures in Boolean Algebras', Trans. Amer. Math. Soc. 64 1948, 467

38. Kelley, J.L., 'Measures in Boolean Algebras', Pacific Jour. Math. 9, 1959, 1165

39. Kappos, D.A., Strukturtheorie der Wahrscheinlichkeitsfelder und -räume, Springer: Berlin 1960

40. Groot de, M., 'Uncertainty, Information and Sequential Experiments', Ann. Math. Statist. 33, 1962,404

41. Groot de, M., 'Optimal Statistical Decisions', McGraw-Hill: New York 1970

42. Birnbaum, A., 'On the Foundations of Statistical Inference', Ann. Math. Statist. 32, 1961, 414

43. McGuire,C.B., 'Comparison of Information Structures', in Decision and Organization, Radner, R. and McGuire, C.B. eds., North Holland,Amsterdam 1972, 101

44. Gottinger, H.W., 'Some Measures of Information arising in Statistical Games', Kybernetik 15, 1974, 111

45. Groot de, M., 'Optimal Statistical Decisions', McGraw-Hill: New York 1970

46. Howard, R.A., 'Information Value Theory', IEEE Trans.Syst. Science and Cyber. SSC-2, 1966, 22

47. Marschak, J., 'Economics of Information Systems', in Frontiers of Quantitative Economics, Intrilligator, M.D. ed., North-Holland, Amsterdam 1971, 31

48. Marschak, J. and Radner, R., Economic Theory of Teams, Yale Univ.Press, New Haven 1972

49. Belis, M. and Guiasu, S., 'A Quantitative-Qualitative Measure of Information in Cybernetic Systems', IEEE Trans. Information Theory IT-14, 1967, 593

50. Guiasu, S., Mathematical Structure of Finite Random Cybernetic Systems, CISM Courses and Lectures No.86, Wien:Springer-Verlag 1971

51. Longo, G., Quantitative-Qualitative Measure of Information, CISM Courses and Lectures No. 138, Wien:Springer-Verlag 1972

52. Marschak, J., 'Optimal Systems for Information and Decision', Techniques of Optimization, Academic Press: New York 1972, 355

53. Marschak, J., 'Limited Role of Entropy in Information Economics', in 5th Conference on Optimization Techniques, Part II, Conti, R. et al. eds., Springer, New York 1973, 264

54. Marschak, J., 'Value and Cost of Information Systems', Working Paper 51, Wirtschaftstheoretische Abt., Universität Bonn, September 1973

55. Gottinger, H.W., 'Computable Organizations - Representation by Sequential Machine Theory', Ann. Systems Research 3, 1973, 81

56. Gottinger, H.W., 'Information Structures in Dynamic Team Decision Problems', to appear in Economic Computation and Economic Cybernetic Studies and Research (Bucharest), 1975.

SELF-ORGANIZING DYNAMICS WITH ENTROPY POTENTIALS

Giacomo DELLA RICCIA*
Ben Gurion University of the Negev
Beer - Sheva (Israel)

1 - Introduction

Since the work of Gibbs we are familiar with the idea of treating the phase space $\Gamma = \{p,q\}$ of a mechanical system S as a sample space where the initial conditions $\omega = (p,q)\varepsilon\Gamma$ of S, at time $t = 0$, are supposed to be chosen at random. To each $\omega\varepsilon\Gamma$ corresponds a curve $\{\omega_t; -\infty<t<\infty\}$ in Γ which describes the time evolution of the system. $\{\omega_t, -\infty<t<\infty\}$ can be viewed as a stochastic process whose sample curves are possible time histories of S. Given an arbitrary measurable function $\Phi(\omega)$ on Γ, we derive from the previous process

* The author wrote these lecture notes while on sabbatical leave and guest of the Laboratorio di Cibernetica del Centro Nazionale delle Ricerche - Arco Felice(Napoli) and is indebted to the members of the Laboratorio for their hospitality.

another stochastic process $\{\Phi_t(\omega);\ -\infty< t<\infty\}$ defined by $\Phi_t(\omega) = \Phi(\omega_{-t})$.

Originally our work was motivated by the desire to reduce the conceptual gap which exists between quantum theory and classical probability theory. In fact the formalism we are going to develop is essentially the same as the one followed in a previous work.[1] However, our main interest here is the study of some self-organizing aspects of a classical dynamics. Generally speaking we shall say that the dynamics of S has self-organizing features if we can find processes $\{\Phi_t(\omega);\ -\infty<t<\infty\}$ with interesting properties like, for instance, a discrete energy spectrum or a periodic behaviour.

We shall see that self-organizing dynamics in the above sense are governed by potentials which are local entropy functions. This, we believe, is an important fact since it relates information theory and dynamics by suggesting that the appearance of structure and organization in a physical or biological system may be the result of a mechanical evolution governed by a potential acting as a local source of information.

As mentioned before our present aim is not to draw conclusions on the foundations of quantum physics, however, we strongly emphasize the surprising fact that in our approach we are naturally forced to use procedures specific to quantum

1 - Della Riccia, G. and Wiener, N., Wave mechanics in classical phase space, Brownian motion and quantum theory, *J. Math. Phys.*, 7, 1372, 1966.

theory. In that connection it is interesting to quote the work of Hall and Collins,[2] and Santos[3] who, in a different context, also developed a quantumlike formulation of stochastic problems not necessarily related to atomic physics.

2 - The wave equation in phase space

Let $\Gamma = \{p,q\}$, where $p=(p_1, \dots, p_n)$ and $q=(q_1, \dots, q_n)$ be the phase space of a mechanical system S whose Hamiltonian is $H = \sum_i p_i^2/2m + F(q)$. Let us indicate by $\omega = (p,q)$ the initial state, at time $t = 0$, of the system and by $\{\omega_t = (p_t(\omega),\ q_t(\omega));\ -\infty < t < \infty\}$ the solution of the equation of motion

$$\begin{aligned} \dot{p} &= -\partial H/\partial q \\ \dot{q} &= \partial H/\partial p \end{aligned} \tag{1}$$

satisfying the initial conditions $p_o(\omega) = p$ and $q_o(\omega) = q$.

Given, at time $t = 0$, an arbitrary function $\Phi(p,q)$ on Γ, we assume that the time evolution of that function is defined by $\Psi(p,q;t) = \Phi(p_{-t}(\omega),\ q_{-t}(\omega))$. From that definition and (1) it follows that Ψ is solution of

$$\partial\Psi/\partial t - [\,H,\ \Psi] = 0, \tag{2}$$

where $[H,\ \Psi] = \sum_i \left(\partial H/\partial q_i\ \partial\Psi/\partial p_i - \partial H/\partial p_i\ \partial\Psi/\partial q_i \right)$ is the usual Poisson bracket and we assume that Φ is sufficiently

2. Hall, H.G., and Collins, R.E., *J. Math. Phys.*, 12, 100,1971.
3. Santos,E., Quantumlike formulation of stochastic problems *J. Math. Phys.*, 15, 1954, 1974.

regular to have derivatives.

Equation (2) is the usual conservation equation of statistical mechanics.

In statistical mechanics one normally deals with solutions of (2) which represent probability density functions $\rho(p,q;t)$: $\rho(p,q;t) \geq 0$ and $\int_\Gamma \rho dpdq = 1$.

We shall instead consider complex-valued square integrable functions $\Psi(p,q;t)$ from which probability density functions can be derived by simply writing $\rho(p,q;t) = |\Psi(p,q;t)|^2$.

We notice that the conservation of the norm of Ψ

$$\int_\Gamma |\Psi(p,q;t)|^2 dpdq = \int_\Gamma |\Phi(p_{-t}, q_{-t})|^2 dpdq = \int |\Phi(p,q)|^2 dpdq$$

is an immediate consequence of Liouville theorem on the invariance of the measure: $dpdq = dp_t dq_t$, $-\infty<t<\infty$. In other words we introduce "probability amplitudes" in phase space and not in configuration space as in quantum theory.

The first problem we want to discuss is the nature of the wave equation for probability amplitudes in phase space. Let us rewrite (2) as follows:

$$\partial\Psi/\partial t - \underset{\sim}{v} \cdot \nabla\Psi = 0 \, . \qquad (3)$$

Equation (3) shows that Ψ propagates like a wave with wave-front velocity $\underset{\sim}{v} = (-\partial H/\partial q, \partial H/\partial p)$ along the trajectories $\{p_t(\omega), q_t(\omega); -\infty<t<\infty\}$. However, we cannot say that (3) is the wave equation of Ψ because of its lack of symmetry in the sense that this equation excludes the existence of waves propagating in opposite directions, that is with velocity $-\underset{\sim}{v}$ instead of $\underset{\sim}{v}$.

In order to have a better understanding of what is involved here, let us for a while consider the elementary problem of vibrating strings. Let $u(x,t)$ represent the disturbance of the amplitude of a vibrating string. It is well known that this disturbance propagates according to the equation:

$$\partial^2 u / \partial t^2 = v^2 \, \partial^2 u / \partial x^2 \, , \tag{4}$$

whose general solution is of the form

$u(x,t) = f(x + vt) + g(x - vt)$ where f and g are arbitrary functions. $f(x + vt)$ represents a disturbance moving, let us say, from left to right and $g(x - vt)$ a disturbance moving from right to left. We notice that $f(x + vt)$ satisfies the equation

$$\partial f / \partial t - v \partial f / \partial x = 0 \, , \tag{5}$$

whereas $g(x - vt)$ satisfies the equation

$$\partial g / \partial t + v \partial g / \partial x = 0 \, . \tag{6}$$

Obviously (3) should be considered as the analogue of (5) which, however. describes only half of the physical possibilities implied by the wave equation (4). That suggests that we should introduce in phase space the analogue of (6), namely

$$\partial \Psi / \partial t + \underset{\sim}{v} \cdot \nabla \Psi = 0 \, . \tag{7}$$

As the combination of (5) and (6) leads to (4), we can derive from (3) and (7) one single equation

$$\partial^2 \Psi / \partial t^2 = \underset{\sim}{v} \cdot \nabla \, (\underset{\sim}{v} \cdot \nabla \Psi) \, ,$$

which becomes, by using the Poisson bracket notation:

$$\partial^2\Psi / \partial t^2 = [H, [H, \Psi]]. \tag{8}$$

The above symmetry argument justifies the choice of (8) as the wave equation in phase space with the understanding that only those solutions which are also solution of (2) are compatible with the dynamics of the system S. For an interpretation of the solutions of (8) which are also solutions of (7) we refer the reader to our previous work.[1]

3 - The energy of a wave in phase space

In order to define the energy of a wave in phase space we shall derive the wave equation (8) from a variational principle. Considering $\Psi(p,q;t)$ as a field, we introduce a Lagrangian density function $\lambda(p,q;t) = \frac{1}{2}A(\dot{\Psi}\dot{\Psi}^* - [H,\Psi]\,[H,\Psi^*])$ where $\dot{\Psi} = \partial\Psi/\partial t$ and $*$ means complex conjugate.
A is a dimension constant which will be fixed later on.
The total Lagrangian is then $\mathcal{L} = \int_\Gamma \lambda(p,q;t)dpdq$ and the total action between two times t_1 and t_2 is $\mathcal{S} = \int_{t_1}^{t_2} L\, dt$. We assume that the principle of least action holds, i.e. that $\mathcal{S}$ must be stationary when Ψ and Ψ^* are varied independently by arbitrary quantities $\delta\Psi$ and $\delta\Psi^*$ vanishing at t_1 and t_2. As a consequence, from a standard calculus of variation, we obtain the wave equation (8).

Let $\pi = \partial\lambda/\partial\dot{\Psi} = \frac{1}{2}A\dot{\Psi}^*$ and $\pi^* = \partial\lambda/\partial\dot{\Psi}^* = \frac{1}{2}A\dot{\Psi}$ be canonical conjugate variables to Ψ and Ψ^*, respectively. Then the Hamiltonian density of the field Ψ is

$$h(p,q;t) = \tfrac{1}{2}A(\dot{\Psi}\dot{\Psi}^* + [H,\Psi]\,[H,\Psi^*])$$

and thus the total energy of Ψ is

$$E = \tfrac{1}{2} A \int_\Gamma (\dot{\Psi}\dot{\Psi}^* + [H,\Psi]\,[H,\Psi^*])\,dpdq.$$

Recalling the condition that Ψ must also be solution of (2), we obtain

$$E = A \int_\Gamma [H,\Psi]\,[H,\Psi^*]\,dpdq.$$

Finally, by repeated integration by parts and using the fact that the integrated parts vanish (because Ψ is assumed to be square-integrable and hence must vanish at infinity), we obtain for the energy of Ψ :

$$E = -A \int_\Gamma \Psi^* \,[H,[H,\Psi]]\, dpdq. \tag{9}$$

Since the energy was obtained by a Lagrangian formalism it is time-invariant; for convenience we shall always compute E at time $t=0$ by using in (9) the initial condition $\Psi(p,q;0) = \Phi(p,q)$.

Let us now study the power spectrum of waves defined by initial conditions of the form

$$\Phi(p,q) = C \exp(-\beta \sum_i p_i^2/2m)\; W(q)\;, \tag{10}$$

where $W(q)$ is a complex-valued square integrable function of configuration space c ($\int_c |W(q)|^2\, dq < \infty$), C is a normalization constant that shall not be written explicitly anymore and β is another constant whose value will be discussed later on. The choice of the functions defined in (10) is motivated by the fact that

$$\Phi_o(p,q) = \exp(-\beta \sum_i p_i^2/2m)\, \exp(-\beta F(q)) = \exp(-\beta H)$$

is one of them and $\rho_o(p,q) = |\Phi_o(p,q)|^2 = \exp(-2\beta H)$

is the thermal equilibrium probability density.
Hence funtions of the type defined in (10) lead to probability densities $\rho(p,q;0) = \exp(-2\beta\sum_i p_i/_{2m})\ |W(q)|^2$ which can be interpreted as perturbations of the thermal equilibrium in which the Gaussian distribution with respect to the momenta coordinates p_i is preserved and only the equilibrium in configuration space is perturbed by replacing

$|W_o(q)|^2 = \exp(-2\beta F(q)$ with any $|W(q)|^2$ such that

$\int_C |W(q)|^2\, dq < \infty$.

To simplify the notation we introduce the dimensionless variables $P_i = (2\beta/_m)^{\frac{1}{2}}\ p_i$, $i = 1, \ldots, n$.

For $H = \sum_i p_i^2/_{2m} + F(q)$ and Φ defined in (10), we find that

$$[H,[H,\Phi]] = \exp(-\sum_i P_i^2/_4)\{1/_{2\beta m}\Delta + 1/_{2m}[\Delta F - \beta\sum_i (\partial F/_{\partial q_i})^2]\}W(q)$$

$$+ \exp(-\sum_i P_i^2/_4)\{\sum_i (P_i^2 - 1)(\partial/_{\partial q_i} + \beta\ \partial F/_{\partial q_i})^2\}\ W(q)$$

$$+ \exp(-\sum_i P_i^2/_4)\{\sum_{\substack{i\ j\\ i\neq j}}\sum P_i P_j (\partial/_{\partial q_i} + \beta\ \partial F/_{\partial q_i})$$

$$(\partial/_{\partial q_j} + \beta\ \partial F/_{\partial q_j})\}\ W(q) .$$

We notice that $\exp(-P_i^2/_4)$, $\exp(-P_i^2/_4)\ P_i$ and $\exp(-P_i^2/_4)(P_i^2 - 1)$ are, respectively, Hermite functions of order zero, one and two of the variable P_i . Hence, when we multiply the previous expression by
$\Phi^* = \exp(-\sum_i P_i^2/_4)\ W^*(q)$ and integrate with respect to the

p variables, it follows from the orthonormal properties of the Hermite functions that the energy integral reduces to

$$E = -A/_{\beta} \int_{C} W^*(q) \, \{ 1/_{2m} \Delta + \beta/_{2m} [\Delta F - \beta \sum_i (\partial F/_{\partial q_i})^2] \} \, W(q) \, dq \, ,$$

where $\Delta = \sum_i \partial^2/_{\partial q_i^2}$ is the Laplacian operator in configuration space.

Let us put

$$\beta /_{2m} [\beta \sum_i (\partial F/_{\partial q_i})^2 - \Delta F] = 1/_{\hbar^2} [V(q) + a] . \qquad (11)$$

The energy becomes

$$E = A/_{\beta \hbar^2} \int W^*(q) \{ -\hbar^2/_{2m} \Delta + V(q) + a \} W(q) \, dq$$

and with $A = \beta \hbar^2$, we obtain

$$E = \int W^*(q) \, (\mathcal{H} + a) \, W(q) \, dq \, , \qquad (12)$$

where $\mathcal{H} = -\hbar^2/_{2m} \Delta + V(q)$ is a Schroedinger type Hamiltonian.

The energy is given as the expectation value of a Hamiltonian operator, exactly as in quantum theory. This striking analogy suggests that we choose $\hbar$ to be the Planck's constant. However, let us notice the important fact that the potential $V(q)$ in the Schroedinger Hamiltonian $\mathcal{H}$ is not the same as the potential $F(q)$ in the classical Hamiltonian H. We shall later on discuss in detail the relation between $F(q)$ and $V(q)$ expressed in (11) and also fix the value of the constant a.

Let us now examine the interesting case where $\mathcal{H}$ has discrete eigenvalues $\{e_k ; k = 0, 1, \ldots\ldots\}$ with corresponding eigenfunctions $\{W_k(q);\ k = 0, 1, \ldots\}$. Using (12) we find that $\Phi_k = \exp(-\beta\sum_i p_i^2/2m)W_k(q)$ has the energy $E_k = e_k + a$ and more generally, that

$\Phi = \exp(-\beta\sum_i p_i^2/2m)\ W(q) = \exp(-\beta\sum_i p_i^2/2m)\ \sum_k c_k W_k(q)$ has the energy $E = \sum_k |c_k|^2\ (e_k + a)$.

This quantization of the energy is one of the self-organizing features we mentioned in the Introduction.

Let us adopt the point of view that in order to characterize the system S we are actually given the Schroedinger potential $V(q)$ and derive from (11) the classical potential $F(q)$. If we make the transformation

$$F(q) = 1/\beta\ \ln W_o(q) \qquad (13)$$

we obtain from (11)

$$-\hbar^2/2m\ \Delta\ W_o(q) + V(q)\ W_o(q) = \mathcal{H} W_o(q) = -a\,W_o(q).$$

This shows us that $-a$ can be any one of the eigenvalues of $\mathcal{H}$ and $W_o(q)$ the corresponding eigenfunction. We shall choose $-a$ to be equal to e_o, the energy of the ground state $W_o(q)$ of $\mathcal{H}$ because of the following interesting implications:

1) The ground state $W_o(q)$, which according to (13) is equal to $W_o(q) = \exp(-\beta F(q))$, will correspond to the wave $\Phi_o = \exp(-\beta\sum_i p_i^2/2m)\exp(-\beta F(q)) = \exp(-\beta H)$ defining the canonical equilibrium $\rho_o(p,q) = |\Phi_o|^2 = \exp(-2\beta H)$ in statistical mechanics. The energy of Φ_o is $E_o = e_o - e_o = 0$.

2) Excited states $W_k(q)$; $k = 1, 2, \ldots,$ will correspond to waves $\Phi_k = \exp(-\beta \sum_i p_i^2/2m)\, W_k(q)$ with positive energies $E_k = e_k - e_o$ defining perturbed densities

$\rho_k(p,q;0) = \exp(-2\beta \sum_i p_i^2/2m)\,|W_k(q)|^2$.

According to (13) and using the more standard notation $\beta = 1/2kT$, where k is the Boltzmann constant (not to be confused with the index k used to label the eigenstates of $\mathcal{H}$) and T is a temperature, we can write

$$H = \sum_i p_i^2/2m + F(q) = \sum_i p_i^2/2m - 2kT\ln W_o(q)$$
$$= \sum_i p_i^2/2m - kT\ln|W_o(q)|^2 .$$

Since $|W_o(q)|^2$ can be interpreted as a probability density function, we can say that $F(q) = -kT\ln|W_o(q)|^2$ is a local entropy function in the configuration space of S. Moreover, if we write

$$H = -kT\ln[\exp(-1/kT \sum_i p_i^2/2m)\,|W_o(q)|^2]$$
$$= -kT\ln|\Phi_o(p,q)|^2$$

we find that the classical potential H itself can be viewed as a local entropy function in the phase space of S or, using a different terminology, as a local source of information.

We have defined explicitly all the quantities and constants introduced up to now except the value of the temperature T of a system S.
In the next section we shall show that physical considerations lead us to fix the value of T by the relation $kT = |e_o|$

where again e_o is the energy of the ground state of the Schroedinger operator $\mathcal{H}$ associated with S.

4 - Periodic waves in phase space

The appearance of discrete modes of oscillation should be considered as a self-organizing aspect of a dynamics. We shall discuss in detail the example of an harmonic oscillator where we shall see that there exists a discrete spectrum of periodic waves. For other dynamical systems we expect in general that the waves will have a continuous frequency spectrum; these will be studied in a future work.

Let S be a mechanical system for which we assume that the potential $V(q)$ defined in (11) is $V(q) = 1/2\ m\ \omega^2\ q^2$ for some fixed angular frequency ω. In other words we assume that the Schroedinger Hamiltonian associated with S according to the formalism we have developed, is that of a quantum oscillator $\mathcal{H} = -\hbar^2/_{2m}\ \Delta + \frac{1}{2}\ m\ \omega^2\ q^2$.
It is well-known that the energy spectrum for that $\mathcal{H}$ is $e_k = (k + 1/2)\ \hbar\ \omega$, $k = 0, 1, \ldots,$ and the corresponding eigenfunctions are

$$W_k(q) = \exp(-\ m\omega\ /_{2\hbar}\ q^2)\ h_k\ [(m\omega/_{2\hbar})^{\frac{1}{2}}\ q]\ , \qquad (14)$$

where $h_k(x)$ is the Hermite polynomial of order k of the variable x. The ground state, in particular, is $W_o(q) = \exp(-\ m\omega\ /_{2\hbar}\ q^2)$ with energy $e_o = 1/_2\ \hbar\omega$.
The classical potential, according to (13), should be $F(q) = -\ 1/_{\beta}\ \ln\ W_o(q) = m\omega/_{2\beta\hbar}\ q^2 = 1/_2\ m\ \nu^2\ q^2$ where $\nu = (\omega\ /_{\beta\hbar})^{\frac{1}{2}}$.

Hence the classical Hamiltonian of S is $H = p^2/_{2m} + 1/_2\, m\nu^2 q^2$ which shows that S should be considered as an harmonic oscillator with resonance angular frequency ν.

If we introduce the dimensionless variables $P = (2\beta/_m)^{\frac{1}{2}} p$ and $Q = (2\beta m)^{\frac{1}{2}}\, \nu q$, we find that $H = 1/_\beta (P^2{}_4 + Q^2{}_4)$ and that the Hamiltonian equations of motion are $\dot{P} = -\nu Q$ and $\dot{Q} = \nu P$.

It follows immediately that

$$\Psi_k = \exp[-1/4(P^2 + Q^2)]\,(Q + iP)^k \exp(-ik\nu t) \qquad k = 0, 1, \ldots\ldots \tag{15}$$

is an orthogonal family of periodic waves which are solutions of both the wave equation (8) and equation (2). Expanding the expression $(Q + iP)^k$ and rearranging terms according to Hermite polynomials h of various order we can write (15) as follows

$$\Psi_k(p,q;t) = \Phi_k(p,q)\exp(-ik\nu t) +$$

$$\exp[-1/_4\,(P^2 + Q^2)]\{\textstyle\sum_{j=1}^{k} i^j \binom{k}{j} h_{k-j}(Q)\, h_j(P)\}$$

$$\exp(-ik\nu t),$$

where

$$\Phi_k(p,q) = \exp(-P^2/_4)\exp(-Q^2/_4)h_k(Q) = \exp(-P^2/_4)\,W_k(Q)$$

These Φ_k are the functions we introduced in (10) and the the W_k are precisely the eigenfunctions (14) of the Schroedinger Hamiltonian provided we make

$\nu = (\omega/_{\beta\hbar})^{\frac{1}{2}} = \omega$, that is $1/_\beta = 2kT = \hbar\omega$ or

$kT = 1/2\,\hbar\omega = e_0$ the ground energy of $\mathcal{H}$.

If we now average these waves $\Psi_k(p,q;t)$ over the p variable with Gaussian distribution, we obtain by using the orthogonality of the Hermite functions of different order

$$\overline{\Psi_k(q,t)} = \int \Psi_k(p,q;t)\ \exp(-\beta\ p^2/_{2m})\ dp$$

$$= \int \Phi_k(p,q)\ \exp(-\ ik\omega t)\ \exp(-\beta\ p^2/_{2m})\ dp$$

$$= W_k(Q)\ \exp(-\ ik\omega t) \quad ; \qquad k = 0,\ 1,\ \ldots\ldots$$

These averages are eigensolutions of the time-dependent Schroedinger equation

$$i\ \hbar\ \overline{\partial\Psi_k}/_{\partial t} = (\mathcal{H} - e_o)\ \overline{\Psi_k(q,t)} = E_k\ \overline{\Psi_k(q,t)},$$

where $E_k = e_k - e_o = \hbar\ \omega_k = \hbar k\omega$; $k = 0,\ 1,\ \ldots\ldots$

E_k, according to (12), is the energy of the field $\Phi_k(p,q)$ which appears now as the lowest term in the expansion of $\Psi_k(p,q;t)$ with respect to the Hermite functions of the variable $P = (2\beta/_m)^{\frac{1}{2}}\ p$. We have just shown that the self-organization of the energy spectrum $\{E_k\}$ of functions $\Phi(p,q)$ defined in (10) and the self-organization of the frequency spectrum $\{\omega_k\}$ are related by $E_k = \hbar\ \omega_k$, the fundamental relation of quantum theory.

5 - Conclusion

After we developed our formalism and knowing the kind of results one can expect, we should like now to emphasize the basic ideas on which the whole approach is based.

Given a dynamics defined by the classical Hamiltonian $H = \sum_i p_i^2/2m + F(q)$ of a system S, we consider $W_o(q) = \exp(-\beta F(q))$. If $W_o(q)$ is square-integrable and in that case the dynamics is said to be self-organizing, we build the Schroedinger Hamiltonian $\mathcal{H} = -\hbar^2/2m\ \Delta + V(q)$ such that $\mathcal{H}\,W_o(q) = e_o W_o(q)$ with $1/2\beta = |e_o|$, that is we define a Schroedinger potential $V(q) = \dfrac{\hbar^2/2m\ \Delta W_o + e_o W_o}{W_o}$.

We have seen that one interesting implication is that probability amplitudes in the phase space of S of the form $\Phi(p,q) = (-\beta\sum_i p_i^2/2m)\ W(q)$, $W(q)$ square-integrable, have a discrete wave energy spectrum $\{E_k = e_k - e_o;\ k = 0, 1, \ldots\}$ provided $\mathcal{H}$ has a discrete spectrum $\{e_k;\ k = 0, 1, \ldots\}$. According to this definition, it follows that any quantum mechanical system with Hamiltonian $= -\hbar^2/2m\Delta + V(q)$, having bound states $\{W_k(q);\ k = 0, 1, \ldots\}$ can be associated with the self-organizing dynamics of a system S whose potential is given by $F(q) = -1/\beta\ \ln W_o(q)$, $1/2\beta = |e_o|$. Moreover, in the particular case of an harmonic oscillator, we have found that there exist waves $\Psi(p,q;t)$ in the phase space of S such that

$$W(q,t) = \int\Psi(p,q;t)\,\exp(-\beta\sum_i p_i^2/2m)\,dp$$

are solutions of the time-dependent Schroedinger equation $i\hbar\, \partial W/\partial t = \mathcal{H} W$. A question to be examined in future work is wether a similar result holds in the phase space of the self-organizing system associated with other quantum mechanical systems. A positive answer to that question would suggest the fundamental fact that the system S has a physical reality and that the quantum dynamics is just an appropriate average of its classical dynamics. At any rate, it remains that the basic relation is $F(q) = - kT \ln |W_o(q)|^2$ which expresses a classical potential as a local entropy or a local source of information.

PHYSICS, STRUCTURE AND INFORMATION

F.J. Evans
Department of Electrical and Electronic
Engineering, Queen Mary College
(University of London), Mile End Road,
LONDON E1 4NS

"Suppose that we were asked to arrange the following in two categories; distance, mass, electric force, entropy, beauty, melody, I think that there are the strongest grounds for placing entropy alongside beauty and melody..... Entropy is only found when the parts are viewed in association, and it is by viewing or hearing the parts in association that beauty and melody are discerned....It is a pregnant thought that one of these associates should be able to figure as a commonplace quantity of Science."

Eddington, The Nature of Physical World, 1929

Introduction

An understanding of the behaviour of physical systems can be achieved both by assumptions concerning the physics of the system to produce a model, and by the measurement of relevant variables during some chosen behavioural experiment. In the first, the value of the model will rest on the validity of any assumptions made for reasons of simplification or expediency, and in the second care must be taken to ensure that the act of measurement itself in no way significantly modifies the system.

Attention to the mathematical structure of system models has always been necessary as a basis for the eventual mathematical *solution* but it is the physical aspects of structure that are those most relevant to the model *formulation* although these must, of course, be reflected in the mathematical form. Ideally the mathematics and the physics should be brought into the closest union, and conveniently it is electric network theory that this occurs most naturally. This is due to their unique property that the physical structure can be related completely to the abstract topology, and this can be represented by a linear graph from which the descriptive equations are systematically derived.

Historically systems have been classified into a large number of categories, not only by discipline but also in terms of their general properties - linear, nonlinear, deterministic, stochastic, lumped, distributed, conservative, dissipative - but these distinctions may not always, in reality, exist. Often the differences are only conceptual, associated with particular forms of analysis or solution, although they may with continual usage have assumed the importance of fact.

It has long been accepted that the concept of entropy has a relevance in information theory, but the nature of this association has been the source of much debate. In recent years the early central role of entropy in classical 'thermostatics' has been extended into the field of non-equilibrium behaviour by modern irreversible thermodynamics. Again, by reference to electrical network forms this can be most easily demonstrated, so that even if the original system under investigation is not itself of this class, an understanding of the 'mechanism' of its behaviour can be obtained by mapping back into a network form. The significance of the concept of entropy in the act of measurement can also be demonstrated from this point of view.

Finally, thermodynamics can make a useful contribution to our understanding of some classes of goal-seeking or self-organising behaviour in which the identification of a significant 'potential function', by which to measure the quality of performance, is required. The existence of certain naturally occurring functions can be demonstrated, and the role of these in the generation of dynamic behaviour made more explicit.

THE CLASSIFICATION OF PHYSICAL VARIABLES

The *dynamic* properties of any system reside in its ability to *store* some entity. By virtue of this storage the system simultaneously acquires energy. Associated with the system there must also be some measure of its size, or 'extent', and this measure governs the degree of storage of which it is capable. Those entities which are stored are therefore termed the 'Extensities' as they are dependent on the system 'extent'. A flow of such extensities is termed a 'Rate' and such a flow is generated by a 'Level' or, more correctly, by a 'Force' or an 'Affinity'. These are independent of the system extent, and are termed 'Intensities'. Almost without exception measurement is concerned with intensities, as they are unaffected by random variation of system extent. Superimposed on this basic classification is another concerned with the fundamental 'duality' that pervades the physical world. If all observers of a particular physical system are to agree on its characteristics there must exist certain properties that are independent of the reference axes from which the measurements were made. These properties are termed the 'invariants' and familiarly in physical systems are recognised as 'energy' and 'power'. However, it is also well known that many, if not all, direct measurements on a system are dependent on the reference axes. If, as is the case, all physical variables are again divided into two sub-classes, co-variant and contra-variant, then the product of a co-variant and a contra-variant generates an invariant. The network concepts of 'throughness' and 'acrossness' (as in current and voltage respectively) are simple reflections of the more rigorous mathematical concepts of 'variance'.

Every extensity is related to an intensity by a simple constitutive relationship (e.g. $\psi=Li$, $M=\rho V$, $q=C_V$), that contains a coefficient representing the extent of the system (e.g. inductance, volume, capacitance). In addition the extensities provide a simple, but rigorous, concept of equilibrium, which can only be said to exist when all extensities are no longer varying (i.e. all rates are zero), and therefore the degree of storage is constant.

This brief descriptive survey on the nature of physical variables is summarised in figure 1 with examples from various types of physical system.

Irreversible thermodynamics has its origin in statistical mechanics where the microscopic aspects of irreversibility are dependent on the time properties of physical variables. These can be demonstrated, to some extent, by a dimensional analysis of the classification structure. If it is postulated that the chosen coordinate has a dimensional structure of (L), then, the generalised dimensional structure is shown in figure 2, which has the same form as figure 1.

The variable classification structure outlined is not restricted to lumped systems, and the extension to distributed systems is clearly demonstrated by allowing more than one independent variable of time, and introducing the spacial variables x,y,z.

The basic structural relationships shown in figure 1 are still preserved, although expanded into tensorial form as shown in figure 3. The upper suffices indicate contra-variance, and the lower suffices co-variance. Such classification has been successfully used to generate scalar functions for use in variational methods applied to field

i	ψ
CURRENT	FLUX
q	v
CHARGE	VOLTAGE

ELECTRICAL

f	x
FORCE	DISPLAC$\overset{T}{=}$
P	v
MOMENT$\overset{M}{=}$	VELOCITY

MECHANICAL

$$\lambda = L\tau$$
$$dE_1 = \tau d\lambda$$

τ	λ
THRO' RATE INTENSITY	ACROSS STATE EXTENSITY
THRO' STATE EXTENSITY	ACROSS RATE INTENSITY
σ	α

$\frac{d}{dt}$

$\frac{d}{dt}$

$$dE_2 = \alpha d\sigma$$
$$\alpha = C\sigma$$

S ENTROPY FLOW	
S ENTROPY	T TEMPER$\overset{E}{=}$

THERMAL

GOODS FLOW	
GOODS	PRICE

ECONOMIC(?)

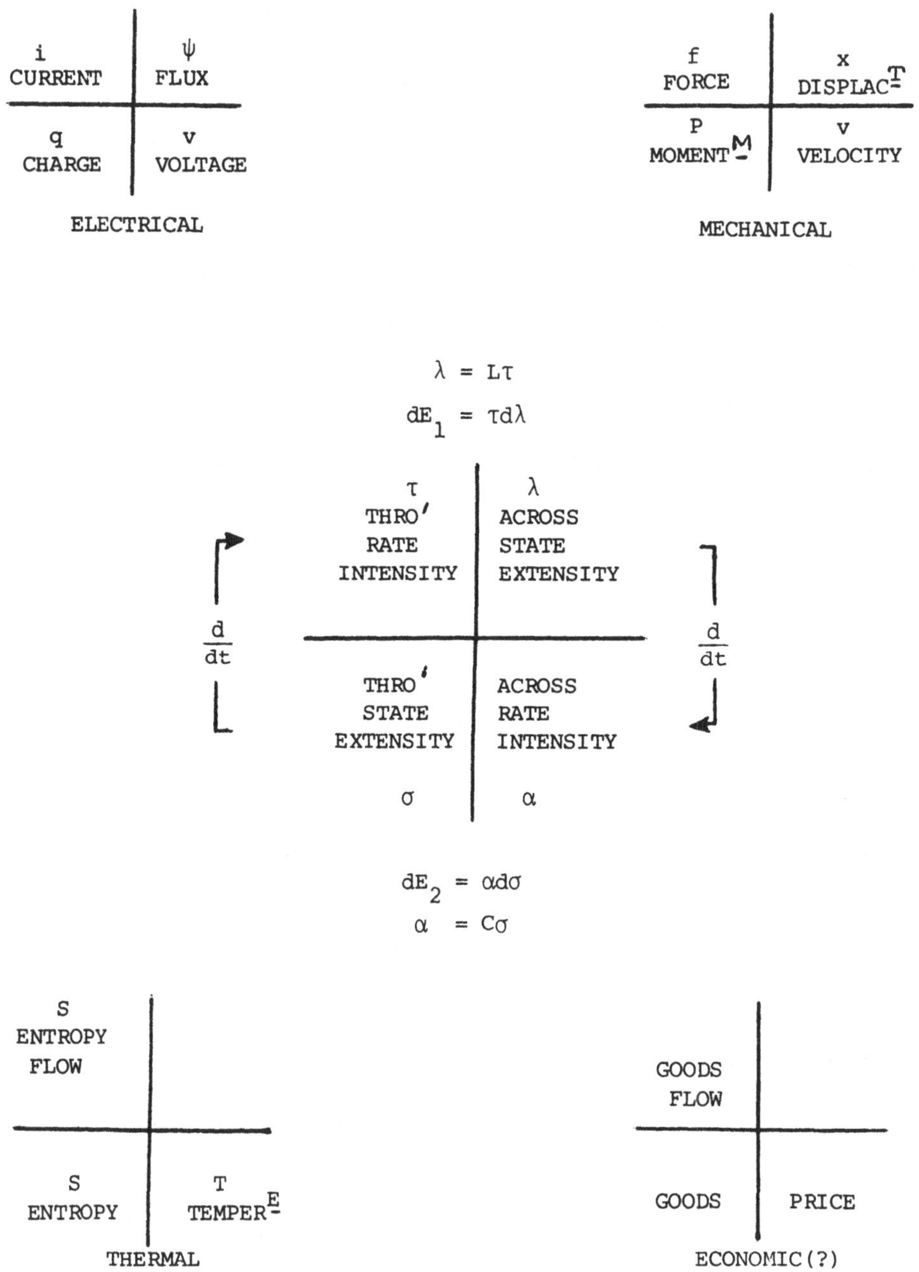

CLASSIFICATION OF PHYSICAL VARIABLES
Fig. 1

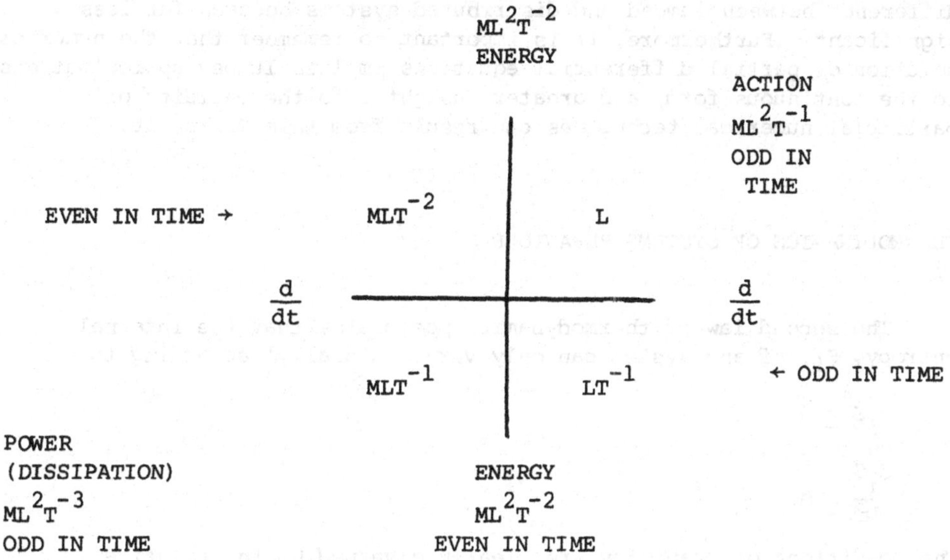

DIMENSIONAL CLASSIFICATION
Figure 2

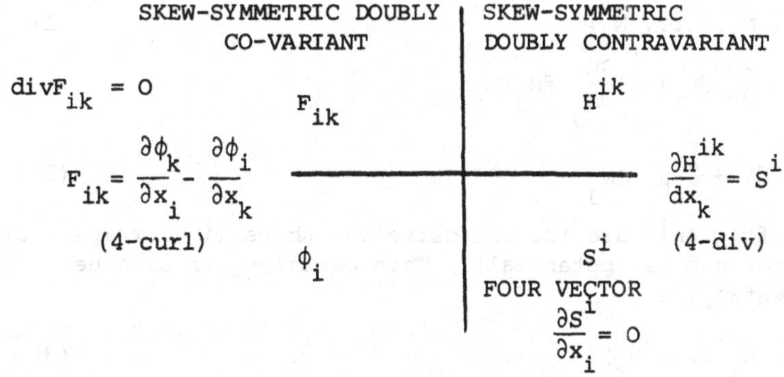

For a general field composed of an irrotational field and a complex lamellar field, there is a simpler form

ϕ becomes a scalar potential

S is considered as a 'source'

VARIABLES FOR DISTRIBUTED SYSTEMS

Figure 3

problems[1]. It should also be noted that the lumped classification is seen as a limited case of the general classification, and the conceptual difference between lumped and distributed systems becomes far less significant. Furthermore, it is important to remember that the numerical solution of partial differential equations implies lumped approximations to the continuous form, and greater insight into the validity of particular numerical techniques can result from this viewpoint.

THERMODYNAMICS OF SYSTEMS BEHAVIOUR

The second law of thermodynamics postulates that the internal entropy, S_i, of any system can only vary 'naturally' according to

$$d_iS \geq 0$$

$$\frac{d_iS}{dt} \geq 0 .$$

The conditions of stability are clearly governed by the relative magnitudes of rate of change of entropy production, and the rate of change of stored energy. Standard texts on thermodynamics[2,3] give the classical relationships and their derivations, but the following summary will suffice.

The total internal energy of a system is a function of the extensive parameters (i.e. entropy, volume, mol number etc.)

$$U = U(S, V, N_1, \dots N_r) \tag{1}$$

$$dU = \frac{\partial U}{\partial S} dS + \frac{\partial U}{\partial V} dV + \sum_1^r \frac{\partial U}{\partial N_j} dN_j$$

$$= TdS - PdV + \sum_1^r \mu_j \, dN_j \quad , \tag{2}$$

in which the coefficients are the intensive variables (i.e. temperature, pressure, electro-chemical potential). This equation can also be solved for the entropy S.

$$S = S(U, V, N_1 \dots N_r) \tag{3}$$

$$= S(X_o, X_1, \dots X_n) \quad \text{say}$$

and

$$dS = \sum_{k=0}^{n} \frac{\partial S}{\partial X_k} dX_k = \sum_{k=0}^{n} F_k dX_k \quad , \tag{4}$$

in which F_k are considered as the generalised forces, or thermodynamic affinities, which drive the process.

The variation of entropy can be written

$$dS = d_e S + d_i S \ , \qquad (5)$$

where $d_e S$ is the entropy supplied from the surroundings, and $d_i S$ is the entropy produced inside the system. Therefore we can say

$$d_i S = \sum_k F_k dX_k$$

$$\text{and } \frac{d_i S}{dt} = \sum_k F_k \frac{dX_k}{dt} = \sum_k F_k J_k = \sigma_s \text{ say.} \qquad (6)$$

There is also another relationship

$$J_k = \Sigma L_{ki} F_i \qquad (7)$$

in which the L_{ki} are the phenomenological coefficients (here considered constant). Furthermore there are distinct physical situations in which

(a) $L_{ki} = L_{ik}$ (The Onsager conditions) (8)

(b) $L_{ki} = -L_{ik}$ (The Casimir consitions) (9)

and these depend on the initial choice of fluxes and affinities, and can be explicitly demonstrated in network theory. If, however, these coefficients are not constant (linear system) we must consider the differential form

$$d\sigma_s = \sum_k F_k dJ_k + \sum_k J_k dF_k$$

$$= d\sigma_J + d\sigma_F \text{ say .} \qquad (10)$$

In the linear case

$$d\sigma_F = d\sigma_J = \tfrac{1}{2} d\sigma_s \ .$$

In the nonlinear case we can also write

$$\sigma_s = \frac{d\sigma_s}{dt} = \sigma_J + \sigma_F \ .$$

The first of these terms σ_J has no sign definite properties but the second σ_F is negative-zero, and therefore possesses a special significance. This inequality is the basic differential law for the time evolution of physical systems to which no exceptions are known in processes with constant boundary conditions. The integral of the differential $d\sigma_F$, if it exists, has been termed the thermo-kinetic potential. Therefore if

$$d\sigma_F = \sum_k J_K \, dF_K$$

$$\sigma_F = \int J dF$$

and

$$J = \text{grad}_F \, \sigma_F . \qquad (11)$$

It is the identification of the function σ_F that is central to the whole analytic problem. Its integrability is related directly to the more well-known concepts of reciprocity and conservation. In a system in which irreversible processes are taking place, the existence of any steady state os dependent on the minimum achievable value of σ_F consistent with the constraints imposed by the constituent nature of the system.

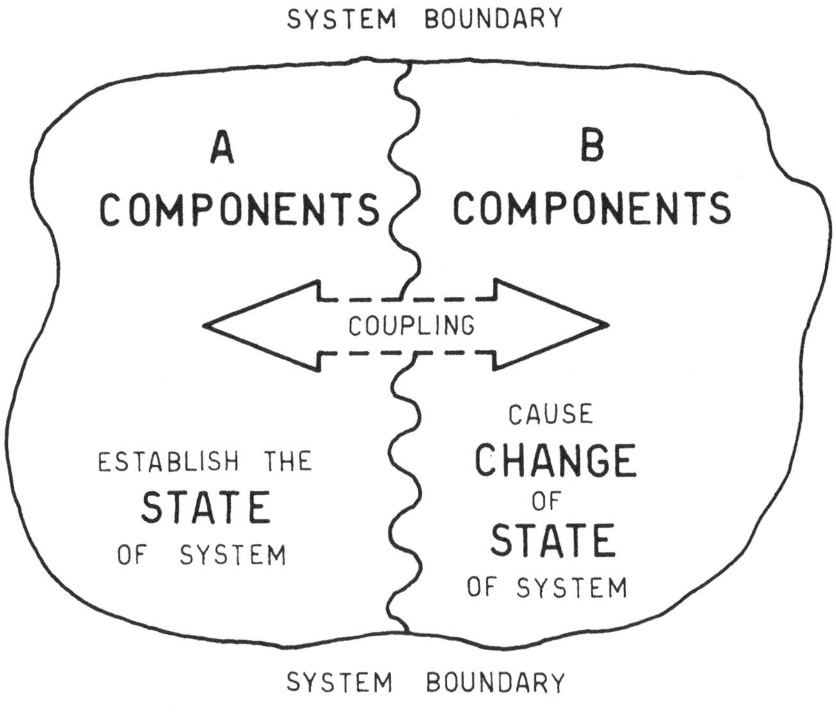

Fig. 4 BASIC SYSTEM PARADIGM

BASIC SYSTEM PARADIGM

A useful basic system paradigm is shown in figure 4. Thermodynamics is concerned with systems that have an interaction with an external environment with respect to the passage of heat, or an application of work. This is conventionally stated in the first law of thermodynamics. We are concerned with similar concepts but the boundaries of the system, and any interaction across these will be re-examined by considering those systems that are bounded and suffer a change of internal energy due to a performance of work.

The two classes of components are shown coupled and this connectivity can be considered as a transformation between variables. The nature of such coupling does, in effect, create functional dependencies which arise due to energy conversion and amplification within the system. It should be noted that the partitioning of the system components suggested here into two sub-systems does not necessarily coincide with the separation of all storage elements from all non-storage elements (i.e. dissipators). For example, it is possible to conceive that in a simple mechanical system, containing only a mass suspended from a spring, the partitioning would, by necessity, separate the mass from the spring. If, on the other hand, this simple system included a frictional damper the subdivision may be accomplished by separating both of the storage devices (mass and spring) from the dissipating element. It is important to realise that the only criterion for the partitioning of a system in this way is that the sub-system A contains at least sufficient of the system to uniquely define its state. There is, therefore, usually more than one way of doing this.

So one can conclude that a study of the transient nature of the system behaviour requires that one firstly identifies an entropic function, defined in terms of a set of measurable intensive coordinates related to the B set of components. Secondly that a final description must be in terms of a set of intensive coordinates related to the A set of components. Implicit in the solution of the problem there is, therefore, a transformation from one set of coordinates to another, and the ability to define all the necessary state functions in terms of either. It is network theory that makes this possible in a clear fashion by its structure and associated well defined analysis.

BASIC NETWORK PROPERTIES

In network theory the choice of sets of independent variables is achieved for any configuration by the division of the network into tree and co-tree (links). It is then possible to write

$$\begin{bmatrix} i_t \\ v_l \end{bmatrix} = \begin{bmatrix} 0 & D \\ -D' & 0 \end{bmatrix} \begin{bmatrix} v_t \\ i_l \end{bmatrix} , \tag{12}$$

in which the suffices refer to tree and link branches, and the matrix D is called the dynamical transformation matrix.

As a result of this equation we have

$$\langle i,v \rangle = 0$$

over all branches and this is known as Tellegen's Theorem, and it states that power is conserved over the whole network. From equation (12) above and the constitutive relationships of the network elements, a set of first order differential equations - known as state space equations can be derived of the form

$$\begin{bmatrix} v_L \\ i_C \end{bmatrix} = \begin{bmatrix} L & 0 \\ 0 & C \end{bmatrix} \begin{bmatrix} \dot{i}_L \\ \dot{v}_C \end{bmatrix} = \begin{bmatrix} -R_t & -a \\ a & -G_l \end{bmatrix} \begin{bmatrix} i_L \\ v_C \end{bmatrix} , \tag{13}$$

in which the suffices L and C refer to inductor and capacitor respectively, and L, C, R and G are diagonal matrices of inductances, capacitances, resistors and admittances respectively. If the following power functions are now defined according to Cherry [4]

$$\text{Content} = G = \int v\,di \tag{14}$$

$$\text{Co-content} = J = \int i\,dv \tag{15}$$

we can clearly write

$$i_t = \text{grad}_{v_t} J_t(v_t) = D\ \text{grad}_{v_l} J_l(v_l) \tag{16}$$

and

$$v_l = \text{grad}_{i_l} G_l(i_l) = -D'\text{grad}_{i_t} G_t(i_t) . \tag{17}$$

Both of these equations are of the form of the earlier thermodynamic equation 11 which was of special significance. In the first case it is the tree currents that are assuming the role of the thermodynamic fluxes, and in the second, it is the link voltages. The choice of a tree might be made so that it is completely resistive, or completely non-resistive so that we should then have respectively

$$v_{Sl} = D'\ \text{grad}_{iRt}[-G_t(i_{Rt})] \tag{18}$$

$$i_{st} = D\ \text{grad}_{vRl}[J_l(v_{Rl})] , \tag{19}$$

in which the suffices S and R refer to storage and resistive elements respectively. Then it is seen that we have achieved the transformation between storage variables and the dissipative variables referred to earlier. However, the correct *physical* assignment of the 'thermo-dynamic' fluxes for networks with mixed storage elements can only be achieved if a preferred tree is chosen containing all the capacitors and all the voltage sources, and a co-tree of all inductors and current sources. The resistors can be allocated as necessary. We shall then derive the equations of the form shown in equations 13, but these cannot be expressed as a pure gradient form, but only in terms of a topologically extended form of the Brayton-Moser mixed potential[5] function P_T where

$$dP_T = -i_t dv_t + v_l di_l$$
$$= -dJ_t + dG_l \quad . \tag{20}$$

We would then have

$$i_{st} = \frac{\partial(P_T)}{\partial i_{sl}}$$
$$i_{st} = \frac{\partial(-P_T)}{\partial v_{st}} \quad . \tag{21}$$

The significance of the potential functions expressed above has been discussed at greater length elsewhere[6], and also their relation to the general variational description of electrical networks and the tensorial field models that result.

For present purposes the foregoing should be taken as minimal evidence of the fact that electrical networks can be described in a thermodynamic manner, and that the 'entropic' function σ_F in equation 11 can be related to definable functions derived from the network. It is clearly necessary to examine that the mathematical conditions for the integrability of such functions do, in fact, exist. At this point it should be noted that these conditions are manifest in the structure of the network equations, which in turn reflect the physical structure of the system itself. It has also been shown elsewhere[7] that, in broad terms, network equations can be derived in the following alternative forms, each of which is associated with a particular potential function, the existence of which demands certain conditions as follows

(i)
$$\begin{bmatrix} v_{Sl} \\ i_{St} \end{bmatrix} = \begin{bmatrix} -R_t & -a \\ a' & -G_l \end{bmatrix} \begin{bmatrix} i_{Sl} \\ v_{St} \end{bmatrix} = \begin{bmatrix} \dfrac{\partial P}{\partial i_{Sl}} \\ -\dfrac{\partial P}{\partial v_{St}} \end{bmatrix} \tag{22}$$

with the condition for the integrability of P

$$\frac{\partial}{\partial v_{St}}\left(\frac{\partial P}{\partial i_{Sl}}\right) = \frac{\partial}{\partial i_{Sl}}\left(\frac{\partial P}{\partial v_{St}}\right) \qquad (23)$$

which is satisfied by the existence of the skew-symmetry. This case corresponds to the choice of a tree containing all capacitors and voltage sources.

(ii)
$$\begin{bmatrix} v_{Sl} \\ v_{St} \end{bmatrix} = \begin{bmatrix} \underset{\sim}{A} \\ \text{SYMMETRIC} \end{bmatrix} \begin{bmatrix} i_{Sl} \\ i_{St} \end{bmatrix} = \begin{bmatrix} \partial G/\partial i_{Sl} \\ \partial G/\partial i_{St} \end{bmatrix} . \qquad (24)$$

In this equation, as the constant A matrix is symmetrical this is sufficient to provide the integrability conditions for the potential function G, which is the system total content as previously defined. This case results from a choice of a completely resistive tree (with voltage sources)

(iii) and (iv) there are two cases dual to those above, one associated with a co-mixed potential function (resulting in two integral equations), and the other with the system total co-content J (for a resistive co-tree)

All of these forms above can be related to those in the thermodynamic equations 11 above. So it can be concluded that the conditions for the existence of the required 'entropic' functions are a reflection of the physical validity of the model. The question then arises 'Under what conditions can equations be presented which could be unacceptable in any given situation?'. In almost all situations such conditions arise due to assumptions about measurement, and the passage of information from one part of the system to the other, but unfortunately the criterion of physical acceptability need not be that which would prevent the equations serving as an approximate model of the system. It could, however, be that which would prevent a description of the system in terms of some meaningful potential function.

COUPLERS AND FUNCTIONAL DEPENDENCY

The conventional transformer can be considered as the archetypal coupler, and its descriptive equation is of the form (when lossless)

$$\begin{bmatrix} v_1 \\ i_1 \end{bmatrix} = \begin{bmatrix} K & 0 \\ 0 & K^{-1} \end{bmatrix} \begin{bmatrix} v_2 \\ i_2 \end{bmatrix} . \qquad (25)$$

This can be generalised, however, to the form

$$\begin{bmatrix} v_1 \\ i_1 \end{bmatrix} = \begin{bmatrix} a_{11} & a_{12} \\ a_{21} & a_{22} \end{bmatrix} \begin{bmatrix} v_2 \\ i_2 \end{bmatrix}, \tag{26}$$

in which, in theory, the elements a_{ij} can have any zero or non-zero values. Then we can define the following classes of dependency[8]

(i) $a_{12} = 0 = a_{21}$ and $a_{22} \neq a_{11}^{-1}$.

A non-conservative transformer type coupler since summation of power over all the ports is not zero.

(ii) $a_{12} = 0 = a_{21}$ and $a_{22} = a_{11}^{-1}$.

A conservative transformer type coupler

(iii) $a_{11} = 0 = a_{22}$ and $a_{21} \neq a_{12}^{-1}$.

A non-conservative, non-reciprocal coupler

(iv) $a_{11} = 0 = a_{22}$ and $a_{21} = a_{12}^{-1}$

A gyrator type coupler.

The coupler concept need not be restricted to a relationship between variables of the same physical nature, but can relate mixed variable sub-systems (e.g. electrical-mechanical). Now clearly if only one element of such a matrix was non-zero, no flow of power would be implied, and a perfect transducer would be indicated. However, such an assumption can destroy, within the equations, the conditions which are demanded by 'physical' reality, apart from those necessary for the description of the system in terms of useful potential functions. This can be illustrated by a simple example.

Consider a simple electrical network as shown in the figure 5

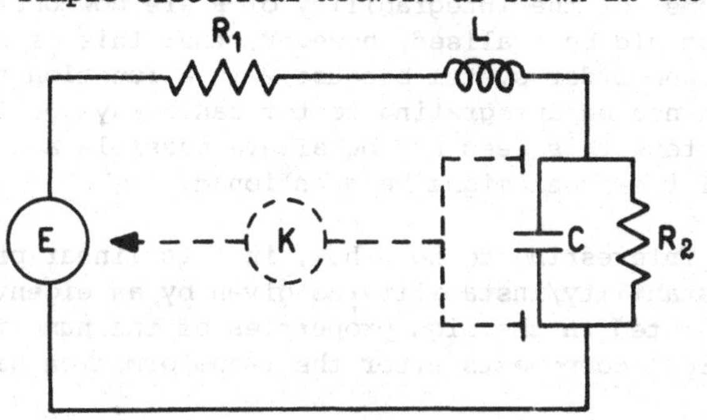

Fig. 5

This network could, with good reason, be considered as a model for a simple d.c. motor (with constant field conditions), in which R_1 and L are the armature electrical parameters, and R_2 and C are the armature mechanical parameters. The equation for this circuit are

$$\begin{bmatrix} L\dot{i}_L \\ C\dot{v}_C \end{bmatrix} = \begin{bmatrix} -R_1 & -1 \\ 1 & -R_2^{-1} \end{bmatrix} \begin{bmatrix} i_L \\ v_C \end{bmatrix} + \begin{bmatrix} E \\ 0 \end{bmatrix} . \tag{27}$$

In these v_C could be considered as the shaft angular velocity, i_L as the armature current, and E as the applied voltage to the armature. If we now close the loop by the simple expedient of adding the condition $E=kv_C$, as shown in the figure by a dotted line, the skew-symmetry is destroyed. Physically this could be considered as a closing of the loop by a perfect tachometer that drew no power from the system (i.e. lossless). So we now have

$$\begin{bmatrix} L\dot{i}_L \\ C\dot{v}_C \end{bmatrix} = \begin{bmatrix} -R_1 & -1+k \\ 1 & -R_2^{-1} \end{bmatrix} \begin{bmatrix} i_L \\ v_C \end{bmatrix} , \tag{28}$$

in which the skew-symmetry has been destroyed. If we now perform a simple variable transformation $v_C^* = (1-k)\, v_C$ we obtain

$$\begin{bmatrix} L\dot{i}_L \\ \dfrac{C}{(1-k)} \dot{v}_C^* \end{bmatrix} = \begin{bmatrix} -R_1 & -1 \\ 1 & \dfrac{-R_2^{-1}}{(1-k)} \end{bmatrix} \begin{bmatrix} i_L \\ v_C^* \end{bmatrix} \tag{29}$$

and we see that the skew-symmetry is restored, and we now write

$$\begin{bmatrix} L\dot{i}_L \\ \dfrac{C}{(1-k)} \dot{v}_C^* \end{bmatrix} = \begin{bmatrix} \dfrac{\partial P}{\partial i_L} \\ -\dfrac{\partial P}{\partial v_C^*} \end{bmatrix} \tag{30}$$

and the conditions for the integrability of P are now once more satisfied. It should be realised, however, that this is only possible here in this second order system because P is a function of only two variables, and hence an integrating factor can always be found. For higher order systems this need not be always possible and the 'physicality' of the model might be questioned.

It is also interesting to note how, in this linear problem, the conditions for stability/instability, as given by an eigenvalue solution, are clearly reflected in the sign properties of the numerical values of the actual physical components after the transformation has been performed.

The problem of integrability can arise easily in models of higher order where the descriptive equations have been supplied in a form in which much valuable physically based structure has already been lost due to previous approximation. It is sometimes possible to restore this to some extent in a quasi-fashion by mapping the problem back into an electrical network form. Nonetheless it is always important to remember that planar electrical networks are fundamentally systems with one degree of freedom, and the problem can be considerably complicated by the need to introduce non-linear coupling devices.

STATE SPACE EQUATIONS

In modern dynamic systems analysis state space models consisting of sets of first order differential equations are used of the form

$$x = Ax + Bu \ .$$

Considering the autonomous case, when $B = 0$, and using the general relationship

$$A = \tfrac{1}{2}(A+A') + \tfrac{1}{2}(A-A')$$

$$= A^{+} + A^{-} \quad \text{say} \ ,$$

in which A^{+} is always symmetric and A^{-} always skew-symmetric, we can see that the velocity vector is now the resultant of two vectors, one of which is orthogonal to the x vector

$$\dot{x} = A\,x + A^{-}\,x$$

and

$$x'.A\,x = 0 \text{ always} \ .$$

Then for a large class of problem - although not for a universal class - a field description, in configuration space, of these differential equations can be proposed. This is possible even if A is not a constant matrix, but satisfies certain other conditions, and this can be considered as an example of the classical Helmholtz theorem that any vector field V can be expressed as

$$V = V_1 + V_2 \ ,$$

where

$$V_1 = \text{grad}\phi$$

and

$$V_2 = \text{curl}\psi$$

and ϕ is a scalar potential and ψ is a vector potential.

It is also necessary that the following conditions also exist

$$\text{curl grad}\phi = 0$$

and

$$\text{div curl } \psi = 0 \,.$$

Mapping the previous equation of the earlier simple electrical network into this form we obtain

$$\begin{bmatrix} \dot{i}_L \\ \dot{v}_C \end{bmatrix} = \begin{bmatrix} L^{-1} & 0 \\ 0 & C^{-1} \end{bmatrix} \left[\begin{bmatrix} -R_1 & 0 \\ 0 & -R_2^{-1} \end{bmatrix} + \begin{bmatrix} 0 & -1 \\ 1 & 0 \end{bmatrix} \right] \begin{bmatrix} i_L \\ v_C \end{bmatrix} \tag{31}$$

and we see that the matrix A^+ is related to all the resistors and the matrix A^- is related to the presence of the storage elements in the system, L and C. Therefore ϕ must be an entropic, or dissipative, function of the form

$$\phi = \tfrac{1}{2} \begin{bmatrix} i_L, & v_C \end{bmatrix} \begin{bmatrix} -R_1 & 0 \\ 0 & -R_2^{-1} \end{bmatrix} \begin{bmatrix} i_L \\ v_C \end{bmatrix} \tag{32}$$

and this will control the general stability properties of the system. The ψ function will be concerned with the periodicity and this can be considered as the generalised 'quadrature' component.

The full implications of this approach and its scope and limitations are fully discussed elsewhere[9], but there is much evidence to show that it enlarges considerably the ability to analyse, in a qualitative sense, a wide class of non-linear problem. Furthermore such a functional form of analysis may, in the future, be directly relatable to a group theoretic approach and a more rigorous algebra of linear operators which could provide further valuable insight.

ENTROPY AND MEASUREMENT

The foregoing has attempted to briefly summarise the role played by entropic functions in the time evolution of dynamic systems. Aspects of this suggest further generalisations concerning the role of entropy in the act of measurement and the interaction of subsystems within larger organisation. In other words the role it performs in the acquisition and the passage of information.

The following presents a condensation of work reported elsewhere[10]. It was shown in figure 1 that, in thermal systems, the basic variables were temperature T, entropy S and entropy flow S. The unique position of the concept of entropy with respect to the notion of information has long been discussed, and here we shall now attempt to support the proposal that the thermal formulation be mapped into a wider generalisation as shown below

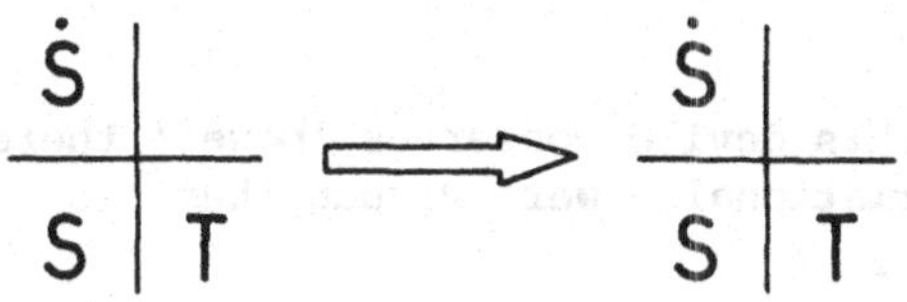

in which I - information - is considered as a generalised, or primitive intensity, embracing all types of measurement. It should therefore follow that entropy be considered as the primitive extensity that spans the whole physical world. It is this universality of information and entropy that will now be emphasised. Because of the need to be universally accommodated there cannot be identified any particular type of entropy storage device (unlike a capacitor, for example, that can be identified as a charge storing device), except the organisation of the system structure itself, by virtue of which the entropy is considered as being accumulated. Entropy is the only extensity that can pass between systems of different classes (e.g. electrical-mechanical). It thereby provides a medium of communication between them and also, of course, between a system and its environment.

Likewise we can consider information as the generalised quantity that can be measured, and due to the relation between it and entropy, it is not possible to obtain any measurement without the system passing entropy to the outside world. It is, as Jaynes has stated, that a system itself may well be reversible but our ability to follow it is not. Engineering and Physics are traditionally concerned with the design and use of measuring instruments that have minimum insertion loss, and therefore the problem of entropy flow is often of no significance. Simple transfer function analysis has, it could be claimed, done a disservice to systems analysis by making it unnecessary to recognise this fact, by only representing uni-directional flows of information. In non-engineering systems, such as economics and social systems, this condition may no longer exist, and the whole problem of optimisation could become a vastly more complicated problem. It is being suggested here that the aspect of uncertainty introduced into large scale information handling systems might be structurally accommodated by the ideas proposed.

Consider a coupler of the transformer type, in which entropy flow and information assume the traditional roles of current and voltage

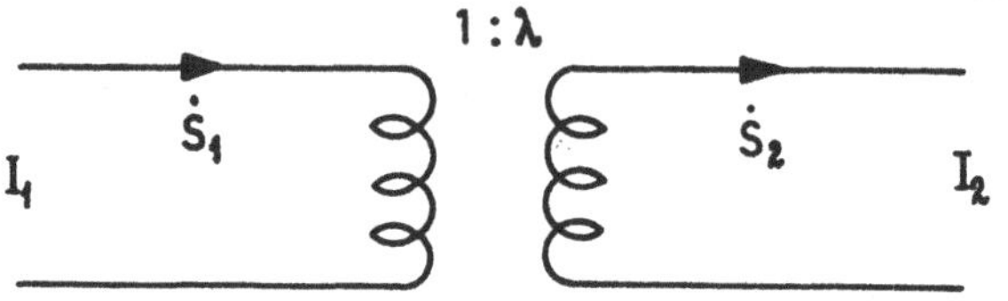

Then, since this device conserves 'power' there will be postulated a quantity, 'Informational power' P, such that

$$P = I_1\dot{S}_1 = I_2\dot{S}_2 \ . \quad (33)$$

The ratio 1:λ can be considered as representing the insertion loss of the measuring device, and it will be assumed that for a perfect device $\lambda = 1$. But in all real situations

$$I_2 = \lambda I_1$$
$$\dot{S}_1 = \lambda\dot{S}_2 \quad (34)$$

and $\lambda < 1$.

Therefore

$$I_2 < I_1$$

and $\dot{S}_2 > \dot{S}_1$.

This concept is in keeping with an earlier one of Thoma[11] used to describe the generation of entropy in thermal systems. Continuing this analogy we can suggest that, in keeping with 'efficiency' definitions for thermal engines, we can define an uncertainty (i.e. an informational efficiency) by

$$\xi = \frac{I_1 - I_2}{I_1} = 1 - \frac{I_2}{I_1} = 1 - \frac{S_1}{S_2}$$

$$= 1 - \lambda . \quad (35)$$

Hence if $\lambda = 1$, when the device is perfect, the uncertainty is zero, and the efficiency therefore, in the normal sense, would be 100%. Any aspect of the design of the measuring device which tends to increase $\dot{S}_2$ must, as in the case of a conventional transformer affect the current (i.e. in this case $\dot{S}_1$) on the primary side.

SOME OPEN QUESTIONS AND FUTURE PATHS

The whole question of information with reference to dynamic systems, or in other words, the development of a dynamic theory of information, brings attention to a number of very fundamental points. Some of these have been briefly discussed above but a recapitulation is probably worthwhile. Most of them arise from the fact that some long cherished concepts are being subjected to close scrutiny, and these mostly concern the conceptual classifications and partitioning that we have imposed on the physical phenomena that we experience. We do this, as stated in the introduction, often for reasons of solution or analysis only, but with continual use they assume an unquestioned reality.

For example linear systems and conservative systems (i.e. lossless systems) never occur in reality, and yet they often hold a signigicant position in our analysis because they possess more tractable forms of solution.

A lumped system is simply a distributed system with one independent variable, and high order lumped systems can be usefully represented by multi-dimensional field models.

A stochastic process with probabilities of unity becomes deterministic without any change of structure. It is not certain that we are always clear wherein lies the uncertainty in a system. Can we always distinguish between systems of constant structure that process information in a deterministic way but are in a random environment, from those which have a random structure and a determined environment?

Is the concept of feedback often reduced to an over-simplified form that bears little resemblance to the reality of measurement and transmission of information?

What can be learned and usefully applied from more classical notions in thermodynamics, not only concerning the more well known concept of entropy, but more generally in relation to the aggregation of information? It has long been recognised that significant scalar potentials exist that provide a measure of system state 'summed' over the whole system (e.g. temperature), and that the total internal energy is a function of the stored 'extensities' - one of which is entropy.

What is the mechanism by means of which information can be extracted from a system?

Is it possible for self-organisation, or self-optimisation, to occur by any other means than the minimisation, or maximisation, of a funadmental potential function? Can such functions be systematically extracted from knowledge of the system structure?

Do we really understand the nature of 'discreteness' in system structure? Is it necessary to maintain an apparent distinction between discreteness in time and discreteness in state? Is there any relation between them?

Many of these questions have been posed, in one form or another, during the past few years, particularly with regard to problems that present themselves in biology, chemical kinetics and economics. Much of this interdisciplinary literature is beginning to exhibit interesting inter-relationships based on a few fundamental sets of concepts. To establish any degree of comparison between different fields it is necessary to formulate an underlying algebraic or geometric structure onto which a reasonably large class of problem can be mapped.

The first attempt was that of Gabriel Kron based on a novel approach to circuit analysis, which he named 'Diakoptics', and a rather unconventional use of the tensor calculus that enabled him to exploit the concepts of transformation, groups and invariance. He was also amongst the first to demonstrate the engineering applications of combinatorial topology and differential geometry. The amazing extent of the applications of Kron's methods can only be fully appreciated by examination of his published work, much of which is collected together in a single volume 'Diakoptics'[12]. It is a remarkable fact that a single conceptual idea can provide a unifying framework for such a diversity of problems that include the solution of non-linear partial differential equations, adaptive control, optimal control and filtering, scattering theory, self-organising automata, some aspects of brain function, and least squares estimation[13,14,15].

The more recent work of Branin[16] extended Kron's ideas to higher dimensional topological structures and provided a direct link-up between network theory and the vector calculus. The structure which Branin proposes was developed independently by Tonti[17,18] and further extended to serve as a formal structure for a very large class of physical theory.

Jumarie[19] has recently proposed new concepts of 'structural entropy', and 'information potential' and also defined an 'information evolution principle'. He proceeds to make tentative correlations between these and the recent, but well known, work of Thom that is now collectively subsumed under the title of 'Catatrophe Theory'. Thom has proposed a qualitative, but well structured, form of analysis which has particular application in the field of biology and the evolutionary processes in living systems. He poses the existence of a class of potential function which governs the whole nature of evolution in time for a given system, and particularly determines the conditions for sudden changes of behaviour.

Also in biology much attention is now being given to possible structures by means of which living organisms maintain a periodicity, by chemical means, even in the absence of apparent environmental stimulation[20]. There are also many provocative questions concerning the transmission of information, not only within a single living cell, but between different cells and also between unconnected organisms. A particularly interesting class of problems concerned with the latter are those related to establishing conditions for entrainment between a population of non-linear oscillators. Goodwin[21] invoked some fairly sophisticated thermodynamic concepts and statistical techniques to further our insight into the temporal and spacial organisation of living cells.

Another interesting development of the last 10 years has grown from the original work of Zadeh[22] on 'Fuzzy Set Theory'. The most recent review of this field is the report on the recent meetings at the 6th IFAC Congress, 1975 on 'Fuzzy Automata and Decision Processes'.[23] It is significant that Aizerman, in a paper presented to this meeting, suggests that our obsession, so far, for the exact explicit solution to problems will need to be replaced by methods of description and analysis more able to accommodate the imprecise boundaries of our knowledge, and the subjective nature of our value judgements and indices of performance. An amalgamation of the type of linguistic description of systems proposed by Zadeh and the qualitative dynamics expressed in terms of informational potential functions would seem to be extremely probable in the future.

Equally probable is the possibility that all of the analytical content of this paper, and the more speculative topics, will eventually become more closely bound by exciting extensions of some well-established concepts, and a strengthening of the underlying algebraic and geometric structure the elements of which are already identifiable.

REFERENCES

1. Jones, D.L. and Evans, F.J., 'A Classification of physical Variables and its Application in variational Methods', *J. Frank. Inst.*, 291, 449, 1971.

2. Callen, H.B., *Thermodynamics*, Wiley, New York, 1960.

3. Prigogine, I., *Introduction to the Thermodynamics of irreversible Processes*, Charles C. Thomas, 1955.

4. Cherry, C., Some general Theorems for Non-linear Networks possessing Reactance, *Phil. Mag.*, 42, 1161, 1951.

5. Brayton, R.K. and Moser, J.K., A Theory of Non-linear Networks, *Quart, Appl. Maths.*, 22, 1, 1964.

6. Jones, D.L. and Evans, F.J., Variational Analysis of Electrical Networks, *J. Frank. Inst.*, 295, 9, 1973.

7. Flower, J.O. and Evans, F.J., Irreversible Thermodynamics and Stability Considerations of Electrical Networks, *J. Frank. Inst.*, 291, 123, 1971.

8. Korn, J., Evans, F.J. and Holding, D.J., Thermodynamics and Field Theory as a Basis for Systems Dynamics, *Physical Structure in Systems Theory,* Van Dixhoorn and Evans, F.J. Eds., Academic Press, 167, 1974.

9. Abd-Ali, A., Fradellos, G. and Evans, F.J., Structural Aspects of Stability in Non-linear Systems, to appear in the *Int. J. of Control* (Parts I and II).

10. Evans, F.J. and Langholz, G., Uncertainty, Measurement and Thermodynamics of Information, *Int. J. Systems Science,* (GB), 6, 281, 1975.

11. Thoma, J.U., Bond Graphs for Thermal Energy Transport and Entropy Flow, *J. Frank. Inst.,* 292, 109, 1971.

12. Kron, G., *Diakoptics*, MacDonald, London, 1963.

13. Lynn, J.W. and Russell, R.A., Kron's Wave Automaton, *Physical Structure in Systems Theory*, Van Dixhoorn and Evans, F.J., Eds., Academic Press, London, 131, 1974.

14. Nicholson, H.H., Structure of Kron's Polyhedron Model and the Scattering Problem, *Proc. IEE*, 120, 1545, 1973.

15. Kron, G., Multidimensional Curve Fitting with self-organising Automata, *J. Math and Anal. and Appl.*, 5, 46, 1962.

16. Branin, F.H., The algebraic topological basis for Network Analogies and the Vector Calculus, Symp. on Generalised Networks, Polytechnic Inst. of Brooklyn, April 1966.

17. Tonti, E., A Mathematical Model for physical Theories, *Rend. Accad. Naz. Linc.*, Serie VIII, LII, 175 and 350, 1972.

18. Tonti, E., On the formal Structure of physical Theories, *Istituto di Matematica del Politecnico di Milano.*

19. Jumarie, G., Structural Entropy, Information Potential, Information Balance and Evolution in self-organising Systems, *Int. J. Systems Sci*, (GB), 5, 953, 1974.

20. Pavlidis, T., *Biological Oscillators, their Mathematical Analysis*, Academic Press, 1974.

21. Goodwin, D., *The Temporal Organisation of Cells*, Academic Press, 1964.

22. Zadeh, L.A., Outline of a New approach to the analysis of complex systems and decision Processes, *IEEE Trans. Systems, Man and Cybernetics*, Vol. SMC-3, January 1973.

23. Mamdani, E.H., Report on the 2nd Round Table discussion on Fuzzy Automata and Decision Processes, *Proc. 6th IFAC Congress*, Boston, 1975, to appear in Automatica.

Part Two

SHANNON THEORY

A GENERALIZATION OF THE RATE - DISTORTION THEORY AND APPLICATIONS

Moshe Zakai and Jacob Ziv
Department of Electrical Engineering
Technion - Israel Institute of Technology
Haifa, Israel.

1. Introduction

We start with the well known model of a communication system:

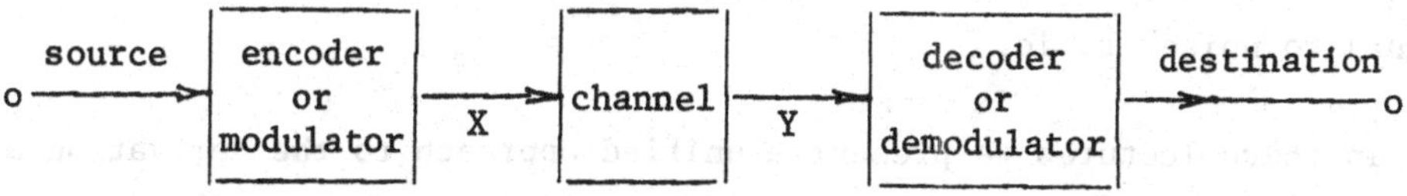

Figure 1

We assume that we have a certain fidelity criterion, namely a numerical criterion for determining how well the system output reproduces its input. The basic problem is to determine the optimal coder and decoder and to evaluate the performance of the optimal system.

This is the basic problem of Information Theory. Exact solutions to this problem are, in general, unknown. The Rate-Distortion theory, which is an important development of Information Theory, provides us with partial solutions to the problem. The Rate Distortion Theory provides us with bounds on the performance of optimal systems; these bounds are asymptotically tight in the sense that they can be approximated by using sufficiently long block codes. We refer the reader to the book by Berger[1] for an exhaustive treatment of the subject.

In communication theory, the encoder or modulator is usually prescribed. In this case the optimal demodulator is, at least in principle, determined explicitly by Bayes rule. An important part of communication theory deals with the evaluation of the performance index for a given modulator. Different setups are considered (such as P.P.M., F.M., Radar, etc.), but the exact evaluation of the performance index is usually difficult or impossible. Here too, bounds on the performance index are of considerable importance. Of particular interest are bounds which are asymptotically tight where "asymptotically" refers to large values of "signal to noise" ratio.

In these lectures we present a unified approach to the derivation of lower bounds on communication and information systems.

Before reviewing the content of the following sections, we give a rough and very short outline of the Rate-Distortion bound of information theory[1]. Let (X,Y) be a pair of discrete valued random variables with a joint probability distribution $P(x,y)$. The mutual information between X and Y is given by

$$I(X,Y) = - \sum_{x,y} P(x,y) \log \frac{P(x)P(y)}{P(x,y)}$$

where $P(x) = \sum_y P(x,y)$, $P(y) = \sum_x P(x,y)$. Let the channel be characterized by the transition probability $P(y|x)$. The channel capacity C is defined as $C = \sup I(X,Y)$ where the supremum is carried over the class of all channel input probabilities $P(x)$ or a subclass satisfying certain constraints (such as an average or peak power constraint). The source U, which is assumed to be discrete, is characterized by a probability distribution $P(u)$. At this point our notation calls for an explanation, we should have used $P_{XY}(x,y)$ and $P_U(u)$ for the channel and source, respectively. Rather than doing this, we use the short-hand notation $P(x,y) \triangleq P_{X,Y}(x,y)$, $P(u) \triangleq P_Y(u)$, etc. This notation will be used throughout the paper.

To the source U, we attach a distortion measure (fidelity criterion) $d(u,v)$ defined on $U \times V$ where V takes values in the same space as U. The rate distortion function associated with the source U is defined by $R(d) = \inf I(U,V)$, where the infimum is taken over all transition probabilities $P(v|u)$ satisfying $Ed(u,v) \leq d$.

The main result of Rate-Distortion theory is the bound

$$R(d) \leq C \qquad (1.1)$$

which leads directly to lower bounds on the achievable distortion[1].

The basic tool in proving (1.1) is the data processing theorem, namely $I(U,V) \leq I(X,Y)$.

In this paper we consider a family of functionals which includes, as a special case, the mutual information functional $I(X,Y)$. We show that the generalized family of functionals satisfies a data processing theorem and this leads to a generalized equivalent of (1.1), thus widening the

In ref. 3, Csizar considered a generalization of $I(X,Y)$ by replacing $-\log\left(\frac{P(x)P(y)}{P(x,y)}\right)$ with a general convex function of $P(x)P(y)/P(x,y)$, and derived a corresponding data processing theorem. The implications to rate distortion theory were not considered in ref. 3. The same idea was introduced independently in ref. 2, where the objective was mainly that of the derivation of a generalized rate distortion bound as a bounding tool on the average distortion. The results presented here generalize considerably the results of refs. 2 and 3, and are applicable to both the information theoretic and communication theoretic models.

In the next section we summarize some properties of convex functions of a single or several real variables, and review the Bayes decision rule. A generalized entropy functional is introduced in Section 3, and a data processing theorem is proved. The results of Section 3 are applied in Section 4 to problems of communication theory. Examples, including new results, are given. Another data processing theorem is proved in Section 5. Section 6 presents new applications to problems of information theory. It is shown in Section 7 that the bounding approach presented here is tight in the sense that the exact optimal solution is included as a special case. Asymptotic results for large coding block lengths are derived in Section 8, where it is shown that the asymptotic optimality of the classical rate distortion bound associated with $I(X,Y)$ is shared by a wide class of other functionals of $P(x)P(y)/P(x,y)$. The treatment throughout the paper is for discrete alphabets. The generalization to general alphabets are considered in Section 9.

2. Some Preliminaries

A. Convex Functions. Let $f(x)$ be a real valued function defined on some interval I of the real line, the interval may be open, half-open or closed finite or infinite. $f(x)$, $x \in I$ is said to be convex if

$$f(\lambda x + (1-\lambda)y) \leq \lambda f(x) + (1-\lambda)f(y)$$

for all x,y in I and all λ in $[0,1]$.

For proofs of the following results and further facts about convex functions, we refer the reader to chapter 1 of ref. 4. If $f''(x)$ exists on an open interval (a,b), then $f(x)$ is convex if and only if $f''(x) \geq 0$ on (a,b).

Examples: (a) On $I = (-\infty,\infty)$: e^x; e^{-x}; $|x|^\beta$, $\beta \geq 1$; $|x-a|^\beta$, $\beta \geq 1$.

(b) On $I = (0,\infty)$: $-\log x$; $-x^\beta$, $0 < \beta < 1$, x^γ, $\gamma < 0$.

We mention some additional properties: if f and g are convex on I and $\alpha \geq 0$, then $f+g$ and αf are also convex. If g is convex on I, and f is convex on the range of g and increasing (non-decreasing), then $f(g(x))$ is convex. If $f_\alpha(x)$ is an arbitrary collection of convex functions on I and $f(x) = \sup_\alpha f(x)$ let $J = \{x \in I: f(x) < \infty\}$ then J is an interval and f is convex on J.

A very important property of convex functions is the Jensen inequality: If X is a real random variable, and $f(\cdot)$ is convex over the range of X, then $Ef(x) \geq f(Ex)$.

We turn now to convex functions of several variables. C is a convex set in R^n if $\underline{x},\underline{y} \in C$ then $(\lambda\underline{x} + (1-\lambda)\underline{y}) \in C$ for all $\lambda \in [0,1]$.

$f(x)$, $\underline{x} \in C$ is convex over C if $\underline{x}, \underline{y} \in C$, $\lambda \in (0,1)$ implies $f(\lambda \underline{x} + (1-\lambda)\underline{y}) \leq \lambda f(\underline{x}) + (1-\lambda) f(\underline{y})$.

Examples: (a) Let $d(\underline{x})$, $\underline{x} \in R^n$ be a semi norm, namely $d(\underline{x}_1 + \underline{x}_2) \leq d(x_1) + d(x_2)$ and $d(\alpha \underline{x}) = |\alpha| d(\underline{x})$. Then $d(\underline{x})$ is obviously convex, and if $f(x)$ is convex and increasing, $f(d(\underline{x}))$ is also convex.

(b) In particular $\sum_{i=1}^{n} |x_i|^{\beta})^{1/\beta}$, $\beta \geq 1$ is convex and so are $\max_i(x_1,\ldots,x_n)$ and $\max_i(-x_1,-x_2,\ldots,-x_n)$, hence $-\min_i(x_1,\ldots,x_n)$ is convex.

Jensen's inequality goes over to convex functions of several variables, i.e. $Ef(\underline{x}) \geq f(E\underline{x})$, where $E\underline{x} = (Ex_1, Ex_2, \ldots, Ex_n)$.[10]

If $f(\underline{x})$ is convex on an open convex set U, then $f(\underline{x})$ is continuous on U. If $Q_i(\underline{\alpha})$ is convex and $\beta_i \geq 0$, then $\sum_1^N \beta_i Q_i(\underline{\alpha})$ is also convex. If $f(\underline{x})$ has continuous second partial derivatives $\partial^2 F(\underline{x})/\partial x_i \partial x_j$ throughout an open convex set in R^n, then f is convex on U iff the matrix $\partial^2 f/\partial x_i \partial x_j$ is non-negative definite for each $\underline{x} \in U$.

B. Bayes' Decision Rule. Let X and Y be random variables, each taking only finitely many values $X \in \{x_1,\ldots,x_K\}$, $Y \in \{y_1,\ldots,y_N\}$. Consider $P(X)$, $P(Y|X)$ and the risk, cost or loss function $d(x_i,x_j)$, $1 \leq i$, $j \leq K$. We will assume, throughout the paper, that $d(x_i,x_i) = 0$ and $d(x_i,x_j) \geq 0$. Let e_i be a subset of $\{y_1,\ldots,y_N\}$ such that for $Y \in e_i$ we make the decision $\hat{x} = x_i$. If $y_j \in e_i$, the conditional average risk $E(d(x,x_i)|y=y_j) = \sum_x P(x|y_j) d(x,x_i)$. Therefore the minimal average risk decision rule is as follows:

Set $y_j \varepsilon e_{i_o}$ where i_o is characterized by

$$\sum_x P(x|y_j)d(x,x_{i_o}) = \min_i \sum_x P(x|y_j)d(x,x_i) \ . \tag{2.1}$$

Hence $\bar{d}_{min}$, the minimal average risk, is given by

$$\bar{d}_{min} = \sum_y P(y)\min_i\left\{\sum_x P(x|y)d(x,x_i)\right\} \ . \tag{2.2}$$

In particular, for the case where $d(i,i) = 0$ and $d(i,j) = 1$, $i \neq j$, $Ed(\hat{x},x) = P_e$ where P_e denotes the probability of error.

By equation (2.2) for $\bar{d}_{min}$ we have

$$P_e^{min} = \sum_y P(y)\min_i(1 - P(x_i|y) = 1 - \sum_y \max_i P(y)P(x_i|y)$$

$$= 1 - \sum_y \max_i P(y|x_i)P(x_i) \ . \tag{2.3}$$

3. <u>A Generalized Information Functional</u>

Let Z be a random variable taking finitely many values $z_1,z_2,\ldots,z_m$ and let $P(Z)$ be the probability distribution of Z, we assume that $P(z_i) \neq 0$, $1 \leq i \leq m$. Let $\mu(Z)$ be a nonnegative measure on Z, namely $\mu(z)/\sum_1^m \mu(z_i)$ is a probability distribution, and let $Q(\alpha)$ be a convex function, some restrictions on μ and Q will be imposed a little later. We define the generalized entropy of P with respect to μ as

$$H^{Q,\mu}(Z) = \sum_z P(z)Q\left(\frac{\mu(z)}{P(z)}\right) \ . \tag{3.1}$$

Note that in the special case where $Q(\alpha) = -\log\alpha$, $Z = (X,Y)$, $P(Z) = P(X,Y)$, $\mu(X,Y) = P(X)P(Y)$, where $P(x) = \sum_y P(x,y)$, the relative entropy becomes $\sum_x \sum_y P(x,y) \log \frac{P(x,y)}{P(x)P(y)} = E \log \frac{P(Y|X)}{P(Y)}$, namely, the mutual information between the random variables X and Y.

An obvious generalization of (3.1) is the case where $Q(\alpha_1,\dots,\alpha_K)$ is convex in the K variables α_i. We will define H under two sets of assumptions:

A: $Q(\alpha_1,\dots,\alpha_k) = Q(\underline{\alpha})$ is convex on $0 < \alpha_i < \infty$, $i = 1,\dots,K$.
μ_i, $i = 1,\dots,K$ are finite positive measures which are mutually absolutely continuous with respect to P. Since we assumed $P(z_j) \neq 0$, this means that $\mu_i(z_i) \neq 0$ for all i and j.

B: $Q(\underline{\alpha})$ is convex and continuous on $(0 \leq \alpha_i < \infty)$, $i = 1,\dots,K$, and the measures μ_i are finite and nonnegative.

Let $\underline{\mu}$ denote μ_i, $1 \leq i \leq K$ and q will denote the triple $(K, \underline{\mu}(z), Q(\underline{\alpha}))$, then under assumptions A or B define

$$H^q(Z) = EQ\left(\frac{\underline{\mu}(z)}{P(z)}\right) \tag{3.2}$$

where the expectation is with respect to $P(Z)$. A basic property of the functional H^q is the following:

<u>Theorem 3.1</u>. (The weak data processing theorem.) Let $f(z)$ be a real valued function of z, $z = z_i$, $1 \leq i \leq m$. Let $P'(w)$ and $\underline{\mu}'(w)$ be the measures induced on w by $f(z)$, namely $P'(w) = P(f^{-1}(w))$, $\mu_j'(w) = \mu_j(f^{-1}(W))$, then

$$\sum_z P(z)Q\left(\frac{\underline{\mu}(z)}{P(z)}\right) \geq \sum_w P'(w)Q\left(\frac{\underline{\mu}'(w)}{P'(w)}\right)$$

namely $H^q(Z) \geq H^q(W)$, where the index q in the right hand side refers to the q induced by $f(z)$ on the q of the left hand side.

<u>Proof</u>: $P'(w_i) = \sum_{z=f^{-1}(w_i)} P(z)$ and $H^q(Z)$ can be written as

$$H^q(Z) = \sum_{w_i} P'(w_i) \sum_{z=f^{-1}(w_i)} \frac{P(z)}{P'(w_i)} Q\left(\frac{\mu(z)}{P(z)}\right) . \tag{3.3}$$

Consider $\beta_i = \sum_{z=f^{-1}(w_i)} \frac{P(z)}{P'(w_i)} Q\left(\frac{\mu(z)}{P(z)}\right)$.

Since $\sum_{z=f^{-1}(w_i)} \frac{P(z)}{P'(w_i)} = 1$, we have by Jensen's inequality that

$$\beta_i \geq Q\left(\sum_{z=f^{-1}(w_i)} \frac{\mu(z)}{P'(w_i)}\right) = Q\left(\frac{\mu'(w_i)}{P'(w_i)}\right)$$

which proves the theorem, since $H^q(Z) = \sum_i P(w_i)\beta_i$.

4. Application to Communication Theory

Consider the system of figure 1, where the modulator is fixed. We want to derive lower bounds on the minimal average distortion over all demodulators. Assume that u,y,v take values in a finite space. Identifying the pair (U,Y) with z we have by Theorem 3.1

$$H^q(U,Y) \geq H^q(U,V) . \tag{4.1}$$

Let us restrict the class of measures $\mu(u,y)$ to those of the linear form

$$\mu_i(u,y) = \sum_{u'} P(u',y)D(u,u') \tag{4.2}$$

where $D(u,u')$ is an $M \times M$ matrix with nonnegative entries.

Then it follows that $\mu_i(u,v) = \sum_y P(v|y)\mu_i(u,y) = \sum_{u'} P(u',v)D(u,u')$. $D(u,u')$ can be replaced by $D(u,u',P(u),P(u'))$ where $P(u)$ is the probability distribution of the source U.

Examples

1. $\underline{\mu}(u,y) = \mu(u,y) = [\sum_{u'} P(u',y)]P(u) = P(y)P(u)$, which, for $Q(x) = -\log x$ yields $\mathcal{H}^q(U,Y) = I(U,Y) = E \log \frac{P(u,y)}{P(u)P(y)}$.

2. $\underline{\mu}(u_i,y) = P(y,u_{i+K})$, $1 \leq i \leq M$; $u_{M+K} \triangleq u_K$.

3. $\underline{\mu}(u,y) = [\sum_{u'} P(u',y)d(u',u_i)]P(u)$; $1 \leq i \leq M$.

Let us denote the functionals $\mathcal{H}^q(U,Y)$ which are associated with the restriction (4.2) by $I^q(U,Y)$. Then, by (4.1),

$$I^q(U,Y) \geq I^q(U,V) \quad . \tag{4.3}$$

Let d be the average distortion associated with the triple U,Y,V of Figure 1. Also, let, for this system,

$$R^q(d) \triangleq \inf I^q(U,V) \tag{4.4}$$

where the infimum is taken over all $P(v|u)$, satisfying $\sum_{u,v} P(u)P(v|u)d(u,v) \leq d$. Then, by (4.3) and (4.4)

$$I^q(U,Y) \geq R^q(d) \ . \tag{4.5}$$

Obviously, $R^q(d)$ is non-decreasing in d and is <u>independent of the demodulator $v = f(y)$ as well as the probability distribution of the channel $P(y|u)$</u>. The function $R^q(d)$ is completely determined by the probability distribution $P(u)$ and the distortion $d(u,v)$.

On the other hand, $I^q(U,Y)$ is independent of $d(u,v)$ or the demodulator $V = f(y)$, and is determined by $P(y|u)$ and $P(u)$.

Let d^q be the solution to the equation $R^q(d^q) = I^q(U,Y)$, then by (4.5), $d \geq d^q$ (see Figure 2).

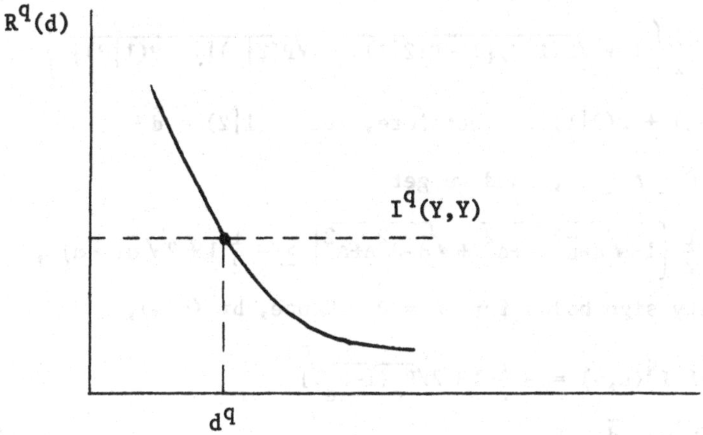

Figure 2

Hence d^q serves as a lower bound on the minimal average distortion, since (4.3) must hold for all possible demodulators.

The key to the application of (4.3) is to find convex functions $Q(\alpha)$ and measures $\mu_j(x,y)$ for which $I^q(U,Y)$ and $R^q(d)$ can be evaluated explicitly or bounded in the proper direction.

Example 1: Consider a channel with a binary input u_1, u_2 and let $P(y|1)$ and $P(y|2)$ denote the probability distribution of the channel output conditioned on the input being u_1 and u_2 respectively. Let $P(u_1) = P(u_2) = \frac{1}{2}$. Set $K = 1$, $\mu(u,y) = P(y|1)P(u)$. Also let $d(u,v) = \begin{cases} 0 ; & u = v \\ 1 ; & u \neq v \end{cases}$. Hence, $\bar{d} = Ed(u,v) = \frac{1}{2}[P(1|2) + P(2|1)]$ is the average probability of error.

Now $$I^q(u,v) = EQ\left(\frac{P(v|1)}{P(v|u)}\right) = \frac{1}{2}Q(1) + \frac{1}{2}P(1|2)Q\left(\frac{P(1|1)}{P(1|2)}\right) + \frac{1}{2}P(2|2)Q\left(\frac{P(2|1)}{P(2|2)}\right)$$
$$= \frac{1}{2}Q(1) + \frac{1}{2}P(1|2)Q\left[\frac{1-P(2|1)}{P(1|2)}\right] + \frac{1}{2}[1-P(1|2)]Q\left[\frac{P(2|1)}{1-P(1|2)}\right].$$

In particular, let $Q(\alpha) = -\alpha^{1/2}$. Then,

$$I^q(u,v) = -\frac{1}{2}\left\{1 + \sqrt{P(1|2)[1-P(2|1)]} + \sqrt{P(2|1)[1-P(1|2)]}\right\} .$$

Now, $\bar{d} = \frac{1}{2}[P(1|2) + P(2|1)]$. Therefore, let $P(1|2) = \bar{d}+\Delta$; $P(2|1) = \bar{d}-\Delta$; $0 \le \Delta \le 1$, and we get

$$I^q(u,v) = -\frac{1}{2}\left\{1+\sqrt{\bar{d}-\bar{d}^2+\Delta+\Delta^2} + \sqrt{\bar{d}-\bar{d}^2-\Delta+\Delta^2}\right\} \ge -\frac{1}{2}\, 1+2\sqrt{\bar{d}(1-\bar{d})} ,$$

where the equality sign holds for $\Lambda = 0$. Hence, by (4.4),

$$R^q(P_e) = \inf_{P(v|u)\,:\,\bar{d} \le P_e} I^q(u,v) = -\frac{1}{2}\{1+2\sqrt{P_e(1-P_e)}\} . \tag{4.6}$$

Now,

$$I^q(U,Y) = -\frac{1}{2}\, Q(1) - \frac{1}{2}\sum_Y \sqrt{P(y|2)P(y|1)} . \tag{4.7}$$

Hence, by (4.5), (4.6) and (4.7)

$$\sqrt{P_e(1-P_e)} \ge \frac{1}{2}\sum_Y \sqrt{P(y|2)P(y|1)} ,$$

which is the Battacharia bound[9]. We leave the following two examples as an exercise:

1. Derive the corresponding bound for $Q(\alpha) = -\log\alpha$ and $\mu(u,y) = P(y|1)P(u)$, $P(u) = \frac{1}{2}$ (the Kullback bound[2]).

2. Show that for $Q(x) = \max(1,x)$, $\mu(u,y) = P(y(1)P(u))$, $P(u) = \frac{1}{2}$, the corresponding lower bound on P_e coincides with the minimal achievable probability of error.

<u>Example 2</u>: Let $\Delta = \frac{A}{2M}$ where M is an integer. Set $U = \{u_i\}$ where $u_i = i\cdot\Delta$, $-M \le i \le M$. Hence, U is a discrete variable taking values in the interval $\left[-\frac{A}{2}, \frac{A}{2}\right]$. Let $P(u)$ be a probability distribution defined on U.

When $\Delta \to 0$ one can think of U as being a discrete approximation to a continuous random variable that takes value in $\left[-\frac{A}{2}, \frac{A}{2}\right]$.

Let

$$d(u,v) = \begin{cases} 0 ; & |u-v| < \frac{\delta}{2} \\ 1 ; & |u-v| \geq \frac{\delta}{2} \end{cases} \tag{4.8}$$

Hence, $\bar{d} = \Pr\left[|\varepsilon| \geq \frac{\delta}{2}\right]$; $\varepsilon = |u-v|$. Furthermore $\overline{\varepsilon^2} = \overline{(u-v)^2} = \int_0^\infty \varepsilon^2 f(\varepsilon) d\varepsilon$ where $f(x) = \frac{d}{dx} \Pr[|\varepsilon| < x]$. Hence, integrating by parts

$$\overline{\varepsilon^2} = \frac{1}{4} \int_0^\infty \delta \Pr\left[|\varepsilon| > \frac{\delta}{2}\right] d\delta . \tag{4.9}$$

Thus, lower bounds on $\bar{d} = \Pr\left[|\varepsilon| \geq \frac{\delta}{2}\right]$ yield corresponding lower bounds on $\overline{\varepsilon^2}$, which will be applicable to parameter-estimation problems. Let $Q(\underline{\alpha}) = \max_i\{\alpha_i; \; i = 1,\dots,D\}$; $D = \frac{A}{\delta}$, where D and δ/Δ are integers. $\underline{\mu}(u,y) = P(u + i\delta;y)$; $i = 1,\dots,D$, where $+$ denotes summation modulo D. Hence

$$I^q(u,v) = \sum_Y \sum_U P(u,y) \max_i \left\{ \frac{P(u+i\delta;y)}{P(u,y)} ; \; i = 1,\dots,D \right\}$$

$$= \sum_U \sum_Y \max_i\{P(u+i\delta;y); \; i = 1,\dots,D\}$$

$$= \sum_U \sum_J P(u+j\delta) \sum_Y \max_i \left\{ \frac{P(u+i\delta;y)}{\sum_j P(u+j\delta)} ; \; i = 1,\dots,D \right\} .$$

Now it follows from (2.3) that for a given U,

$$1 - \sum_Y \max_i \left\{ \frac{P(u+i\delta;y)}{\sum_j P(u+j\delta)} ; \; i = 1,\dots,D \right\}$$

is the minimal probability of error $P_e(D|U)$ associated with a set of

D signals u, $u+\delta, u+2\delta, \ldots$ with a-priori probabilities $\dfrac{P(u+i\delta)}{\sum_j P(u+j\delta)}$.

Hence,

$$I^q(U,Y) = \sum_U \sum_J P(u)+j\delta)[1-P_e(D|u)]$$

$$= D\left[1 - \sum_U \sum_J \frac{1}{D} P(u)+j\delta)P_e(D|u)\right] . \qquad (4.10)$$

Now

$$I^q(U,V) = E \max_i \left[\frac{P(u+i\delta,v)}{P(u,v)} \; ; \quad i = 1,\ldots,D\right]$$

$$\sum_X \sum_V \max_i [P(u+i\ ,v); \quad i = 1,\ldots,D]$$

$$= \frac{A}{\delta} \sum_V \sum_{U=v-\frac{\delta}{2}}^{v+\frac{\delta}{2}} \max_i [P(u+i\ ),V); \quad c = 1,\ldots,D]$$

$$\geq D \sum_V \sum_{\eta=-\frac{\delta}{2}}^{\delta/2} P(\eta+u,v)$$

$$= D \sum_V P(v)\Pr\left|\,|\varepsilon| < \frac{\delta}{2}|v|\right| \; ; \quad \varepsilon = u-v$$

$$= D\left[1-\Pr\left|\,|\varepsilon| \geq \frac{\delta}{2}\right|\right] . \qquad (4.11)$$

Hence, $R^q(d)$ for $d(u,v)$ given by (4.8) satisfies

$$R^q(d) \geq D[1-\bar{d}] . \qquad (4.12)$$

Therefore by (4.10) and (4.12)

$$\bar{d} = \Pr\left[|u-v| \geq \frac{\delta}{2}\right] \geq \sum_U \sum_{j=1}^{D} \frac{1}{D} P(u+j\delta)P_e(D|u) , \qquad (4.13)$$

where $\delta = \dfrac{A}{D}$.

In the special case where u is distributed uniformly in $\left[-\frac{A}{2}, \frac{A}{2}\right]$ $P(u) = P(u+j\delta)$, $j = 1,\dots,D$. Hence,

$$\Pr\left[|u-v| \geq \frac{\delta}{2}\right] \geq E\, P_e(D|u);\quad \delta = \frac{A}{D} \quad . \tag{4.14}$$

The bound (4.14) was first derived in ref. 6, using a different bounding technique. Furthermore, it is shown in ref. 6 that (4.14) is an achievable bound. (On the other hand, the more general bound (4.13) is new to the best of our knowledge.) Now, similar to (4.14), it can be shown that for a uniformly distributed u and any δ, such that $\frac{A}{D} \leq \delta < \frac{A}{D-1}$, $\Pr\left[|u-v| \geq \frac{\delta}{2}\right] \geq E\, Pe(D-1|u)$. Since $Pe(D-1|u) \geq Pe(2|u)$ we have $\Pr\left[|u-v| \geq \frac{\delta}{2}\right] \geq E\, Pe(2|u)$; $0 \leq \delta < \frac{A}{2}$, where $Pe(2|u)$ is the probability of error associated with the equiprobable transmission of u and $u+\delta$.

Applying (4.9) yields

$$\overline{\varepsilon^2} = E|u-v|^2 \geq \frac{1}{4}\int_0^{A/2} \delta E\, Pe(2|u)d\delta \quad . \tag{4.15}$$

The bound (4.15) was derived in refs. 7 and using different bounding techniques, and is considered to be one of the tightest bounds for the mean square error associated with parameter estimation.

Clearly, one can apply (4.9) to (4.13) in order to get new bounds for cases where u is not distributed uniformally.

5. The Strong Data Processing Theorem

Consider the communication system of figure 1. Let $P(u)$, $P(x|u)$, $P(y|x)$, denote the probability distribution of the source and the transition probabilities of the encoder and the channel respectively, $v = f(y)$ characterizes the decoder. Note that for the system of Fig. 1,

$P(y|x,u) = P(y|x)$. Let $\mu_i(x,y)$ be positive measures which are absolutely continuous with respect to $P(x,y)$. We impose the additional condition on $\mu_i(x,y)$:

$$\mu_i(x,y) = \mu_i(y|x)P(x) \tag{5.1}$$

where $P(x) = \sum_u P(x|u)P(u)$.

We define $H^q(X,Y)$, $H^q((U,X),Y)$ and $H^q(U,Y)$ as follows:

$$H^q(X,Y) = \sum_{x,y} P(x,y)Q\left(\frac{\underline{\mu}(y|x)P(x)}{P(x,y)}\right)$$

$$H^q((U,X),Y) = EQ\left(\frac{\underline{\mu}(y|x)}{P(y|x,u)}\right) = \sum_{u,x,y} P(u,x,y)Q\left(\frac{\underline{\mu}(y|x)}{P(y|x,u)}\right)$$

and $$H^q(U,Y) = \sum_{u,y} P(u,y)Q\,\frac{\underline{\mu}(y|u)}{P(y|u)}$$

where $\underline{\mu}(y|u) = \sum_x P(x|u)\underline{\mu}(y|x)$.

Theorem 5.1

$$H^q(X,Y) \geq H^q(U,Y) \quad .$$

Proof: Since for the communication system of figure 1 $P(y|x,u) = P(y|x)$, it follows immediately that $H^q((U,X),Y) = H^q(X,Y)$.

On the other hand,

$$H^q((U,X),Y) = \sum_{u,y} P(u,y)\left(\sum_x P(x|u,y)Q\left(\frac{\underline{\mu}(y|x)}{P(y|x)}\right)\right)$$

and by Jensen's inequality

$$H^q((U,X),Y) \geq \sum_{u,y} P(u,y)Q\left(\sum_x \frac{\underline{\mu}(y|x)P(x|u,y)}{P(y|x)}\right) \quad .$$

Consider now the argument of $Q(\cdot)$.

$$\sum_x \frac{\mu(y|x)P(x|u,y)}{P(y|x)} = \sum_x \frac{\mu(y|x)P(x|u,y)P(u,x)}{P(u,x,y)}$$

$$= \sum_x \frac{\mu(y|x)P(x|u)P(u)}{P(u,y)} = \frac{\sum_x \mu(y|x)P(x|u)}{P(y|u)} \quad .$$

Hence

$$H^q(X,Y) = H^q((U,X),Y) \geq H^q(U,Y) \qquad (5.2)$$

which completes the proof.

Combining (5.2) with the weak data processing theorem of Section 3, we have

$$H^q(X,Y) \geq H^q(U,V) \quad . \qquad (5.3)$$

6. Application to Information Theory

In this section we consider the model of Figure 1, where both the coder and decoder are subjected to optimization. Two bounding techniques will be presented which will be named "Approach I" and "approach II". The classical rate distortion bound will be shown to be special cases of both approaches.

Approach I: Let $\mu_i(x,y)$ be of the form

$$\mu_j(x,y) = \sum_{x'} P(y|x')D_j(x,x',P(x),P(x'))$$

where D_j is an $M \times M$ matrix with nonnegative entries as in Section 4. For a given system $(P(u),P(x|u),P(y|x),v = f(y))$ we have, as in Section 4,

$$H^q(X,Y) = I^q(X,Y) \geq I^q(X,V) = EQ\left(\frac{\mu(x,v)}{P(x,v)}\right) \quad .$$

Now let $R^q(d) = \inf I^q(X,V)$, where the infimum is taken over all admissible $P(x|u)$, $P(v|x)$ satisfying $\sum_{v,u,x} d(u,v)P(x|u)P(u)P(v|x) \leq d$ namely, q, $P(u)$ are kept constant while the infimum is taken over all admissible channels, modulators and demodulators.

Now, define $C^q = \sup I^q(X,Y)$, where the supremum is taken over all possible channel input distributions $P(x)$. Obviously, $R^q(d) \leq C^q$ and the application of this result to the derivation of lower bounds on d is the same as in Section 4.

In the special case where $K = 1$ and $\mu(x,y) = P(y)P(x)$, we can apply theorem 5.1, thus $I^q(X,V) \geq I^q(U,V)$. In this case $R^q(d)$ can be redefined to be $\inf I^q(U,V)$ where the infimum is taken over all $P(v|u)$ satisfying $\sum_{u,v} P(v|u)P(u)d(u,v) \leq d$. This special case was treated in ref. 2, in particular for $Q(\alpha) = -\log \alpha$, $R^q(d) \leq C^q$ reduces to the classical rate distortion bound.

Example

Let $k = 1$, $Q(\alpha) = \alpha^{-1}$; $\mu(x,y) = P(x)P(y)$. Consider the "source coding problem" where the channel is an M-inputs, M-outputs, noiseless channel. The source is assumed to be memoryless. Hence

$$I^q(X,Y) = \sum_x P(x)Q(P(x)) = \sum P(x)\frac{1}{P(x)} = M .$$

Hence, $C^q = M$. Therefore, $M \geq E\left(\frac{P(\underline{v})}{P(\underline{v}|\underline{u})}\right)^{-1}$, where $\underline{v}$ and $\underline{u}$ are n-dimensional vectors.

Now, let $M = e^{nR}$. Then, by a convexity argument,

$$e^{R} \geq \left[E\left(\frac{P(\underline{v})}{P(\underline{v}|\underline{u})}\right)^{-1}\right]^{\frac{1}{n}} \geq E\left[\left(\frac{P(\underline{v})}{P(\underline{v}|\underline{u})}\right)^{-\frac{1}{n}}\right]$$

$$= E\, e^{\frac{1}{n}\log\frac{P(\underline{v}|\underline{u})}{P(\underline{v})}} = e^{I(\underline{u},\underline{v})} E\, e^{\left[\frac{1}{n}\log\frac{P(\underline{v}|\underline{u})}{P(\underline{v})} - I(\underline{u},\underline{v})\right]} \qquad (6.1)$$

where $I(\underline{u},\underline{v}) = E\,\frac{1}{n}\log\frac{P(\underline{v}|\underline{u})}{P(\underline{v})}$ is the classical average mutual information. At this point, note that the classical rate distortion bound for this problem is $R(d) \leq R$, where

$$R(d) = \inf E\,\frac{1}{n}\log\frac{P(\underline{v}|\underline{u})}{P(\underline{v})} = \inf E\log\frac{P(v|u)}{P(v)},$$

where the infimum is carried over all $P(\underline{v}|\underline{u})$ satisfying $\sum_{u,v} P(u)P(v|u)d(u,v) \leq d$, since the infimum in the n-vector case is achieved by a memoryless channel. Hence, by (6.1) and the classical rate distortion bound $C^{q} = e^{R} \geq e^{R(d)+\Theta(n)}$, where

$$\Theta(n) = \log E\, e^{\left[\frac{1}{n}\log\frac{P(\underline{v}|\underline{u})}{P(v)} - I(\underline{u},\underline{v})\right]}.$$

Since, by convexity $\Theta(n) \geq 0$, the bound (6.1) is tighter than (6.2) for all finite n.

Furthermore, (6.1) can be used to derive lower bounds on the rate of convergence of the average distortion associated with block-coding of length n to its asymptotic value (which is the solution of $R(d) = R$).

<u>Approach II</u>: Consider the system of Figure 1 with a deterministic modulator $x = g(u)$ ($g(\cdot)$ may be many to one). Let $u_1,\ldots,u_{k-1}$ be $k-1$ elements of the source alphabet, and let $x_j = g(u_j)$. Let $\underline{\mu}$ be

as follows: $\mu_j(x,y) = P(x)P(y|x_j)$, $j = 1,2,\dots,k-1$; $\mu_k(x,y) = P(x)P(y)$. Note that (5.1) is satisfied. By theorem 3.1,

$$\sum_{x,y} P(x,y)Q\left(\frac{P(y|x_1)}{P(y|x)},\dots,\frac{P(y|x_{k-1})}{P(y|x)},\frac{P(y)}{P(y|x)}\right)$$

$$\geq \sum_{x,v} P(x,v)Q\left(\frac{P(v|x_1)}{P(v|x)},\dots,\frac{P(v|x_{k-1})}{P(v|x)},\frac{P(v)}{P(v|x)}\right).$$

Denoting the left hand side of the last inequality by a, we have by theorem 5.1:

$$a \geq \sum_{u,v} P(u,v)Q\left(\frac{P(v|x_1)}{P(v|u)},\dots,\frac{P(v|x_{k-1})}{P(v|u)},\frac{P(v)}{P(v|u)}\right).$$

Note that $P(v|x_j)$ can be replaced by $P(v|u_j)$, where $x_j = g(u_j)$, therefore

$$\sum_{x,y} P(x,y)Q\left(\frac{P(y|x_1)}{P(y|x)},\dots,\frac{P(y|x_{k-1})}{P(y|x)},\frac{P(y)}{P(y|x)}\right)$$

$$\geq \sum_{u,v} P(u,v)Q\left(\frac{P(v|u_1)}{P(v|u)},\dots,\frac{P(v|u_{k-1})}{P(v|u)},\frac{P(v)}{P(v|u)}\right).$$

In order to obtain results which are independent of the particular modulator, multiply both sides of the last inequality by $P(u_1)\cdot P(u_2)\cdot \dots \cdot P(u_{k-1})$, and sum over $u_1,\dots,u_{k-1}$, hence

$$\sum_{x,x_1,\dots,x_{k-1},y} P(y|x)P(x)P(x_1)\dots P(x_{k-1})Q\left(\frac{P(y|x_1)}{P(y|x)},\dots,\frac{P(y|x_{k-1})}{P(y|x)},\frac{P(y)}{P(y|x)}\right)$$

$$\geq \sum_{u,u_1,\dots,u_{k-1},y} P(v|u)P(u)P(u_1)\dots P(u_{k-1})Q\left(\frac{P(v|u_1)}{P(v|u)},\dots,\frac{P(v|u_{k-1})}{P(v|u)},\frac{P(v)}{P(v|u)}\right) \quad (6.2)$$

Denoting the left hand side by $I^q(X,Y)$ and the right hand side by $I^q(U,V)$, we have by (5.4): $I^q(X,Y) \geq I^q(U,V)$. Define now,

$C^q = \sup I^q(X,Y)$ where the supremum is taken over all admissible $P(x)$, and $R^q(d) = \inf I^q(U,V)$ where the infimum is taken over all $P(v|u)$ such that $\sum_{u,v} P(u)P(v|u)d(u,v) \leq d$. Then

$$C^q \geq R^q(d) . \tag{6.3}$$

Note that C^q is independent of the modulator, source and demodulator, while $R^q(d)$ is independent of the modulator, channel and demodulator. The application of this inequality to the derivation of bounds is as explained in Section 4.

The classical rate distortion bound is the special case of (6.3), where $I(x,y) = -E \log \frac{P(y)}{P(y|x)}$, the generalization of ref. 2 deals with the case where $-\log \frac{P(y)}{P(y|x)}$ is replaced by $Q \frac{P(y)}{P(y|x)}$ which is also a special case of (6.3).

Example

In this example U is a random variable which is uniformly distributed in $[-1/2, 1/2]$. The channel is the white Gaussian channel: $y(t) = s(t,x) + n(t)$, $t \in [0,T]$ where $n(t)$ is white Gaussian noise with the two sided spectral density N_o and $s(t,x)$ is a waveform associated with the input x. The energy of $s(t,x)$ is

$E(x) = \int_0^T s^2(t,x)dt$. We impose the restriction $E\,E(x) = \int_{-\infty}^{\infty} p(x)E(x)dx \leq E_o$.

We will assume that the definitions and results obtained for finite alphabets go over to the general case for a justification of this assumption, see Section 9. Let $Q(\alpha) = -\alpha^{1/2}$ and $d(u,v) = (u-v)^2$. Note that since $p(u) = 1$, $p(u|v) = p(u,v)$. In the following lines, the integration is over $[-1/2,1/2]$ unless otherwise specified. Let $d = \iint (u-v)^2 p(u,v)\,du\,dv$, then

$$
\begin{aligned}
-I^q(U,V) &= \iiint p(v|u)p(u)p(u_1)\sqrt{\frac{p(v|u_1)}{p(v|u)}}\,du\,du_1\,dv \\
&= \int\left[\int p(u)\sqrt{p(v|u)}\,du\right]^2 dv \\
&= \int\left[\int \sqrt{p(u,v)}\,du\right]^2 dv \\
&= \int\left[\int \frac{1}{\sqrt{d+(u-v)^2}} \cdot \sqrt{(d+(u-v)^2 p(u,v)du}\right] dv \\
&\le \int\left[\int_{-\infty}^{\infty} \frac{du}{d+(u-v)^2} \cdot \int (d+(u-v)^2)p(u,v)\,du\right] dv \\
&= \frac{\pi}{\sqrt{d}}\,(d+d) = 2\pi\sqrt{d}\,.
\end{aligned}
\tag{6.4}
$$

Hence, $R^q(d) \le -2\pi\sqrt{d}$. Turning to the channel, let

$$s_o(t) = \int_{-\infty}^{\infty} s(t,x)p(x)\,dx \quad \text{and} \quad E(x,x_1) = \int_{-}^{\infty} s(t,x)s(t,x_1)\,dt\,.$$

In order to evaluate $-\sum P(x,y)p(x_1)\sqrt{\frac{P(y|x_1)}{P(y|x)}}$ note that $P(y|x_1)/P(y|x)$ is the likelihood ratio, $\Lambda(y)$, for detecting whether the received waveform $y(\cdot)$ was $y(t) = s(t,x_1) + n(t)$ or $y(t) = s(t,x) + n(t)$.

It is well known that

$$\Lambda(y) = \frac{P(y|x_1)}{P(y|x)} =$$

$$\mathrm{Exp}\left\{\frac{1}{N_o}\int_o^T y(t)\cdot s(t,x_1)dt - \frac{1}{N_o}\int_o^T y(t)s(t,x)dt - \frac{1}{2N_o}E(x_1) + \frac{1}{2N_o}E(x)\right\} .$$

We have to average $-\Lambda^{1/2}(y)$ under the hypothesis that $y(t) = s(t,x) + n(t)$. We therefore replace $y(t)$ by $s(t,x) + n(t)$.

$$\Lambda(y) = \mathrm{Exp}\left\{\frac{1}{N_o}\int_o^T n(t)(s(t,x_1) - s(t,x))td \right.$$

$$\left. + \frac{1}{N_o}E(x,x_1) - \frac{1}{N_o}E(x) - \frac{1}{2N_o}E(x_1) + \frac{1}{2N_o}E(x)\right\} .$$

Averaging $\Lambda^{1/2}$ over $n(t)$, (recall that if θ is Gaussian $(0,\sigma^2)$ then $Ee^{\theta} = e^{\sigma^2/2}$):

$$\mathrm{Exp}\left\{\frac{1}{8N_o}(E(x) + E(x_1) - 2E(x,x_1)) + \frac{1}{2N_o}E(x,x_1) - \frac{1}{4N_o}E(x) - \frac{1}{4N_o}E(x_1)\right\}$$

$$= \mathrm{Exp}\left\{\frac{1}{4N_o}E(x,x_1) - \frac{1}{8N_o}E(x) - \frac{1}{8N_o}E(x_1)\right\} .$$

Therefore

$$C^q = \sup\left\{-E\ \mathrm{Exp}\left\{\frac{1}{8N_o}(2E(x,x_1) - E(x) - E(x_1))\right\}\right\} ,$$

where the expectation is with respect to $p(x)\cdot p(x_1)$ and the supremum is over all $p(x)$ on $s(t,x)$ satisfying the average power constraint. By the Jensen inequality

$$C^q \le \sup\left\{-\mathrm{Exp}\ E\left[\frac{1}{8N_o}(2E(x,x_1) - E(x) - E(x_1)\right]\right\} .$$

Now, $E\,\mathcal{E}(x) \leq \mathcal{E}_o$, $E\,\mathcal{E}(x_1) \leq \mathcal{E}_o$, and $E\,\mathcal{E}(x,x_1) = \int_o^T s_o^2(t)dt \geq 0$.

Hence $C^q \leq -\text{Exp} - \frac{E_o}{4N_o}$ and $R^q(d) \leq C^q$ implies

$$d \geq \frac{1}{4\pi^2} \text{Exp} - \frac{E_o}{2N_o} \quad . \tag{6.5}$$

Remarks:

1. Note that the bound remains the same if the average power constraint $E\,\mathcal{E}(x) \leq \mathcal{E}_o$ is replaced by $\mathcal{E}(x) \leq \mathcal{E}_o$ for all x.

2. In the classical case $(I(X,Y) = -E \log P(y)/P(y|x))$, $C = \mathcal{E}_o/2N_o$ and $R(d) \approx -\frac{1}{2}\log 2\pi ed$ (for $d \ll 1$), hence $d \geq (2\pi e)^{-1}$ $\text{Exp} - \frac{\mathcal{E}_o}{N_o}$; Note the difference in the exponents of this bound and the result of the present example (since this example deals with a block-length of one).

3. A comparison between (6.5) and other bounds has been carried out by D. Endelman in an M.Sc. (Faculty of Electrical Engineering, Technion - Israel Institute of Technology). The other bounds were the classical rate distortion bound and the case $K = 1$, $Q(\alpha) = \alpha\log\alpha$, $\mu(x,y) = P(y)P(x)$. (6.5) turned out to be the best bound.

7. Tightness of the Bounding Techniques

Let $\bar{d}_{min}$ be the minimal achievable average distortion for a given channel and source. Let q^d be a lower bound on $\bar{d}_{min}$ resulting for a particular choice of q resulting from the appropriate application of data processing theorem (Section 4 or Approach I of Section 6, depending on whether the modulator is predetermined or is subjected to optimization). The supremum of d^q over all admissible choices of q is also a lower bound on $\bar{d}_{min}$. In this section, we show that the bounding techniques suggested in Section 4 and Approach I of Section 6 are tight in the following sense:

<u>Theorem 7.1</u>: $\sup d^q = \bar{d}_{min}$, where the supremum is taken over all admissible choices of q.

<u>Remark</u>: This theorem is an existence theorem since the optimal system (the optimal demodulator and also, if applicable, the optimal modulator) are used to construct the optimal q.

<u>Proof</u>: Consider, first, the case where the modulator is given in Section 4.

Let $K = M$ where M is the cardinality of the input alphabet. Let $Q(\underline{\alpha}) = -\min_j (\alpha_j;\ 1 \le j \le M)$ and $\mu_i(u,y) = P(u) \sum_{u'} P(y|u')P(u')d(u',u_i)$, then

$$R^q(d) = -\sup E\left\{\min_i \left(\frac{P(u) \sum_{u'} P(v|u')P(u')d(u',u_i)}{P(u,v)}\right)\right\},$$

where the supremum is over all $P(v|u)$, such that

$\sum_{u,v} P(u) \cdot P(u) \cdot P(v|u)d(u,v) \le \bar{d}$. Hence,

$$R^q(d) \ge -\sup E\left(\frac{P(u)\sum_{u'} P(v|u')P(u')d(u',v)}{P(u,v)}\right) = -\sup \sum_{u,v} P(u) \sum_{u'} P(u',v)d(u',v)$$

$$= -\sup \sum_u P(u)\left(\sum_{u',v} P(u',v)d(u',v)\right) = -\sup \bar{d}.$$

Hence,

$$R^q(d) \geq -\bar{d} \ . \tag{7.1}$$

On the other hand,

$$I^q(U,Y) = -E \min_i \frac{\sum_{u'} P(y|u')P(u')d(u',u_i)}{P(y|u)}$$

$$= - \sum_{u,y} P(u)P(y) \min_i \sum_{u'} P(u'|y)d(u',u_i)$$

$$= - \sum_{y} P(y) \min_i \sum_{u'} P(u'|y)d(u',u_i) \quad .$$

Hence, by (2.2), $I^q(U,Y) = -\bar{d}_{min}$, therefore for the q chosen we obtain the bound $\bar{d} \geq \bar{d}_{min}$ where $\bar{d}$ min is the minimal achievable distortion, which proves the theorem for this case.

Turning now to the case where both the modulator and demodulator are subject to optimization as in Section 6, let

$$\mu_j(x,y) = \left[\sum_{x'} \sum_{u} P(x',y) \frac{1}{P(x')} \tilde{P}(x'|u)\tilde{P}(u)d(u,u_j)\right] P(x) \tag{7.2}$$

where $\tilde{P}(x'|u)$ and $\tilde{P}(u)$ are probabilities which will be specified later. Let K be the cardinality of U an $Q(\underline{\alpha}) = -\min_j \alpha_j$. Therefore,

$$I^q(X,Y) = -E \min_j \frac{\mu_j(x,y)}{P(x,y)} = -\sum_x P(x) \sum_y \min_j \frac{\mu_j(x,y)}{P(x)} \quad . \tag{7.3}$$

Note that $\mu_j(x,y)/P(x)$ is independent of x and therefore $I^q(x,y)$ is independent of $P(x)$. Thus,

$$I^q(X,Y) = -\sum_y \min_j \frac{\mu_j(x,y)}{P(x)} \tag{7.4}$$

and

$$C^q = I^q(X,Y) \tag{7.5}$$

for any $P(x)$.

In the special case where $\tilde{P}(u) = P(u)$ and $\tilde{P}(x|u)$ is the $P(x|u)$ of the optimal encoder (modulator), it follows from (7.2) and (7.3) that

$$I^q(X,Y) = -\sum_y \min_j \left\{ \sum_u P(y|u)P(u)d(u,u_j) \right\} \tag{7.6}$$

where $P(y|u)$ is the one associated with the optimal encoder. Hence by (2.2), (7.5) and (7.6)

$$C^q = -\bar{d}_{min} .$$

Note that because of (7.6), R^q for this case is lower-bounded by the same bound as the one given in (7.1). Since $C^q \geq R^q(d)$, $\bar{d} \geq \bar{d}_{min}$ which proves the theorem.

8. Asymptotic Optimality for Large Block-Length

In Section 7 it was demonstrated that there exists a $q = \{K, Q(\alpha), \mu(x,y)\}$ for which $R^q \leq C^q$ yields a tight bound on the average distortion, since the solution of $R^q(d) = C^q$ is identical with the minimum achievable average distortion. However, it can be evaluated only if the optimal encoder and decoder are known.

It was demonstrated in Section 6 that the class of functionals for which $K = 1$, $\mu(x,y) = P(x)P(y)$, yields a bound $R^q(d) \leq C^q$ which is completely independent of the modulator and the demodulator.

Furthermore, it is well known[1] that the classical rate-distortion theory {i.e. $K = 1$, $Q(\alpha) = -\log\alpha$, $\mu(x,y) = P(x)P(y)$} yields a lower bound on the average distortion, which is asymptotically optimal as the coding block-length approaches infinity.

In this section it is demonstrated that the asymptotic optimality of the classical rate-distortion theory is shared with a class of functionals of $\frac{\mu(x,y)}{P(x,y)} = \frac{P(x)P(y)}{P(x,y)}$.

Let $Q(\alpha)$ be a convex decreasing function of α that is also a convex function of x where $\alpha = e^{-x}$. These conditions are satisfied by any $Q(\alpha)$ such that $Q'(\alpha) < 0$, $Q''(\alpha) > 0$ and $\alpha Q''(\alpha) > -Q'(\alpha)$. Note that $Q(\alpha^{1/n})$ is also convex, where n is an integer.

Examples: 1.) $Q(\alpha) = -\log\alpha$; 2.) $Q(\alpha) = x^{-\rho}$, $\rho > 0$, etc.

Now let $\underline{x} = (x_1, \ldots, x_i, \ldots, x_n)$ and

$$EI_n^q(\underline{X},\underline{Y}) = EQ\left[\left(\frac{P(\underline{x})P(\underline{y})}{P(\underline{x},\underline{y})}\right)^{1/n}\right] = EQ\left[\left(\frac{P(\underline{y})}{P(\underline{y}\ \underline{x})}\right)^{1/n}\right]$$

and let

$$C_\infty^q = \lim_{n\to\infty} \sup_{P(x)} I_n^q(\underline{X},\underline{Y}) = \lim_{n\to\infty} C_n^q; \quad R_\infty^q = \lim_{n\to\infty} R_n^q .$$

We show in this section that $C_\infty^q = Q(e^{-C}) \geq R_\infty^q \geq Q(e^{-R(d)})$ where C and $R(d)$ are the classical capacity and rate-distortion function respectively. For n vectors $\underline{x}$ and $\underline{y}$, define the compositions $c(x)$ and $c(x,y)$:

$$c(x) = \frac{1}{n}\sum_{i=1}^{n} \delta(x_i - x); \quad \delta(a)\begin{cases} 0, & a \neq 0 \\ 1, & a = 0 \end{cases}; \quad c(x,y) = \frac{1}{2}\sum_{i=1}^{n} \delta(x_i - x)\delta(y_i - y);$$

$$c(y|x)c(x) = c(x,y); \quad \sum_y c(x,y) = c(x); \quad \sum_x c(x) = 1 .$$

Assume that $P(\underline{y}|\underline{x}) = \prod_{i=1}^{n} P(y_i|x_i)$ (memoryless channel). Hence,

$$P(\underline{y}|\underline{x}) = e^{n\sum_{x,y} c(x,y)\log P(y|x)} \tag{8.1}$$

Assume now that some probability distribution $P_1(\underline{x})$ maximizes $I_n^q(\underline{X},\underline{Y})$, and let $F(\underline{x})$ be a permutation operator on the n-vectors $\underline{x}$, then $P_1(F(\underline{x}))$ is also a maximizing distribution for $I_n^q(X,Y)$. Let $P_o(\underline{x}) = \frac{1}{N(F)}\sum_F P_1(F(\underline{x}))$, where the summation is carried over all the $N(F)$ possible permutations. Then $P_o(\underline{x})$ is a maximizing probability distribution for $I_n(\underline{X},\underline{Y})$.

It should be noted that the set of all vectors $\underline{x}$ which are characterized by the same $c(x)$ are all equiprobable relative to $P_o(x)$. Hence,

$$P(y) = \sum_{\underline{x}} P(y|x)P(x) = \sum_{c'} \frac{1}{N[c'(x)]}\left[\sum_{\underline{x}:c(x)=c'} e^{n\sum_{X,Y} c'(x)c(y|x)\log P(y|x)}\right]P(c'(x))$$

where $P(c'(x)) = \Pr[\underline{x} : c(x) = c']$, and where $N(c(x))$ is the number of n-vectors $\underline{x}$ which are characterized by $c(x)$.

Denote

$$P(\underline{y}|c'(x)) = \frac{1}{N[c'(x)]}\sum_{\underline{x}:c(x)=c'} e^{n\sum_{x,y} c'(x)c(y|x)\log P(y|x)}$$

$$P(\underline{y}) = \sum P(c(x))P(\underline{y}|c(x)) .$$

Consider the memoryless probability distribution $P_m(\underline{x}) = \prod_i P(x_i)$. Then, for this distribution too, all vectors which are characterized by the same $c(x)$ are equiprobable. Furthermore,

$$P_m(\underline{y}) = \sum_{\underline{x}} P_m(\underline{x})P(\underline{y}|\underline{x}) = \sum_{c} P_m(c(x))P(\underline{y}|c(x)) .$$

Furthermore, for large n $P_m(\underline{y}) \simeq e^{-nH_{P(x)}(y)}$ where $H_{P(x)}(y) \triangleq -\sum_y \sum_x P(x)P(y|x)\log \sum_x P(y|x)P(x)$, and for $\delta > 0$

$$\lim_{n\to\infty} P_m[|c(x) - P(x)| > \delta] = 0 . \tag{8.2}$$

Now, for any $\underline{x}$ such that $c(x) > 0$, and any $\delta > 0$,

$$\lim_{n\to\infty} \Pr[|c(y|x) - P(y|x)| > \delta] = 0 . \tag{8.3}$$

Hence, since $|P(y|x)\log P(y|x) < \max_{x,y} P(y|x)|\log P(y|x)|$, is bounded, it follows that for any δ' and for large enough n

$$P(\underline{y}|c(x)) \geq e^{n[\sum_x c(x)\sum_y P(y|x)\log P(y|x) - \delta']} .$$

Now, let δ be a positive number such that $\frac{1}{\delta}$ is an integer, and let

$$\hat{c}(x) \triangleq \frac{1}{N(x)} \sum_{x:|c(x)-j\delta/2|\leq\delta/2} c(x) \quad ; \quad j = 1,3,5,\dots , \tag{8.4}$$

where $N(x)$ is the number of letters x for which $|c(x) - j\frac{\delta}{2}| \leq \frac{\delta}{2}$.

Then, it can be shown that for any δ'' and for large enough n and small enough δ, $P(\underline{y}|c(x)) = P(\underline{y}|\hat{c}(x))e^{-n\delta''}$. Thus,

$$P(\underline{y}) = \sum_{c'(x)} P(c(x)')P(\underline{y}|c'(x)) \geq P(\hat{c}(x)P(\underline{y}|\hat{c}(x)e^{-n\delta''}$$

where $\hat{c}(x)$ corresponds to the vector $\underline{x}$ on which $P(\underline{y}|\underline{x})$ is conditioned.

Let $\hat{P}_m(\underline{x}) = \prod_i P(x_i)$, where $P(x) = \hat{c}(x)$. Then it follows from (8.1), (8.2) and (8.3) that for any positive Δ and for large enough n

$$\left[\frac{P(\underline{y})}{P(\underline{y}|\underline{x})}\right]^{1/n} \geq \left(e^{-H_{\hat{c}(x)}(y)-H_{\hat{c}(x)}(y|x)]-\Delta} - \Delta\right) \cdot P(\hat{c}(x))^{1/n} \tag{8.5}$$

where $H_{c(x)}(y|x) = -\sum_Y \sum_X c(x)P(y|x)\log P(y|x)$.

Now, by (4) and (5)

$$I^q(\underline{X},\underline{Y}) = \sum_{\hat{c}} P(\hat{c}(x))E_{c(x)}Q\left[\left(\frac{P(\underline{y})}{P(\underline{y}|\underline{x})}\right)^{1/n}\right]$$

$$\leq \Pr[\hat{c}(x) < \delta^2] \cdot Q\left[\frac{\min_{x,y} P(y|x)}{\max_{x,y} P(y|x)}\right]$$

$$+ \Pr[\hat{c}(x) \geq \delta^2] \cdot \sup_{\hat{c}(x)} Q\left[\left(e^{-I_{\hat{c}(x)}(x,y) - \Delta} - \Delta\right)e^{-2/n \log\delta}\right],$$

where $I_{\hat{c}(x)}(x,y) = H_{\hat{c}(x)}(y) - H_{\hat{c}(x)}(y|x)$. Hence, it follows that

$$C_\infty^q = \sup_{\hat{c}(x)} Q\left[e^{-I_{\hat{c}(x)}(x,y)}\right] = Q[e^{-C}], \tag{8.6}$$

where $C = \max_{P(x)} \sum P(x)P(y|x) \log \frac{P(y|x)}{P(y)}$, which is the classical channel capacity.

Furthermore, C_∞^q is achieved by $P_o(\underline{x}) = \prod_{i=1}^n P_o(x_i)$ where P_o is the one that achieves C. On the other hand, since $Q(e^{-x})$ is assumed to be a convex function of x, hence

$$I^q(U,V) = EQ\left[\left(\frac{P(\underline{v})}{P(\underline{v}|\underline{u})}\right)^{1/n}\right] = EQ\left[e^{-\frac{1}{n}\log\frac{P(\underline{v}|\underline{u})}{P(\underline{v})}}\right] \geq EQ\left[e^{-\frac{1}{n}I(\underline{u},\underline{v})}\right]$$

where $I(\underline{u},\underline{v})$ is the classical mutual information $I(\underline{u},\underline{v}) = E\log\frac{P(\underline{v}|\underline{u})}{P(\underline{v})}$.

Hence, if the source is assumed to be memoryless we have, for any n, $R^q(d) \geq \left[Q(e^{-R(d)})\right]$, where $R(d)$ is the classical rate-distortion function.

Hence, by (8.6) $C^q_\infty = Q\left[e^{-C}\right] \geq R^q(d) \geq Q\left[e^{-R(d)}\right]$, and since $Q(\alpha)$ is a decreasing function of α, $C \geq R(d)$, which is the classical Rate-Distortion Bound.

9. Extension of the Information Functional and Data Processing Theorems to General Alphabets

In this section, we extend the results of Sections 3 and 5 to general alphabets. The extension of the bounding techniques of Sections 4 and 6 is straightforward, and will not be discussed here.

Let $(\Omega,\mathcal{B})$ be a measurable space, let P be a probability measure on $(\Omega,\mathcal{B})$, and let μ_i, $i = 1,\dots,k$ be finite positive measures on $(\Omega,\mathcal{B})$, which are mutually absolutely continuous with respect to P, and let $Q(\alpha_1,\dots,\alpha_k)$ be a convex function on $0 < \alpha_i < \infty$, $1 \leq i < k$. Let q denote the triple $(K,\underline{\mu},Q)$.

<u>Definition</u>: The generalized entropy of P with respect to q is defined as

$$\mathcal{H}^q(P) = \sup \sum_j P(E_j)Q\left(\frac{\underline{\mu}(E_j)}{P(E_j)}\right), \tag{9.1}$$

where the supremum is taken over all finite $\mathcal{B}$ measurable partitions of Ω such that $P(E_j) \neq 0$ for all j.

Lemma 9.1: $\mathcal{H}^q(P) \geq Q(\underline{\mu}(\Omega))$.

Proof: By Jensen's inequality

$$\sum_j P(E_j) Q\left(\frac{\mu_i(E_j)}{P(E_j)}\ ;\ 1 \leq j \leq k\right) \geq Q\left(\sum_j \mu_i(E_j);\ \ 1 \leq j \leq k\right) = Q(\underline{\mu}(\Omega)) .$$

Lemma 9.2: If $f(\omega) = \tilde{\omega}$ is a measurable function from $(\tilde{\Omega},\mathcal{B})$ to $(\tilde{\Omega},\mathcal{B})$, $\tilde{P}$, $\tilde{\mu}_i$ are the measures induced on $(\tilde{\Omega},\tilde{\mathcal{B}})$ by P and μ_i, and q $\tilde{q} = (K,\tilde{\underline{\mu}},Q)$ then $\mathcal{H}^q(P) \geq \mathcal{H}^q(\tilde{P})$.

The proof is the same as the proof given in ref. 2.

Lemma 9.3: The summation in the right hand side of (9.1) is not decreased when a finite $\mathcal{B}$ measurable partition $\{E_i\}$, of Ω is replaced by a finite $\mathcal{B}$ measurable subpartition $\{E_i'\}$ of $\{E_i\}$ where $P(E_i') \neq 0$ for all i.

Proof: Let $E, E', E'' \in \mathcal{B}$, $E = E' \cup E''$, $E' \cap E'' = \phi$, $P(E') \neq 0$, $P(E'') \neq 0$, then by convexity

$$P(E)Q\left(\frac{\mu_j(E)}{P(E)}\ ;\ j = 1,\dots,k\right) \leq P(E')Q\left(\frac{\mu_j(E')}{P(E')}\ ;\ 1 \leq j \leq k\right)$$
$$+ P(E'')Q\left(\frac{\mu_j(E'')}{P(E'')}\ ;\ 1 \geq j \geq k\right) ,$$

which proves the lemma.

Theorem 9.1:

$$\mathcal{H}^q(P) = \int_\Omega Q(\underline{\rho}(\omega)dP(\omega) \qquad (9.2)$$

where $\rho_j(\omega) = (d\mu_j/dP)(\omega)$ is the Radon-Nykodym derivative of μ_j with respect to P.

Proof: Consider the partition $A_i \in \mathcal{B}$, $P(A_i) \neq 0$, $i = 1,\ldots,n$ which achieves $\mathcal{H}^q(P)$ within an ε. Then

$$\int_{A_i} Q(\underline{\rho}(\omega)dP(\omega) \geq P(A_i)Q \int_{A_i} \underline{\rho}(\omega) \frac{dP(\omega)}{P(A_i)} = P(A_i)Q \frac{\underline{\mu}(A_i)}{P(A_i)} .$$

Therefore $h \geq \mathcal{H}^q(P) - \varepsilon$ where h is the right hand side of (9.2).

Conversely, let $\{E_i^n\}$ be a sequence of positions such that

$H_n = \sum_i P(E_i^n)Q\left(\frac{\underline{\mu}(E_i')}{P(E_i^n)}\right)$ converges to $\mathcal{H}^q(P)$ as $n \to \infty$. Define

$\rho_j^n(\omega) = \frac{\mu_j(E_i^n)}{P(E_i^n)}$, where E_i^n is the E_i^n such that $\omega \in E_i^n$. Therefore,

$H_n = \int_\Omega Q(\underline{\rho}^n(\omega))dP(\omega)$. It follows from the martingale convergence theorem

that $\rho_j^n(\omega) \xrightarrow{a.s} \rho_j(\omega)$ (c.f. Doop, 343-4). The convexity of Q implies that Q is continuous, therefore $Q(\rho_j^n(\omega), 1 \leq j \leq k) \xrightarrow{a.s} Q(\mu_j(\omega), 1 \leq j \leq k)$ as $n \to \infty$. Assuming first that Q is bounded from below, it follows by Fatou's Lemma that $\mathcal{H}^q(P) = \lim_{n\to\infty} H_n \geq \int_\Omega Q(\underline{\rho}(\omega))dP(\omega) = h$, which proves that theorem for Q bounded from below, since we have shown that $h \geq \mathcal{H}^q(P) - \varepsilon$.

In order to remove the restriction that $Q(\underline{\alpha})$ is bounded from below, let $Q_N(\underline{\alpha}) = \max(-N, Q(\underline{\alpha}))$. Then $Q_N(\underline{\alpha})$ is convex and bounded from below.

Furthermore, by monotone convergence

$$\int_{\Omega} Q_N(\underline{\rho}(\omega))dP(\omega) \longrightarrow \int_{\Omega} Q(\underline{\rho}(\omega))dP(\omega) \tag{9.3}$$

as $N \to \infty$. Consider the partition A_i which, as in the beginning of the proof achieves $H^q(P)$ within an ε, for N large enough

$$\sum_i P(A_i)Q\frac{\underline{\mu}(A_i)}{P(A_i)} = \sum_i P(A_i)Q\frac{\underline{\mu}(A_i)}{P(A_i)} \tag{9.4}$$

and theorem 9.1 follows from (9.3) and (9.4).

Let $(X,\mathcal{B}_X)$ and $(Y,\mathcal{B}_Y)$ be two measurable spaces. $P(dy|x)$ and $\mu_j(dy|x)$, $j = 1,2,\dots,k$ are, for every fixed $B \in \mathcal{B}_Y$ measurable functions on $(X,\mathcal{B}_X)$, for every fixed $x \in X$, $P(dy|x)$ is a probability measure on $(Y,\mathcal{B}_Y)$ and $\mu_j(dy|x)$ are finite positive measures on $(Y,\mathcal{B}_Y)$. Let $P(dx,dy) = P(dy|x)P_X(dx)$, $\mu_j(dx,dy) = \mu_j(dy|x)P_X(dx)$.

We assume that the measures $\mu_j(dx,dy)$ are equivalent to $P(dx,dy)$ and $\frac{d\mu_j}{dP} = \rho_j(x,y)$. Let $x = g(u)$ be a deterministic modulator, where $g(\cdot)$ is a measurable function from $(U,\mathcal{B}_U)$ to $(X,\mathcal{B}_X)$. For every $B_x \in \mathcal{B}_X$, $P_X(B_X) = P_U(g^{-1}(B_x))$. The measure P_{UY} induced on $(U\times Y,\ \mathcal{B}_U\times\mathcal{B}_Y)$ is as follows. Let $D \in \mathcal{B}_U\times\mathcal{B}_Y$, $D_U = (y\colon (u,y) \in D)$, then, as in Section III of [2],

$$P_{UY}(D) = \int_U P_{XY}(D_u|g(u))P_U(du); \qquad \underline{\mu}_{UY}(D) = \int_U \underline{\mu}_{XY}(D_u|g(u))P_u(du);$$

$$\frac{d\underline{\mu}_{UY}}{dP_{UY}}(u,y) = \underline{\rho}(g(u),y) .$$

It follows by the same arguments as in Section III of ref. 2, that for a deterministic modulator

$$H^q(X,Y) = H^q(U,Y) . \tag{9.5}$$

Combining this with Lemma 9.2 for a deterministic demodulator yields

$$H^q(X,Y) \geq H^q(U,V) . \tag{9.6}$$

Remarks:

1. Lemma (9.2) is the extension of the weak data processing theorem of Section 3, eq. (9.5) is the extension of the result of Section 5 for a deterministic modulator.

2. The results of this section can be shown to hold under the following modified assumptions: $Q(\underline{\alpha})$ is convex and continuous on $0 \leq \alpha_i < \infty$ and the requirement $\mu_j \sim P$ is relaxed to $\mu_j << P$.

3. The main differences between the treatment in ref. 2 and the one given in this Section are as follows. In ref. 2, $Q(\alpha)$ was considered only for scalar α, Q was required to satisfy $\alpha Q(1/\alpha) \to 0$ as $\alpha \to 0$. On the other hand, no requirements of the type $\mu \sim P$ and $\mu << P$ were made in ref. 2.

References

1. Berger, T., *Rate Distortion Theory*, Prentice Hall, New Jersey, 1971.

2. Ziv, J., Zakai, M., On functionals satisfying a data-processing theorem, *IEEE Trans. on Inf. Th.*, IT-19, 275, 1973.

3. Csiszar, I., A class of measures of informativity of observation channels, *Periodica Mathematica Hungacrica*, 2, 191, 1972.

4. Roberts, A.W., Varberg, D.E., *Convex Functions*, Academic Press, London, 1973.

5. Van Trees, H.L., *Detection, Estimation and Modulation*, Wiley, New York, 1968; Vol. I.

6. Wyner, A.D., Ziv. J., On communication of analog data from a bounded source space, *Bell Syst. Tech. J.*, 48, 3139, 1969.

7. Bellini, S., Tartara, G., Bounds on error in signal parameter estimation, *IEEE Trans. on Communications*, 340, 1974.

8. Chazan, D., Ziv, J., Zakai, M., Improved lower bounds on signal parameter estimation, *IEEE Trans. on Inf. Th.*, IT-21, 90, 1975.

9. Kailath, T., The divergence and Bhattachayya distance measures in signal selection, *IEEE Trans. Commun. Technol.*, COM-15, 52, 1967.

10. Neveu, J., *Mathematical Foundations of the Calculus of Probability*, Holden-Day, San Francisco, 1965.

THE AEP PROPERTY OF RANDOM SEQUENCES AND APPLICATIONS TO INFORMATION THEORY: PART I BASIC PRINCIPLES

Jack Keil Wolf
Department of Electrical and Computer Engineering
University of Massachusetts
Amherst, Massachusetts 01002

Consider a biased coin with probability of heads p. If p does not equal 0 or 1, there is not much that one can say with certainty about a single toss of the coin. However, for a sequence of N independent tosses, if one chooses N large enough one can make statements about the composition of this sequence which will be true with probability as close to 1 as desired. Specifically if R_N is the relative frequency of heads in a sequence of N tosses (that is, R_N = Number of heads/N) and $\varepsilon > 0$, then

$$P_r[|R_N - p|>\varepsilon] \leq e^{-N\delta(\varepsilon,p)}$$

where $\delta(\varepsilon,p)$ is positive and depends on ε and p but not on N. Thus for N large enough the probability that R_N differs from p in absolute value by more than ε can be made very small. This is a consequence of the Chernoff bound and the law of large numbers.

The asymptotic equipartition property (AEP) is a statement regarding long sequences of random variables. In these notes we will consider the consequences to be formed by independent drawings from a fixed distribution. (Such sequences are said to be i.i.d. - the components are independent and identically distributed). However, it is known that the AEP holds for much more general classes of sequences which include ergodic and even some nonstationary sequences.

There are many forms of stating the AEP but all have the following in common. Let X be a discrete random variable with pdf $p_X(x)$ where $x \varepsilon \mathcal{X}$. Let the size of the alphabet $\mathcal{X}$ be $|\mathcal{X}|$. The $|\mathcal{X}|^N$ possible sequences of length N can be divided into two sets. All the sequences in the first set have approximately the same probability. Furthermore the sum of the probabilities of the sequences in the first set is almost 1. Finally tight upper and lower bounds are known for the number of sequences in the first set and this number is usually much less than $|\mathcal{X}|^N$, the total number of sequences. Thus, although this set contains relatively few of the sequences, it has almost all the probability.

The sequences in this first set are often called "typical sequences" (while the sequences in the other set are called "nontypical sequences"). A common misconception is that the sequences with the highest probability are typical sequences. This is not always the case. Some nontypical sequences may have higher probability than the typical ones. For example, if one tosses a coin N times and if on each toss, p is the probability of obtaining a head, then the typical sequences are those sequences with approximately pN heads. The most probable sequence (if $p < 1/2$) is the sequence of all tails which is a nontypical sequence.

There are many different definitions of typical sequences. The one alluded to above is that the typical sequences have the "right" composition. That is, the relative frequencies of each of the symbols in a typical sequence are close to the probabilities of these symbols. In the next section where typical sequences are formally defined, a different approach will be taken. In this approach, typical sequences are those sequences whose probability is close to some pre-chosen number. There is a close relationship between these approaches but they are not identical. However either can be used to develop a useful theory.

The applications of the AEP to problems in information theory all center on the ideas that we need only worry about typical sequences and can ignore the nontypical ones. Every now and then a nontypical sequence will arise and we will be fooled. However, this occurs with probability very close to 0. Furthermore we can control this probability by choosing N appropriately. Specifically, by choosing N large enough, we can make this probability smaller than any $\varepsilon>0$.

In all but the simplest application we will require the AEP for sets of sequences rather than for a single sequence. Thus, following Cover[1] and Forney[2] we will develop the AEP for sets of sequences. The notation is that of Cover.[1]

Jointly Typical Sequences

Let $\{X^{(1)},X^{(2)},\ldots,X^{(k)}\}$ denote a finite collection of discrete random variables with some fixed joint pdf $p_{X^{(1)}X^{(2)}\ldots X^{(k)}}(x^{(1)},x^{(2)},\ldots, x^{(k)})$. For ease of notation we will sometimes write this and all subsequent pdf's without the subscripts - that is, $p(x^{(1)},x^{(2)},\ldots,x^{(k)})$. Let S denote an ordered subset of these random variables and let $\bar{s}$ be a vector formed from N independent drawings of the random variables in question. Thus if $\bar{S} = (S_1,S_2,\ldots,S_N)$, then $P_r[\bar{S} = \bar{s}] = \prod_{i=1}^{N} P_r[S_i = s_i]$. We now define $A_\varepsilon(X^{(1)},X^{(2)},\ldots,X^{(k)})$, the set of "jointly ε-typical" N-sequences $(\bar{x}^{(1)},\bar{x}^{(2)},\ldots,\bar{x}^{(k)})$ as $A_\varepsilon(X^{(1)},X^{(2)},\ldots,X^{(k)}) = \{(\bar{x}^{(1)},\bar{x}^{(2)},\ldots,\bar{x}^{(k)}): \left| -\frac{1}{N}\log P_r[\bar{S} = \bar{s}] - H(S)\right| \leq \varepsilon$ for all $\bar{S} \subseteq \{\bar{X}^{(1)},\bar{X}^{(2)},\ldots \bar{X}^{(k)}\}\}$. Here $\bar{s}$ denotes the ordered set of sequences in $\{\bar{x}^{(1)},\bar{x}^{(2)},\ldots,\bar{x}^{(k)}\}$ corresponding to $\bar{S}$. H(S) is defined as $\sum_s P_r[S = s] \log_2 \frac{1}{P_r[S=s]}$.

Thus for example if k=3, and we let $(X^{(1)},X^{(2)},X^{(3)}) = (X,Y,Z)$, then

$$A_\varepsilon(X,Y,Z) = \{(\bar{x},\bar{y},\bar{z}):\ E_{xyz} \cap E_{xy} \cap E_{xz} \cap E_{yz} \cap E_x \cap E_y \cap E_z\}$$

where

$$E_{xyz} = \text{event } \left| -\frac{1}{N}\log P_r[\bar{X}=\bar{x},\ \bar{Y}=\bar{y},\ \bar{Z}=\bar{z}] - H(X,Y,Z)\right| \leq \varepsilon$$

$$E_{xy} = \text{event } \left| -\frac{1}{N}\log P_r[\bar{X}=\bar{x},\ \bar{Y}=\bar{y}] - H(X,Y)\right| \leq \varepsilon$$

$$E_{xz} = \text{event } \left| -\frac{1}{N}\log P_r[\bar{X}=\bar{x},\ \bar{Z}=\bar{z}] - H(X,Z)\right| \leq \varepsilon$$

$$E_{yz} = \text{event } \left| -\frac{1}{N}\log P_r[\bar{Y}=\bar{y},\ \bar{Z}=\bar{z}] - H(Y,Z)\right| \leq \varepsilon$$

$$E_{x} = \text{event } \left| -\frac{1}{N}\log P_r[\bar{X}=\bar{x}] - H(X)\right| \leq \varepsilon$$

$$E_{y} = \text{event } \left| -\frac{1}{N}\log P_r[\bar{Y}=\bar{y}] - H(Y)\right| \leq \varepsilon$$

$$E_{z} = \text{event } \left| -\frac{1}{N}\log P_r[\bar{Z}=\bar{z}] - H(Z)\right| \leq \varepsilon$$

Note that if $(\bar{x},\bar{y},\bar{z}) \in A_\varepsilon(X,Y,Z)$, then $(\bar{x},\bar{y}) \in A_\varepsilon(X,Y)$, $(\bar{x},\bar{z}) \in A_\varepsilon(X,Z)$, $(\bar{y},\bar{z}) \in A_\varepsilon(Y,Z)$, $\bar{x} \in A_\varepsilon(X)$, $\bar{y} \in A_\varepsilon(Y)$ and $\bar{z} \in A_\varepsilon(Z)$.

Returning to the general case of k random variables, the AEP now states that for any $\varepsilon>0$, there exists an N ($N=N(\varepsilon)$), such that for every subset S of the random variables $(X^{(1)},X^{(2)},\ldots,X^{(k)})$,

1. $\sum_{\bar{s}\in A_\varepsilon(S)} P_r[\bar{S}=\bar{s}] \geq 1 - \varepsilon$

2. For all $\bar{s}\in A_\varepsilon(S)$, $2^{-N(H(S)+\varepsilon)} \leq P_r[\bar{S}=\bar{s}] \leq 2^{-N(H(S)-\varepsilon)}$

3. $(1-\varepsilon)\, 2^{N(H(S)-\varepsilon)} \leq |A_\varepsilon(S)| \leq 2^{N(H(S)+\varepsilon)}$.

The proof is given by Cover.[1] Here, $A_\varepsilon(S)$ denotes A_ε restricted to the coordinates corresponding to S and $|A_\varepsilon(S)|$ is the cardinality of the set $A_\varepsilon(S)$. Note that (2) is just a restatement of the definition of $A_\varepsilon(S)$ and that (3) follows directly from (1) and the fact that the sum of the probabilities in (1) is upper bounded by the value 1. The only interesting part of the proof is the proof of (1) which follows from the law of large numbers.

For the special case of k=3, we have from the AEP that for any $\varepsilon>0$, there exists an N such that

1. $$\sum_{A_\varepsilon(X,Y,Z)} P_r[\bar{X}=\bar{x},\ \bar{Y}=\bar{y},\ \bar{Z}=\bar{z}] \geq 1 - \varepsilon$$

$$\sum_{A_\varepsilon(X,Y)} P_r[\bar{X}=\bar{x},\ \bar{Y}=\bar{y}] \geq 1 - \varepsilon$$

$$\sum_{A_\varepsilon(X,Z)} P_r[\bar{X}=\bar{x},\ \bar{Z}=\bar{z}] \geq 1 - \varepsilon$$

$$\sum_{A_\varepsilon(Y,Z)} P_r[\bar{Y}=\bar{y},\ \bar{Z}=\bar{z}] \geq 1 - \varepsilon$$

$$\sum_{A_\varepsilon(X)} P_r[\bar{X}=\bar{x}] \geq 1 - \varepsilon$$

$$\sum_{A_\varepsilon(Y)} P_r[\bar{Y}=\bar{y}] \geq 1 - \varepsilon$$

$$\sum_{A_\varepsilon(Z)} P_r[\bar{Z}=\bar{z}] \geq 1 - \varepsilon$$

2. For $(\bar{x},\bar{y},\bar{z}) \varepsilon A_\varepsilon(X,Y,Z)$, $2^{-N(H(X,Y,Z)+\varepsilon)} \leq P_r[\bar{X}=\bar{x},\bar{Y}=\bar{y},\bar{Z}=\bar{z}] \leq 2^{-N(H(X,Y,Z)-\varepsilon)}$

For $(\bar{x},\bar{y}) \varepsilon A_\varepsilon(X,Y)$, $2^{-N(H(X,Y)+\varepsilon)} \leq P_r[\bar{X}=\bar{x},\bar{Y}=\bar{y}] \leq 2^{-N(H(X,Y)-\varepsilon)}$

For $(\bar{x},\bar{z}) \varepsilon A_\varepsilon(X,Z)$, $2^{-N(H(X,Z)+\varepsilon)} \leq P_r[\bar{X}=\bar{x},\bar{Z}=\bar{z}] \leq 2^{-N(H(X,Z)-\varepsilon)}$

For $(\bar{y},\bar{z}) \varepsilon A_\varepsilon(Y,Z)$, $2^{-N(H(Y,Z)+\varepsilon)} \leq P_r[\bar{Y}=\bar{y},\bar{Z}=\bar{z}] \leq 2^{-N(H(Y,Z)-\varepsilon)}$

For $(\bar{x}) \varepsilon A_\varepsilon(X)$, $2^{-N(H(X)+\varepsilon)} \leq P_r[\bar{X}=\bar{x}] \leq 2^{-N(H(X)-\varepsilon)}$

For $(\bar{y}) \varepsilon A_\varepsilon(Y)$, $2^{-N(H(Y)+\varepsilon)} \leq P_r[\bar{Y}=\bar{y}] \leq 2^{-N(H(Y)-\varepsilon)}$

For $(\bar{z}) \varepsilon A_\varepsilon(Z)$, $2^{-N(H(Z)+\varepsilon)} \leq P_r[\bar{Z}=\bar{z}] \leq 2^{-N(H(Z)-\varepsilon)}$

3. $(1-\varepsilon)\, 2^{N(H(X,Y,Z)-\varepsilon)} \leq |A_\varepsilon(X,Y,Z)| \leq 2^{N(H(X,Y,Z)+\varepsilon)}$

$(1-\varepsilon)\, 2^{N(H(X,Y)-\varepsilon)} \leq |A_\varepsilon(X,Y)| \leq 2^{N(H(X,Y)+\varepsilon)}$

$(1-\varepsilon)\, 2^{N(H(X,Z)-\varepsilon)} \leq |A_\varepsilon(X,Z)| \leq 2^{N(H(X,Z)+\varepsilon)}$

$(1-\varepsilon)\, 2^{N(H(Y,Z)-\varepsilon)} \leq |A_\varepsilon(Y,Z)| \leq 2^{N(H(Y,Z)+\varepsilon)}$

$(1-\varepsilon)\, 2^{N(H(X)-\varepsilon)} \leq |A_\varepsilon(X)| \leq 2^{N(H(X)+\varepsilon)}$

$(1-\varepsilon)\, 2^{N(H(Y)-\varepsilon)} \leq |A_\varepsilon(Y)| \leq 2^{N(H(Y)+\varepsilon)}$

$(1-\varepsilon)\, 2^{N(H(Z)-\varepsilon)} \leq |A_\varepsilon(Z)| \leq 2^{N(H(Z)+\varepsilon)}$

In (3), $|A_\varepsilon(X,Y,Z)|$ are the number of $(\bar{x},\bar{y},\bar{z})$ sequences which are in $A_\varepsilon(X,Y,Z)$, $|A_\varepsilon(X,Y)|$ denotes the number of $(\bar{x},\bar{y})$ sequences which are in $A_\varepsilon(X,Y)$, etc.

One somewhat confusing fact is that although $\bar{x}$ may be a typical sequence, it may have a very atypical composition. For example let X take on the values (0,1,2) with probabilities (2/3,1/6,1/6). A sequence consisting of 2/3N 0's and 1/3N 1's will be typical but will not have the expected composition of roughly 2/3N 0's, 1/6N 1's and 1/6N 2's.

Two Random Variables

For k=2, with two random variables $(X^{(1)},X^{(2)}) = (X,Y)$ we can give a simple pictorial description of typical sequences. Referring to Figure 1, we label the rows of the array by all $|\mathcal{X}|^N$ possible $\bar{x}$-vectors, $\bar{x}_1,\bar{x}_2,\ldots$ and the columns of the array by all $|\mathcal{Y}|^N$ possible $\bar{y}$-vectors, $\bar{y}_1,\bar{y}_2,\ldots$. We put a dot in the ith row and jth column if and only if $(\bar{x}_i,\bar{y}_j)\in A_\varepsilon(X,Y)$. Furthermore we order the rows and columns so that the elements of $A_\varepsilon(X,Y)$ crowd the upper left corner of the array.

For each $\bar{y}$, let the set of $\bar{x}$ that are jointly ε-typical with that $\bar{y}$ be denoted as $T_{\bar{y}}$. Thus

$$T_{\bar{y}} = \{\bar{x} : (\bar{x},\bar{y})\in A_\varepsilon(X,Y)\}.$$

We can now show

Lemma 1: $|T_{\bar{y}}| \leq 2^{N(H(X|Y)+2\varepsilon)}$

Proof: The lemma is trivially true for $\bar{y}\notin A_\varepsilon(Y)$ since then $T_{\bar{y}} = 0$. Thus assume $\bar{y}\in A_\varepsilon(Y)$. Then

$$1 = \sum_{\bar{x}} p(\bar{x}|\bar{y}) = \sum_{\bar{x}} \frac{p(\bar{x},\bar{y})}{p(\bar{y})} \geq \sum_{\bar{x}\in T_{\bar{y}}} \frac{p(\bar{x},\bar{y})}{p(\bar{y})}$$

$$\geq \sum_{\bar{x}\in T_{\bar{y}}} \frac{2^{-N(H(X,Y)+\varepsilon)}}{2^{-N(H(Y)-\varepsilon)}} = |T_{\bar{y}}|\ 2^{-N(H(X|Y)+2\varepsilon)}$$

Dividing by $2^{-N(H(X|Y)+2\varepsilon)}$ completes the proof.

This lemma shows that there are at most $2^{N(H(X|Y)+2\varepsilon)}$ dots in each column. In a similar fashion we can show that there are at most $2^{N(H(Y|X)+2\varepsilon)}$ dots in each row. It does not appear, however, that there is a corresponding lower bound on the number of dots in each row and column (for those rows and columns containing dots). One can obtain such a lower bound if one defines typical sequences in terms of their composition but this approach is not followed here.

Another interesting fact concerning the array in Figure 1 is the density of dots in the upper left hand corner of the array. Specifically consider only those rows corresponding to $\bar{x}$ sequences in $A_\varepsilon(X)$ and only those columns corresponding to $\bar{y}$ sequences in $A_\varepsilon(Y)$. The number of points in the lattice formed by the intersection of these rows and columns, L_ε, is bounded as

$$(1-\varepsilon)^2\ 2^{N(H(X)+H(Y)-2\varepsilon)} \leq L_\varepsilon \leq 2^{N(H(X)+H(Y)+2\varepsilon)}$$

However the number of "dots" in this lattice, $|A\ (X,Y)|$, is bounded as

$$(1-\varepsilon)\ 2^{N(H(X,Y)\ -\ \varepsilon)} \leq |A_\varepsilon(X,Y)| \leq 2^{N(H(X,Y)\ +\ \varepsilon)}$$

The density of "dots" in this lattice, $\frac{|A_\varepsilon|}{L_\varepsilon}$, is then bounded as

$$(1-\varepsilon)\ 2^{-N(I(X;Y)+3\varepsilon)} \leq \frac{|A_\varepsilon|}{L_\varepsilon} \leq 2^{-N(I(X;Y)-3\varepsilon)}\ (1-\varepsilon)^{-2}$$

where $I(X;Y) = H(X) + H(Y) - H(X,Y)$ is the mutual information between X and Y.

It will now be shown that the "dots" are uniformly distributed in this lattice. That is, if one chooses an $\bar{x}$ sequence at random (that is, with probability $p(\bar{x})$) and a $\bar{y}$ sequence at random (with probability $p(\bar{y})$), the probability that the pair $(\bar{x},\bar{y})$ will be jointly typical is upper and lower bounded by the same bounds as for $\frac{|A_\varepsilon|}{L_\varepsilon}$. Thus for large N, this probability is just the density of the "dots".

Proof

$$|A_\varepsilon(X,Y)|\,2^{-N(H(X)+\varepsilon)}2^{-N(H(Y)+\varepsilon)} \le \sum_{(\bar{x},\bar{y})\varepsilon A_\varepsilon(X,Y)}\sum p(\bar{x})\,p(\bar{y})$$

$$\le |A_\varepsilon(X,Y)|\,2^{-N(H(X)-\varepsilon)}2^{-N(H(Y)-\varepsilon)}$$

$$(1-\varepsilon)\;2^{-N(I(X;Y)+3\varepsilon)} \le \sum_{(\bar{x},\bar{y})\varepsilon A_\varepsilon(X,Y)}\sum p(\bar{x})\;p(\bar{y}) \le 2^{-N(I(X;Y)-3\varepsilon)}$$

We next show a remarkable construction due to Cover.[3] Let B_1, B_2, ..., B_M, $M=2^{NR_X}$ be a random partition of X^N. That is, assign each $\bar{x}$ in X^N to one of the B_i, independently and with equal probability. Specifically let $P_r[\bar{x}\varepsilon B_i] = \frac{1}{M}$ for i=1,2,...,M and for all $\bar{x}$ in X^N. We define the event G as

G: $(\bar{X},\bar{Y})\varepsilon A_\varepsilon(X,Y)$ and there exist an $\bar{x}'$, such that $(\bar{x}',\bar{Y})\varepsilon A_\varepsilon(X,Y)$ and $\bar{x}'$ and $\bar{X}$ are in the same partition.

We now show the following

Theorem: $P_r[G] \le 2^{N(H(X|Y)+2\varepsilon-R_X)}$

Proof

$$P_r[G] = \sum_{(\bar{x},\bar{y})\varepsilon A_\varepsilon(X,Y)} p(\bar{x},\bar{y})\;P_r[\exists\bar{x}' \ne \bar{x},\ \bar{x}'\varepsilon\, T_{\bar{y}},\ \bar{x} \text{ and } \bar{x}' \text{ are in the same partition}]$$

$$\leq \sum_{(\overline{x},\overline{y})\varepsilon A_\varepsilon(X,Y)} p(\overline{x},\overline{y}) \sum_{\substack{\overline{x}'\neq\overline{x}\\ \overline{x}'\varepsilon T_{\overline{y}}}} P_r[\overline{x}' \text{ is in same partition as } \overline{x}]$$

$$= \sum_{(\overline{x},\overline{y})\varepsilon A_\varepsilon(X,Y)} p(\overline{x},\overline{y}) \sum_{\substack{\overline{x}'\neq\overline{x}\\ \overline{x}'\varepsilon T_{\overline{y}}}} 2^{-NR_X}$$

$$\leq \sum_{(\overline{x},\overline{y})\varepsilon A_\varepsilon(X,Y)} p(\overline{x},\overline{y}) \; |T_{\overline{y}}| \; 2^{-NR_X}$$

$$\leq \sum_{(\overline{x},\overline{y})\varepsilon A_\varepsilon(X,Y)} p(\overline{x},\overline{y}) \; 2^{N(H(X|Y)+2\varepsilon)} \; 2^{-NR_X}$$

$$\leq 2^{N(H(X|Y)+2\varepsilon-R_X)}.$$

Since in the above theorem we have calculated the average probability of G over all partitions, there surely is a deterministic choice of these partitions that have this property. We thus see that if we choose $R_X > H(X|Y)+2\varepsilon$, we can partition the $\overline{x}$ sequences so that the total probability of more than one $\overline{x}$ sequence in a partition being jointly typical with any $\overline{y}$ sequence is as small as we desire. Such a partitioning is shown in Figure 2. Note that we need only assign $\overline{x}$ sequences from $A_\varepsilon(X)$ to partitions. The other $\overline{x}$ sequences do not play any role in the theorem. Note that the average number of typical $\overline{x}$ sequences in each set B_i is $|A_\varepsilon(X)|/2^{NR_X}$. Thus at least one set B_i contains $|A_\varepsilon(X)|/2^{NR_X} \geq (1-\varepsilon)\, 2^{N(H(X)-2\varepsilon-R_X)}$ typical $\overline{x}$ sequences. Since we want to choose $R_X > H(X|Y)+\varepsilon$ let us choose $R_X = H(X|Y)+\varepsilon_1$, $\varepsilon_1>\varepsilon$. Then, at least one B_i contains at least $(1-\varepsilon)\, 2^{N(H(X)-2\varepsilon-H(X|Y)-\varepsilon_1)} = (1-\varepsilon)\, 2^{N(I(X;Y)-2\varepsilon-\varepsilon_1)}$ $\overline{x}$ sequences from $A_\varepsilon(X)$.

We complete this section by proving the following

Theorem: For any $\varepsilon>0$, $\delta>0$, there exists an N and a set of $M=2^{N(I(X;Y)+4\varepsilon)}$ $\bar{y}$ sequences, say $\bar{y}_1,\bar{y}_2,\ldots,\bar{y}_M$, such that for every $\bar{x}$, $(\bar{x},\bar{y}_i)\varepsilon A_\varepsilon(X,Y)$ for at least one $\bar{y}_i$ except for a set of $\bar{x}$ of total probability less than δ.

Proof We first choose the M $\bar{y}$ sequences independently according to the distribution $p_{\bar{Y}}(\bar{y})$. For any such $\bar{y}$ and any $\bar{x}$ chosen in accordance with the distribution $p_{\bar{X}}(\bar{x})$, the probability that $(\bar{x},\bar{y})$ are jointly typical is bounded as

$$(1-\varepsilon)\ 2^{-N(I(X;Y)+3\varepsilon)} \le \sum_{(\bar{x},\bar{y})\varepsilon A_\varepsilon(X,Y)}\sum p(\bar{x})\ p(\bar{y}) \le 2^{-N(I(X;Y)-3\varepsilon)}$$

Let J be the set of $\bar{x}$'s defined as

$$J = \{\bar{x} : (\bar{x},\bar{y}_1)\notin A_\varepsilon(X,Y) \cap (\bar{x},\bar{y}_2)\notin A_\varepsilon(X,Y) \ldots \cap (\bar{x},\bar{y}_M)\notin A_\varepsilon(X,Y)\}$$

Then

$$\sum_{\bar{x}\varepsilon J} p_{\bar{X}}(x) = P_r[(\bar{x},\bar{y}_1)\notin A_\varepsilon(X,Y) \cap (\bar{x},\bar{y}_2)\notin A_\varepsilon(X,Y) \ldots \cap (\bar{x},\bar{y}_M)\notin A_\varepsilon(X,Y)]$$

$$= \prod_{i=1}^{M} P_r[(\bar{x},\bar{y}_i)\notin A_\varepsilon(X,Y)]$$

$$= \prod_{i=1}^{M} \left[1 - P_r[(\bar{x},\bar{y}_i)\varepsilon A_\varepsilon(X,Y)]\right]$$

$$\le \prod_{i=1}^{M} (1 - (1-\varepsilon)\ 2^{-N(I(X;Y)+3\varepsilon)})$$

$$= (1 - (1-\varepsilon)\ 2^{-N(I(X;Y)+3\varepsilon)})^M$$

$$\le e^{-M(1-\varepsilon)\ 2^{-N(I(X;Y)+3\varepsilon)}}$$

$$= e^{-2^{N(I(X;Y)+4\varepsilon-I(X;Y)-3\varepsilon)}(1-\varepsilon)}$$

$$= e^{-2^{N\varepsilon}(1-\varepsilon)}$$

For N large enough, this probability is less than any $\delta>0$. Since this result holds for a random choice of the $\bar{y}_i$, there must be a deterministic choice that has the same property.

Acknowledgment

This work was partially supported by the Air Force Office of Scientific Research, Air Force Systems Command, USAF under Grant No. AFOSR-74-2601 and partially by the National Science Foundation under Grant ENG 73-08235.

References

1. Cover, T., "An achievable rate region for the broadcast channel," IEEE Transactions on Information Theory, vol. IT-21, 399, July 1975.

2. Forney, D., "Information theory," unpublished notes for a course at Stanford University, Winter, 1972.

3. Cover, T., "A proof of the data compression theorem of Slepian and Wolf for ergodic sources," IEEE Transactions on Information Theory, vol. IT-21, 226, March 1975.

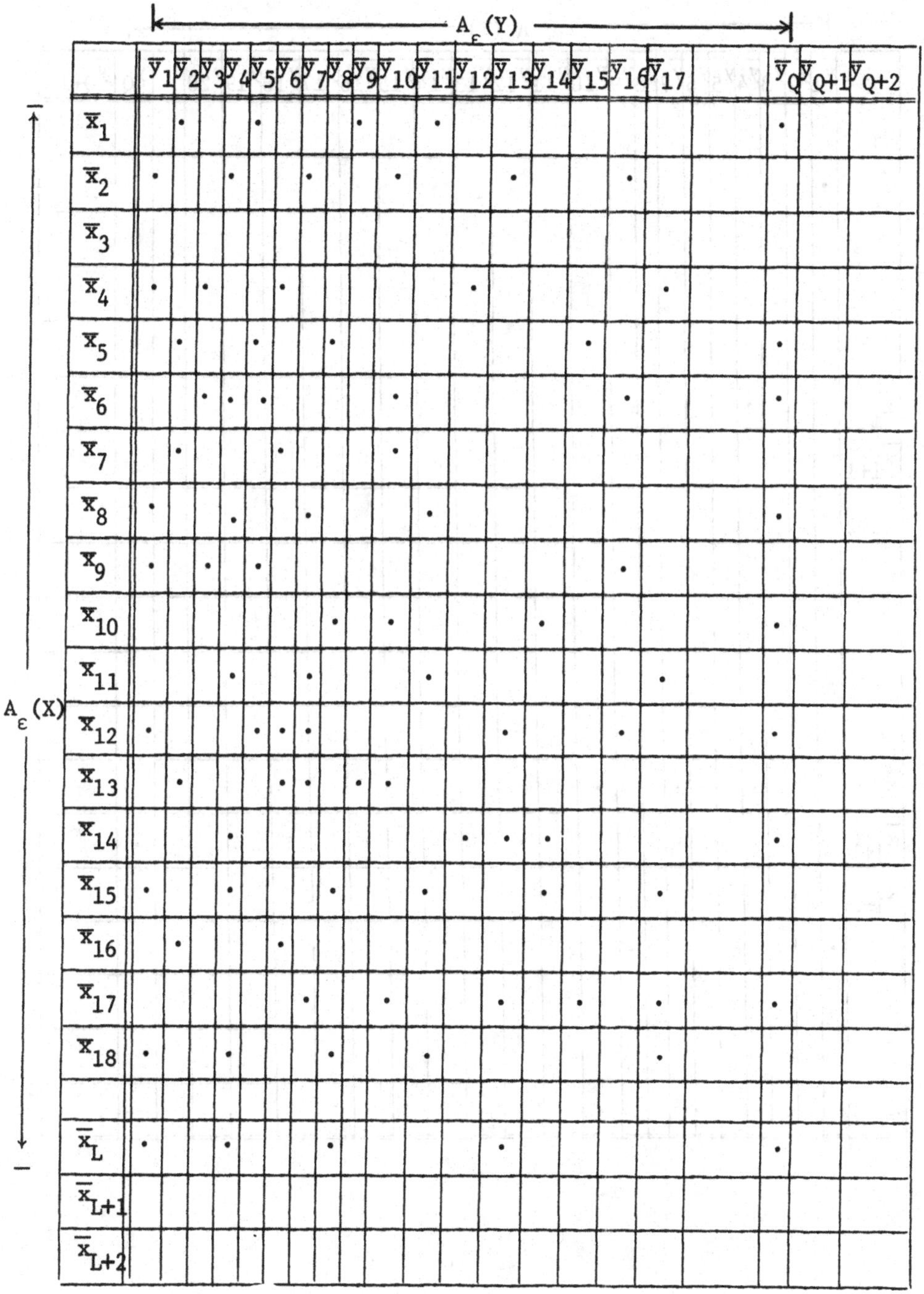

Figure 1. Typical $(\overline{X},\overline{Y})$ Sequences

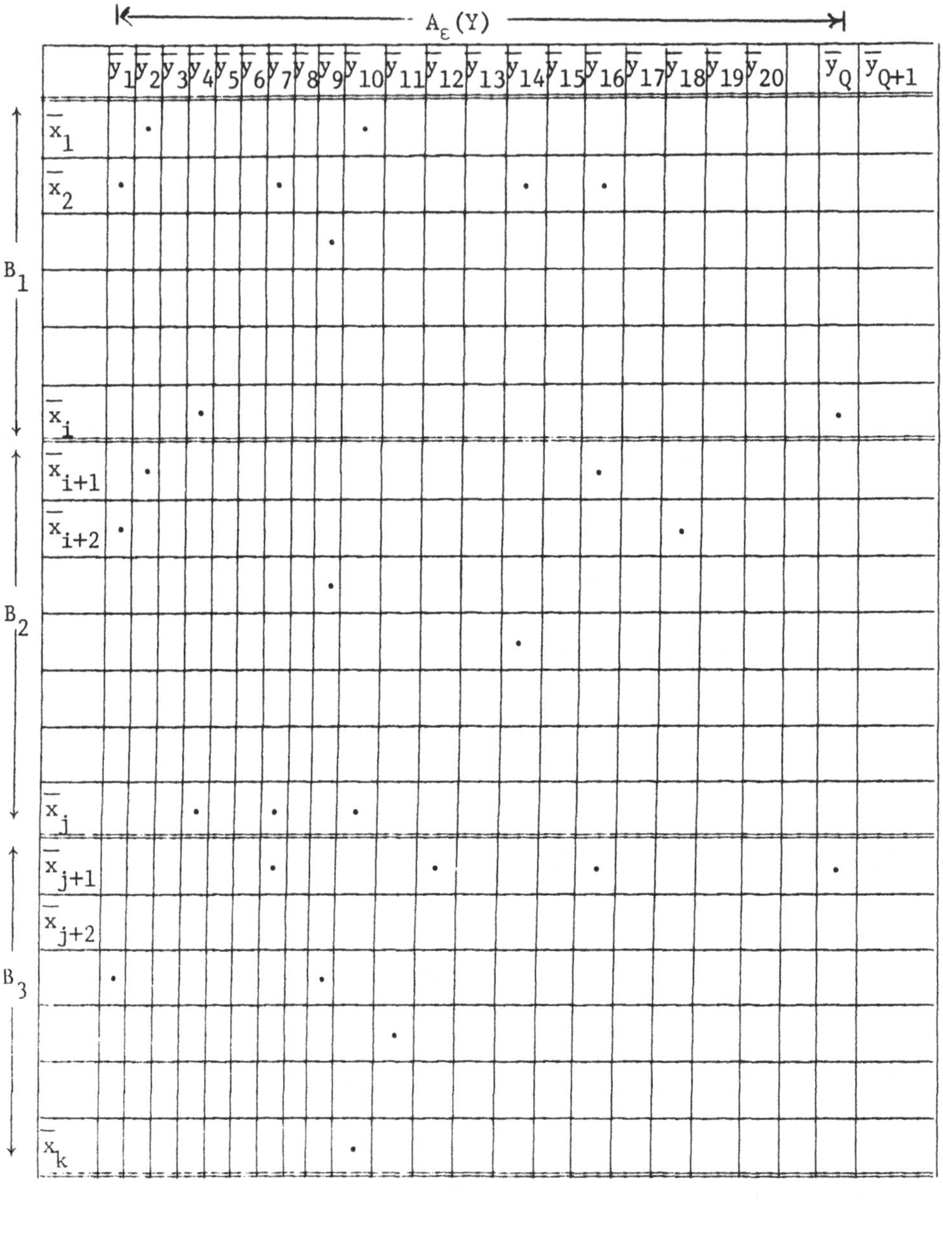

Figure 2. Partition of Typical $(\bar{X},\bar{Y})$ Sequences

THE AEP PROPERTY OF RANDOM SEQUENCES AND APPLICATIONS TO INFORMATION THEORY: PART II SINGLE-USER COMMUNICATIONS

Jack Keil Wolf
Department of Electrical and Computer Engineering
University of Massachusetts
Amherst, Massachusetts 01002

The single-user communication problem introduced by Shannon is concerned with reliably transmitting information from a single source to a single destination via a noisy communications channel. The block diagram of this system is shown in Figure 1. This block diagram has been called the "coat of arms" of the information theorist.

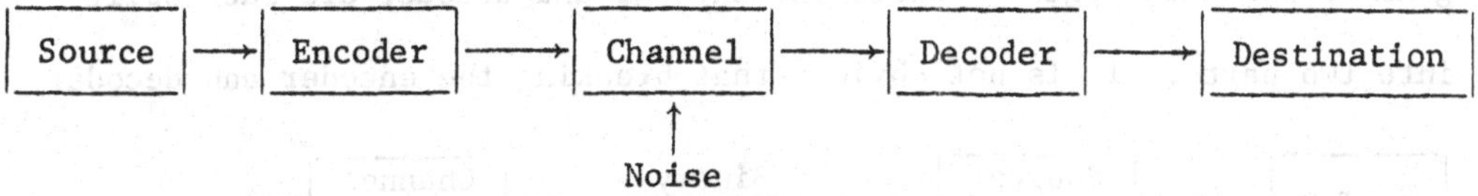

Figure 1. Single-User Communication System

The source originates the information to be transmitted. We shall consider only <u>finite, discrete, memoryless sources</u>. These sources produce symbols from a finite alphabet $\{1,2,\ldots,L\} = \mathcal{U}$ at a rate of ρ_s per second. Each $\frac{1}{\rho_s}$ seconds, the source produces an output U which takes values from the set $\mathcal{U}$ in accordance with the distribution $p_U(\mu)$. Successive outputs are statistically independent.

The memoryless assumption is a poor one for most real sources. However, it is known that the basic concepts are the same for sources with memory--only the mathematics and verbal description are more complicated for the situation when memory is present.

We first assume that we desire that an almost perfect reproduction of the source output be available at the destination. Thus, if the output of the source for $T = \frac{N}{\rho_s}$ seconds is the vector $\overline{U} = (U_1, U_2, \ldots, U_N)$ and if the input to the destination is the vector $\overline{\hat{U}} = (\hat{U}_1, \hat{U}_2, \ldots, \hat{U}_N)$ we will be interested in the probability that $\overline{U} \neq \overline{\hat{U}}$: namely

$$P_e = P_r[\hat{U}_1 \neq U_1 \quad \text{or} \quad \hat{U}_2 \neq U_2 \quad \text{or} \quad \ldots \quad \text{or} \quad \hat{U}_N \neq U_N]$$

We first ignore the effects of noise and ask the question: What is the minimum number of binary digits required to faithfully represent the source output $\overline{U} = (U_1, U_2, \ldots, U_N)$? What we have in mind is a block diagram as shown in Figure 2 where the encoder and decoder are each split into two parts. It is not obvious that breaking the encoder and decoder

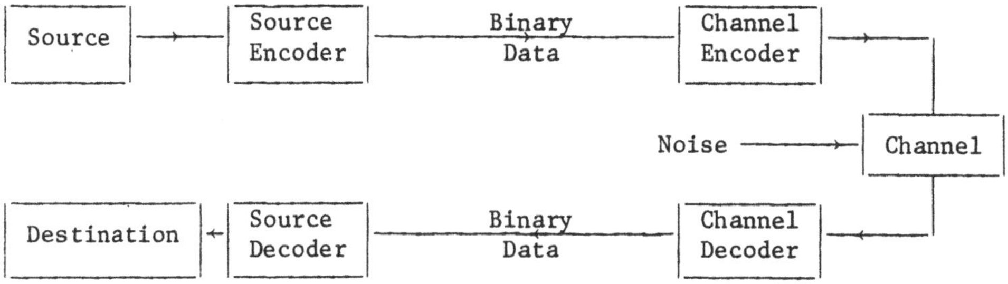

Figure 2. Single-User System with Split Encoder and Decoder

into two parts is a good thing to do. One of the most important results of information theory is that nothing is lost in this interpretation.

Define $H(U) = \sum_{\mu \in U} p_U(\mu) \log_2 \frac{1}{p_U(\mu)}$. H(U) is called the entropy of the source. We now prove the

Source Coding Theorem: For any $\varepsilon>0$, there is an N sufficiently large such that blocks of N source letters can be encoded into $N[H(X)+\varepsilon]$ binary symbols in a one-to-one manner except for a set of source symbols whose total probability is less than ε.

Proof: From the AEP we know that there exists a set of vectors

$$A_\varepsilon(U) = \{\bar{\mu} : \left| -\frac{1}{N} \log P_r[\bar{U} = \bar{\mu}] - H(U) \right| \leq \varepsilon\}$$

such that for any $\varepsilon>0$ there exists an N such that

$$\text{a.} \quad \sum_{\bar{\mu} \in A_\varepsilon(u)} P_r[\bar{U} = \bar{\mu}] \geq 1 - \varepsilon$$

and

$$\text{b.} \quad |A_\varepsilon(U)| \leq 2^{N(H(U)+\varepsilon)}$$

Our encoding scheme is to enumerate the vectors $\bar{\mu}$ in $A_\varepsilon(U)$ and represent each one by the binary expansion of its enumeration. Part (b) ensures us that $N(H(U)+\varepsilon)$ binary digits are sufficient for this purpose. Part (a) tells us that the total probability of those sequences not taken care of is $< \varepsilon$. Q.E.D.

In an actual system we would map all the nontypical source outputs to some common binary number -- say all zeros. Then at the decoder when the source decoder receives all zeros it would output an arbitrary N-tuple--say the first typical sequence. This is the only time an error event occurs, and the probability of this event is less than ε.

A more general situation is when we do not insist that the input to the destination be an exact reproduction of the source output but rather we allow some distortion in the reproduction. Certainly we should be able to get away with fewer binary digits if we are satisfied with a more course representation of the source output. The input letters to the destination may even be from a different alphabet than the source alphabet, say $\hat{U} = \{\hat{1},\hat{2},\ldots,\hat{L}\}$. For every pair of letters μ and $\hat{\mu}$, μ from the source alphabet U and $\hat{\mu}$ from the destination alphabet $\hat{U}$ we define a finite non negative number called the distortion and written $d(\mu,\hat{\mu})$. We assume $d(\mu,\hat{\mu})<\infty$ for all μ and $\hat{\mu}$. The distortion between N-vectors $\overline{\mu}$ and $\overline{\hat{\mu}}$, written $d(\overline{\mu},\overline{\hat{\mu}})$, is defined as

$$d(\overline{\mu},\overline{\hat{\mu}}) = \sum_{i=1}^{N} d(\mu_i,\hat{\mu}_i).$$

Thus, the distortion between vectors is taken as the sum of the distortion between their components.

If we assume an arbitrary conditional probability function $p_{\hat{U}|U}(\hat{\mu}|\mu)$, that together with the probability distribution of the source $p_U(\mu)$, allows us to define a mutual information $I(U;\hat{U})$ between U and $\hat{U}$, as

$$I(U;\hat{U}) = \sum_{\mu}\sum_{\hat{\mu}} p_{\hat{U}|U}(\hat{\mu}|\mu)p_U(\mu) \log_2 \frac{p_{U|\hat{U}}(\mu|\hat{\mu})}{p_U(\mu)} .$$

and an average distortion, $\overline{d}$, as

$$\overline{d} = \sum_{\mu}\sum_{\hat{\mu}} p_{\hat{U}|U}(\hat{\mu}|\mu)p_U(\mu)d(\mu,\hat{\mu}).$$

The so-called rate distortion function R(d) is now defined for all $d \geq 0$ as

$$R(d) = \min_{\substack{p_{\hat{U}|U}(\hat{\mu}|\mu) \\ \overline{d} \le d}} I(U;\hat{U})$$

We now give a partial proof of the

Rate Distortion Theorem: For any $\varepsilon>0$, $\varepsilon'>0$ and $\delta>0$, there exists an N sufficiently large such that blocks of N source letters can be encoded into $N[R(d)+\varepsilon]$ binary symbols and these binary symbols can be converted into blocks of N destination letters and such that the distortion between the source sequence and destination sequence is less than $N[d+\varepsilon']$ except for a set of source sequences whose total probability is less than δ.

Proof: Since $p_U(\mu)$ is fixed by the source, if we choose an arbitrary $p_{\hat{U}|U}(\hat{\mu}|\mu)$, we have a joint distribution $p_{U,\hat{U}}(\mu,\hat{\mu})$. We know from the last theorem of Part I that one can choose $M = 2^{N(I(U;\hat{U})+\varepsilon)}$ vectors $\overline{\hat{\mu}}$ such that almost every $\overline{\mu}$ is jointly typical with at least one of these vectors. The total probability of those $\overline{\mu}$'s not having this property is less than δ. One can show that the distortion between any jointly typical $\overline{\mu}$ and $\overline{\hat{\mu}}$ is close to $N\,\overline{d}$. The proof is not given here. Since the above holds for any $p_{\hat{U}|U}(\hat{\mu}|\mu)$, it holds for that conditional probability that maximizes $I(U;\hat{U})$ subject to the constraint that $\overline{d} \le d$. Q.E.D.

In the previous two theorems we have examined how we can convert source data to binary digits and then back into a form suitable for the destination. We now concern ourselves with transmitting this binary data over a noisy communication channel. The channel accepts inputs from a finite alphabet $\mathcal{X}$, one input every $\frac{1}{\rho_c}$ seconds. For each input symbol $x \in \mathcal{X}$, it produces an output symbol y from the finite alphabet $\mathcal{Y}$. The noise in the channel causes the outputs to be random. The distribution for the output random variable Y given an input X = x is $p_{Y|X}(y|x)$. Successive outputs are assumed independent. That is

$$p_{\overline{Y}|\overline{X}}(\overline{y}|\overline{x}) = \prod_{i=1}^{n} p_{Y|X}(y_i|x_i).$$

Our scheme for transmitting over the channel is as follows

1. Every $T = \frac{n}{\rho_c}$ seconds, the encoder selects an n-tuple $\overline{x}_i$ from the set of distinct n-vectors $\{\overline{x}_1, \overline{x}_2, \ldots, \overline{x}_K\}$, $K = 2^{nR}$. (Note that $R = \frac{1}{n} \log_2 K$).

2. The channel converts the transmitted vector to the sequence $\overline{y}$.

3. The decoder upon observing $\overline{y}$, chooses the vector $\overline{x}_i$ which it believes was transmitted. If the vector selected by the decoder is not the transmitted vector we say an error has occurred. We are interested in the probability of error, P_e, when the transmitted vectors are chosen with equal a priori probability.

If we choose a distribution for the input symbols $p_X(x)$, this distribution along with the conditional probability $p_{Y|X}(y|x)$ of the channel allows us to calculate I(X;Y). We define the channel capacity C as

$$C = \max_{p_X(x)} I(X;Y)$$

We now prove the

Channel Coding Theorem: For any $\varepsilon>0$, if $R < C - \varepsilon$, there exists an n, a set of code words $\{\bar{x}_1, \bar{x}_2, \ldots, \bar{x}_K\}$, and a decoder such that the probability of error is no more than 2ε.

Proof: Refer to the partitions discussed in Part I and choose as our code words the vectors in the set containing at least $2^{n(I(X;Y)-\varepsilon)}$ vectors. Use the following rule for the decoder. For a received vector $\bar{y}$, decode to that $\bar{x}_i$ such that $(\bar{x}_i, \bar{y}) \varepsilon A_\varepsilon(X,Y)$. If no $\bar{x}_i$ exists for which this is true or if more than one exists such that this is true decode to $\bar{x}_1$.

An error will occur in decoding if one of the following two events occurs.

E_1 = {the transmitted vectors and the received vector are not jointly typical}

E_2 = {some other code word is jointly typical with the transmitted vector}

From Part I, we know that $P_r[E_2] \le e^{-n\varepsilon}$ so this probability can be made as small as desired by choosing n large enough so it can be made less than ε. We also know that $P_r[E_1] \le \varepsilon$. Thus the total probability of error is no more than 2ε. Q.E.D.

Putting the source coding and channel coding theorem together, we see that we can reliably transmit data with negligibly small error from a source to a destination if $(H(U)+\varepsilon)\rho_s < (C-\varepsilon)\rho_c$. If we are willing to allow a distortion d in our reproduction we then use the rate distortion theorem and the channel coding theorem to state that acceptable transmission is possible if

$$(R(d) + \varepsilon)\, \rho_s < (C - \varepsilon)\rho_c.$$

Acknowledgment

This work was partially supported by the Air Force Office of Scientific Research, Air Force Systems Command, USAF under Grant No. AFOSR-74-2601 and partially by the National Science Foundation under Grant ENG 73-08235.

THE AEP PROPERTY OF RANDOM SEQUENCES AND APPLICATIONS TO INFORMATION THEORY: PART III MULTI-USER COMMUNICATIONS

Jack Keil Wolf
Department of Electrical and Computer Engineering
University of Massachusetts
Amherst, Massachusetts 01002

The multi-user communication problem is concerned with transmitting information from several sources to several destinations. Shannon[1] introduced the problem of a two-way channel as a model of two people communicating with one another. Subsequently many other researchers have considered this and other models of multi-user communications. Two surveys of these results have been given by Wolf[2] and Wyner.[3] Current interest in this problem stems from possible applications to communication networks (e.g., computer-communication networks).

We will consider several of these network configurations and prove positive coding theorems for these configurations via the A.E.P.

Source Coding with Side Information

Let us first consider the configuration shown in Figure 1. Source 1

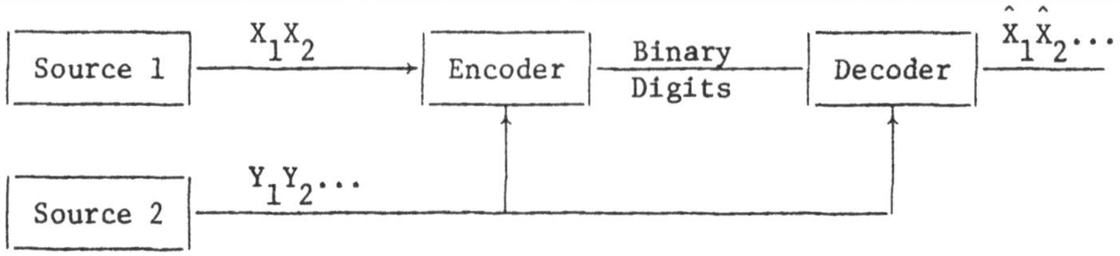

Figure 1. Source Coding with Side Information Known to Encoder and Decoder.

is producing a sequence of random variables $X_1X_2\ldots$ while source 2 is simultaneously producing a sequence of random variables $Y_1Y_2\ldots$. The random variables X and Y are governed by a joint distribution $p_{XY}(x,y)$ and the sequences are produced by independent drawings from this distribution. The encoder upon observing a sequence of N X's and N Y's produces a stream of binary digits. The decoder upon observing this stream of binary digits must produce an estimate sequence $\hat{X}_1\hat{X}_2\ldots\hat{X}_N$. The probability of error P_e is

$$P_e = P_r[\hat{X}_1 \neq X_1 \quad \text{or} \quad \hat{X}_2 \neq X_2 \quad \text{or} \quad \ldots \quad \text{or} \quad \hat{X}_N \neq X_N]$$

It is easy to prove the

Source Coding Theorem for Side Information Known to Encoder and Decoder: For any $\varepsilon>0$, there is an N sufficiently large such that blocks of N source letters from sources 1 and 2 can be encoded into $N[H(X|Y)+2\varepsilon]$ binary symbols and such that the decoder upon observing these binary digits and N letters from source 2 can reproduce the source letters $\overline{X}$ except for a set of source letters with total probability less than ε.

Proof From the AEP we know that the probability that the two source output sequences $(\overline{X},\overline{Y})$ do not belong to $A_\varepsilon(X,Y)$ is less than ε. If

$(\overline{X},\overline{Y}) \in A_\varepsilon(X,Y)$, than $|T_y|$ the number of $\overline{X}$ sequences jointly typical with each typical $\overline{y}$ is bounded as

$$|T_y| \le 2^{N(H(X|Y) + 2\varepsilon)}$$

The encoder merely sends the binary expansion of the enumeration of the $\overline{X}$ sequence, having observed the $\overline{Y}$. The decoder, knowing $\overline{Y}$ and the number of the $\overline{X}$ sequence jointly typical with it can produce the correct $\overline{X}$ sequence. The scheme fails only if the $\overline{X}$ and $\overline{Y}$ are not jointly typical--an event which occurs with probability less than ε.

We now consider an almost identical situation--however, now the side information is unavailable to the encoder as shown in Figure 2

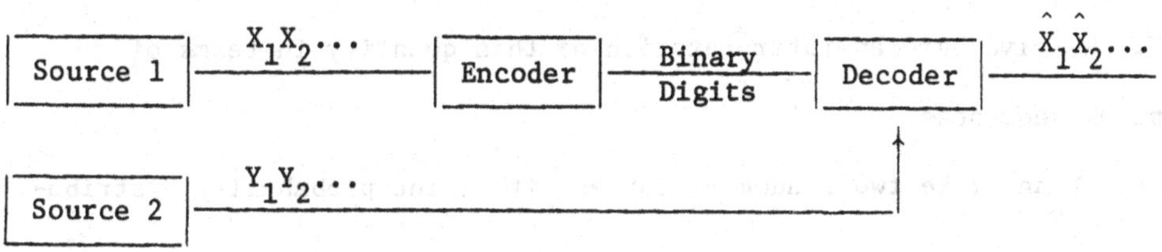

Figure 2. Source Coding with Side Information Known Only to Decoder

The surprising thing is that the same theorem holds in this situation. That is, we have the

<u>Source Coding Theorem for Side Information Known Only to Decoder</u>[4-5]

For any $\varepsilon>0$ and $\delta>0$ there is an N sufficiently large such that blocks of N letters from source 1 can be encoded into $N[H(X|Y)+\varepsilon]$ binary symbols and such that the decoder upon observing these binary digits and the corresponding N letters from source 2 can reproduce the source letters from source 1 except for a set of source letters with probability less than δ.

Proof Our scheme for encoding and decoding is different now. We use the partition of the $\overline{X}$ sequences described in Part 1. Upon observing $\overline{X}$ the encoder tells the decoder the binary expansion of which partition $\overline{X}$ belonged. (All $\overline{X}$ sequences are in a unique partition and there are $M = 2^{NR_X} = 2^{N(H(X|Y)+\varepsilon_1)}$ such partitions.) The decoder upon observing $\overline{Y}$ and knowing to which partition $\overline{X}$ belonged can correctly identify $\overline{X}$ except for a set of $\overline{X}$ of total probability less than δ.

Q.E.D.

Common Information

Wyner[6] has given two strong arguments for a quantity C(X,Y) (to be defined) to be the common information of two discrete random variable X and Y. We give here an interpretation of this quantity in terms of ε-typical sequences.

Let X and Y be two random variables with joint probability distribution

$$p_{XY}(x,y) = P_r[X = x, Y = y], \quad x\varepsilon\mathcal{X}, \ y\varepsilon\mathcal{Y}$$

where $\mathcal{X}$ and $\mathcal{Y}$ are finite sets. Let W be an auxiliary random variable which takes on values in the finite set $\mathcal{W}$ and let X and Y be conditionally independent given W. That is,

$$p_{XYW}(x,y,w) = p_{X|W}(x|w)p_{Y|W}(y|w)p_W(w) \qquad \text{all } w\varepsilon\mathcal{W}, \ x\varepsilon\mathcal{X}, \ y\varepsilon\mathcal{Y},$$

and $\sum_w p_{XYW}(x,y,w) = p_{XY}(x,y)$.

Define C(X,Y), the common information between X and Y as

$$C(X,Y) = \min I\,(X,Y;W)$$

where the minimum is taken over all distributions satisfying the above conditions. We now give an interpretation of C(X,Y) in terms of typical sequences.

First let X and Y be statistically independent random variables. The reader may verify that if we consider sequences of length N for X and Y, $(\bar{x},\bar{y}) \varepsilon A_\varepsilon(X,Y)$ if and only if $\bar{x} \varepsilon A_\varepsilon(X)$ and $\bar{y} \varepsilon A_\varepsilon(Y)$. Thus for the case that X and Y are independent, the table of jointly typical sequences can be arranged in the rectangular lattice as shown in Figure 3.

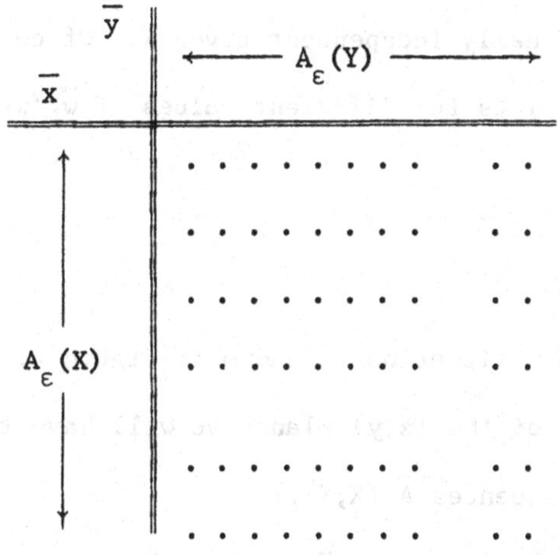

Figure 3. Pattern of Typical $(\bar{X},\bar{Y})$ Sequences if X and Y are Independent

Note that if X and Y are independent C(X,Y) = 0 since we can choose W independent of X and Y in which case

$$I(X,Y;W) = 0$$

and the conditions required by our minimization are satisfied (i.e., X and Y are conditionally independent given W).

Now consider an (X,Y) pair of random variables that are not statistically independent. The pairs of $(\bar{x},\bar{y})$ sequences which are jointly ε-typical form a pattern which is not a rectangular lattice but is as shown in Figure 1 of part I. Now consider a triple of random variables (X,Y,W) where X and Y are conditionally independent given W. Consider the sets of jointly typical sequences $(\bar{x},\bar{y})$ which are jointly typical with a given typical $\bar{w}$. That is, define

$$T_{\bar{w}} = \{(\bar{x},\bar{y}) : (\bar{x},\bar{y},\bar{w}) \varepsilon A_\varepsilon(X,Y,W)\}$$

Note that the pattern of $T_{\bar{w}}$ for every $\bar{w} \varepsilon A_\varepsilon(W)$ is that of a rectangular lattice since X and Y are conditionally independent given W. Of course, this lattice contains different points for different values of $\bar{w}$ $(\bar{w} \varepsilon A_\varepsilon(W))$ but

$$\bigcup_{\bar{w} \varepsilon A_\varepsilon(W)} T_{\bar{w}} = A_\varepsilon(X,Y)$$

A three dimensional picture of this situation is shown in Figure 4. If we project all the dots to one of the (x,y) planes we will have the pattern of dots for the typical sequences $A_\varepsilon(X,Y)$.

Treating (X,Y) as one random variable and W as the other random variable we know from the last theorem of part I that we can choose $M = 2^{N(I(X,Y;W)+4\varepsilon)}$ $\bar{w}$ sequences such that for every $(\bar{x},\bar{y}) \varepsilon A_\varepsilon(X,Y)$, $(\bar{x},\bar{y},\bar{w}) \varepsilon A_\varepsilon(X,Y,W)$ for at least one of these $\bar{w}$ sequences except for a set of probability less than δ.

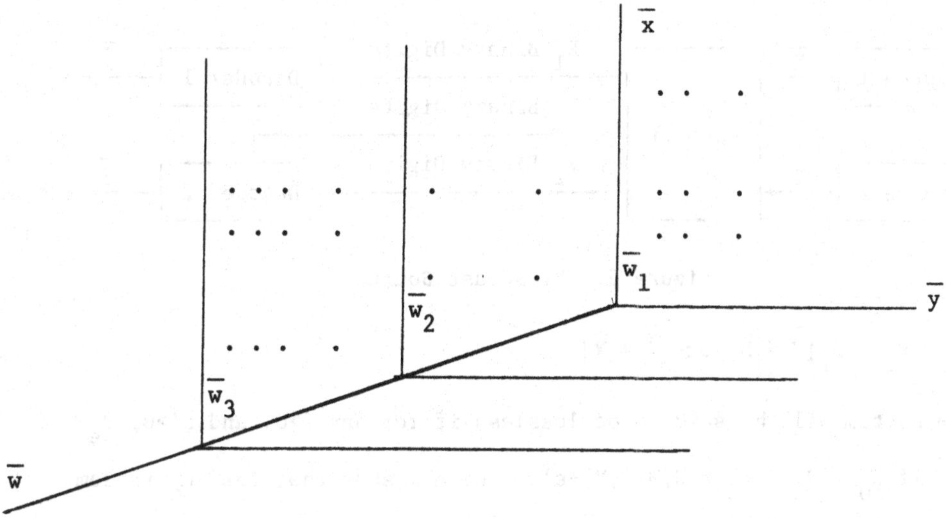

Figure 4. Three Dimensional Picture of Typical $(\bar{x},\bar{y},\bar{z})$ sequences.

Thus we claim that the common information between two random variables is the minimum number of binary digits required to index rectangular lattice points such that the union of these rectangular lattices gives all typical $(\bar{x},\bar{y})$ sequences except for a set with probability less than δ.

<u>Broadcast Source</u>

One of the justifications for the definition of common information given by Wyner is the source coding configuration given below in Figure 5. This system which was studied by Gray and Wyner[7]. Sources 1 and 2 produce random sequences as described in the previous section. The encoder takes N-vectors of $\bar{x}$ and $\bar{y}$ and produces three binary vectors. Decoder 1 upon observing the top two binary vectors produces an estimate of $\bar{x}$. Decoder 2 observing the bottom two binary vectors produces an estimate of $\bar{y}$. The probability of error P_e is defined as

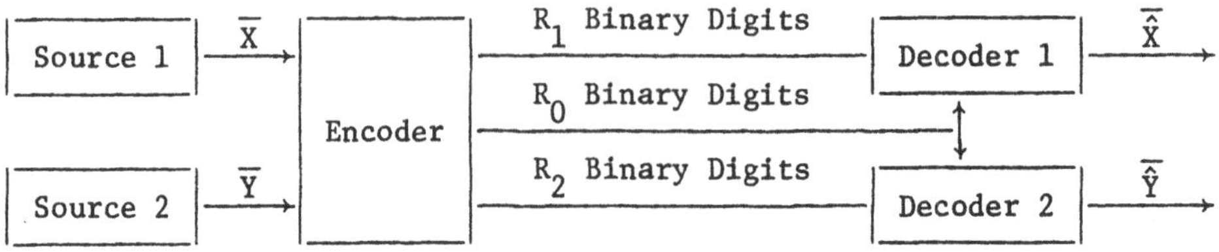

Figure 5. Broadcast Source

$$P_e = P_r[\hat{\bar{X}} \neq \bar{X} \text{ or } \hat{\bar{Y}} \neq \bar{Y}]$$

The system will be said to be lossless if for any $\delta>0$, and $\varepsilon'>0$, $P_e \leq \delta$ and if $R_0 + R_1 + R_2 = N[H(X,Y)+\varepsilon']$. We now show that for any random variable W such that $P_{XYW}(x,y,w) = P_{X|W}(x|w)P_{Y|W}(y|w)P_W(w)$, and $\sum_w P_{XYW}(x,y,w) = P_{XY}(x,y)$, a lossless system exists with

$$R_0 = N[I(X,Y;W)+4\varepsilon]$$

$$R_1 = N[H(X|W)+\varepsilon]$$

$$R_2 = N[H(Y|W)+\varepsilon]$$

Proof The encoding scheme is as follows. The encoder sends over the center channel the binary enumeration corresponding to the common information. We know that

$$|T_{\bar{w}}| \leq 2^{N[H(X,Y|W)+\varepsilon]} = 2^{N[H(X|W)+\frac{\varepsilon}{2}]}\, 2^{N[H(Y|W)+\frac{\varepsilon}{2}]}$$

so that $N[H(X,Y|W)+\varepsilon]$ bits need be sent over the other two channels to specify $(\bar{X},\bar{Y})$. For any $\bar{w}\varepsilon A_\varepsilon(W)$, let us define two new sets $R_{\bar{w}}$ and $S_{\bar{w}}$ as

$$R_{\bar{w}} = \{\bar{x}: (\bar{x},\bar{w})\varepsilon A_\varepsilon(X,W)\}$$

$$S_{\bar{w}} = \{\bar{y}: (\bar{y},\bar{w})\varepsilon A_\varepsilon(Y,W)\}$$

Since X and Y are conditionally independent given W,

$$T_{\bar{w}} = R_{\bar{w}} \times S_{\bar{w}}.$$

That is, for any $\bar{w}\varepsilon A_\varepsilon(W)$, $(\bar{x},\bar{y})\varepsilon T_{\bar{w}}$ if and only if $\bar{x}\varepsilon R_{\bar{w}}$ and $\bar{y}\varepsilon S_{\bar{w}}$. It is easy to see that

$$|R_{\bar{w}}| \leq 2^{N[H(X|W)+\varepsilon]}$$

$$|S_{\bar{w}}| \leq 2^{N[H(Y|W)+\varepsilon]}$$

Then our encoding scheme is to first choose $\bar{w}$ and send its enumeration over the center channel. For this $\bar{w}$, send the enumeration of $\bar{x}$ in $R_{\bar{w}}$ over the top channel and send the enumeration of $\bar{y}$ in $S_{\bar{w}}$ over the bottom channel. The system is lossless since the sum of the binary digits required is correct and the decoders can choose the correct $\bar{x}$ and $\bar{y}$ except for a probability of error $< \delta$.

Other Configurations

Cover[8] gives a coding theorem for the broadcast channel using a typical sequence argument. A block diagram of this system is shown below in Figure 6.

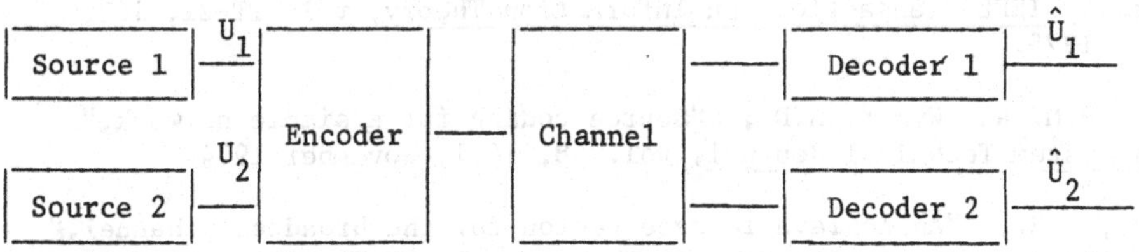

Figure 6. Broadcast Channel

His results are not repeated here. It appears that coding theorems for other configurations of multi-users can also be derived in terms of typical sequences.

ACKNOWLEDGMENT

This work was partially supported by the Air Force Office of Scientific Research, Air Force Systems Command, USAF under Grant No. AFOSR-74-2601 and partially by the National Science Foundation under Grant ENG 73-08235.

References

1. Shannon, C.E., "Two-way communication channels," Proc. of Fourth Berkeley Symposium on Mathematical Statistics and Probability, vol. 1, 611, 1961.

2. Wolf, J.K., "Multiple-user communications," National Telecommunications Conference, Atlanta, Georgia, 1973.

3. Wyner, A.D., "Recent results in the Shannon theory," IEEE Transactions on Information Theory, vol. IT-20, 2, January 1974.

4. Slepian, D. and Wolf, J.K., "Noiseless coding of correlated information sources," IEEE Transactions on Information Theory, vol. IT-19, 471, July 1973.

5. Cover, T.M., "A proof of the data compression theorem of Slepian and Wolf for ergodic sources," IEEE Transactions on Information Theory, vol. IT-21, 226, March 1975.

6. Wyner, A.D., "The common information of two dependent random variables," IEEE Transactions on Information Theory, vol. IT-21, 163, March 1975.

7. Gray, R.M. and Wyner, A.D., "Source coding for a simple network," Bell System Technical Journal, vol. 58, 1681, November 1974.

8. Cover, T.M., "An achievable rate region for the broadcast channel," IEEE Transactions on Information Theory, vol. IT-21, 399, July 1975.

CONSTRUCTIVE CODES FOR MULTI-USER COMMUNICATION CHANNELS

Jack Keil Wolf
Department of Electrical and Computer Engineering
University of Massachusetts
Amherst, Massachusetts 01002 USA

In these notes several constructive coding schemes are presented for specific multi-user communication channels. Both the multi-access channel and the broadcast channel will be considered.

No claims are made regarding the optimality of these schemes. The reason for considering them is that the codes are constructive. This is in contrast to the random coding proofs given to establish the capacity region for these channels.

Multiple-Access Channel

The multiple-access channel has been considered by Liao,[1] Slepian and Wolf,[2] Ahlswede,[3] Van der Meulen[4] and Ulrey.[5] Referring to the block diagram of Figure 1, every N time units source 1 produces a message U_1 and source 2 produces a message U_2. Message U_1 and U_2 are

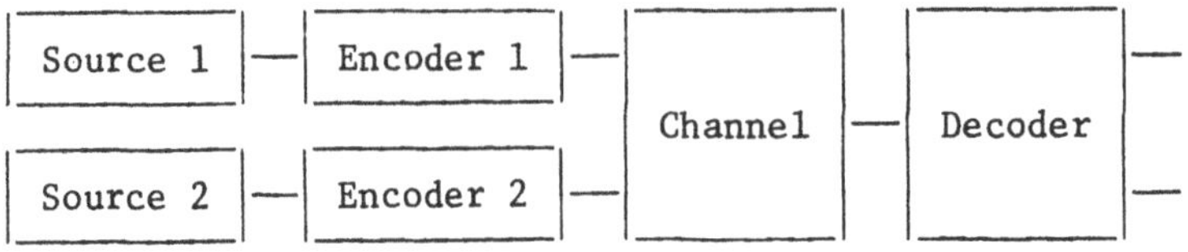

Figure 1. The Multiple Access Channel

statistically independent, random variables which are uniformly distributed over the sets $\{1,2,\ldots,M_1 = 2^{NR_1}\}$ and $\{1,2,\ldots,M_2 = 2^{NR_2}\}$ respectively. Every time unit the channel accepts a pair of inputs $\{x_1,x_2\}$ and produces the output y. The inputs and output are assumed to be elements of the finite sets $\mathcal{X}_1$, $\mathcal{X}_2$ and $\mathcal{Y}$. The channel is described by the conditional probabilities $P_{Y|X_1,X_2}(\cdot|\cdot,\cdot)$. Furthermore the channel is assumed to be memoryless. For each output U_1 of source 1, encoder 1 produces a sequence of N channel inputs from the set $\mathcal{X}_1$. Simultaneously, encoder 2 produces a sequence of N channel inputs from the set $\mathcal{X}_2$ for each output U_2 from source 2. The decoder after observing N channel outputs from the set $\mathcal{Y}$ produces two estimates $\hat{U}_1$ and $\hat{U}_2$. If the system is working well, the estimates $\hat{U}_1$ and $\hat{U}_2$ will equal the source outputs U_1 and U_2. The measure of goodness of the system is the probability of error, P_e, given as

$$P_e = P_r\{\hat{U}_1 \neq U_1 \text{ or } \hat{U}_2 \neq U_2\}.$$

It has been shown that for certain values of R_1 and R_2, the probability of error can be made as small as desired if N is allowed to be very large. The capacity region R, is defined as the set of all allowable rates (R_1,R_2) for which this is the case. A specification of the capacity region in terms of conditional and unconditional mutual information is known.

Noiseless Erasure Channel

We now focus on a particular channel, termed the noiseless erasure channel. The alphabets for this channel are $X_1 = X_2 = \{0,1\}$ and $Y = \{0,1,e\}$. The conditional probabilities describing this channel are

$$1 = P_{Y|X_1X_2}(0|0,0) = P_{Y|X_1X_2}(e|0,1) = P_{Y|X_1X_2}(e|1,0) = P_{Y|X_1X_2}(1|1,1)$$

while all other conditional probabilities are zero. The capacity region for this channel is known to be the shaded region shown in Figure 2.

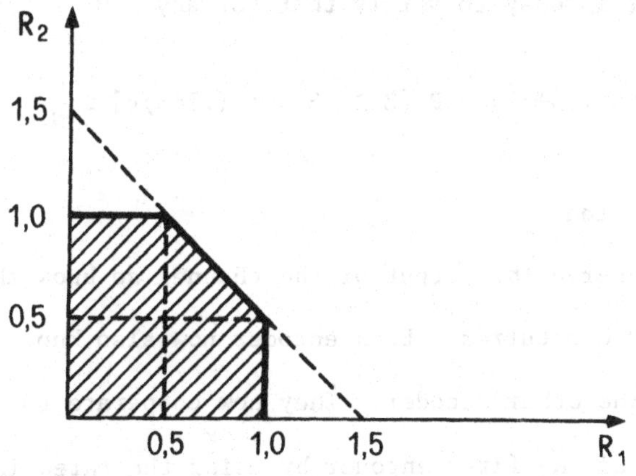

Figure 2. Capacity Region for Noiseless Erasure Channel.

Gaarder and Wolf[6] have given a constructive coding scheme which demonstrates that if two noiseless feedback paths connect the output of the channel to the two encoders, the probability of error can be made vanishingly small for the rate pair $(R_1,R_2) = (.76,.76)$. This rate pair falls outside the capacity region. The result is somewhat surprising since the capacity of a single-input, single-output, discrete, memoryless channel is not increased by the use of a noiseless feedback link.

The coding scheme is as follows:

1. Let N be a large integer such that $(.76)N = K$, K an integer. Each encoder first transmits its respective message by sending K uncoded binary digits.

2. The decoder observes the output of the channel and knows all message bits corresponding to channel outputs of 0 or 1. However for those positions where the channel output was "e", the decoder only knows the input symbols were complements of each other. The number of "e"'s in the output is a random variable, say Z. From the law of large numbers it is easy to verify that for any $\varepsilon>0$

$$P_r[Z \geq (.76N)(.5+\varepsilon)] = P_r[Z \geq .38N + (.76N)\varepsilon] \leq \frac{C}{N}$$

where C is a constant.

3. Both encoders observe the output of the channel so know the positions where the output e occurred. Each encoder now also knows the message transmitted by the other encoder. They now cooperate to send the missing symbols of the first encoder by using the three input pairs (0,0), (0,1), (1,1) all of which are received error free at the receiver. This transmission requires QN channel input where $Q = \frac{Z}{N} \log_3 2$. But

$$P_r[Q \geq .24] = P_r[Z \geq N(.3803] \leq \frac{C}{N}$$

where C is a constant. If $Q \leq .24$, the total transmission requires $\leq N$ bits and no error occurs. Thus by choosing N large enough, the probability of error can be made vanishingly small.

Kasami and Lin[7] have given a simple scheme for N=2 which achieves the rate pair $(R_1,R_2) = (.5,.792)$ with zero probability of error. Encoder 1 uses one of the two code words (0 0) or (1 1) while encoder 2 uses one of the three code words (0 0), (0 1) or (1 0). The following table shows that this coding scheme leads to unambiguous decoding.

	(0 0)	(1 1)
(0 0)	(0 0)	(e e)
(0 1)	(0 e)	(e 1)
(1 0)	(e 0)	(1 e)

This code is a special case of a scheme which achieves the rate pair $(R_1,R_2) = (\frac{1}{N}, \frac{1}{N}\log_2(2^N-1))$. Here the first encoder uses the two code words $(\overbrace{0\ 0\ 0\ \ldots\ 0}^{N})$ and $(\overbrace{1\ 1\ 1\ \ldots\ 1}^{N})$ and the second encoder uses all binary N-tuples except $(\overbrace{1\ 1\ 1\ \ldots\ 1}^{N})$. Again unambiguous decoding results.

Another interesting pair of codes given by Kasami and Lin achieve the rate pair $(R_1,R_2) = (\frac{K}{N}, \frac{1}{N}\log_2(2^{N-K+1}-1))$. Here, encoder 1 uses the code words of a Hamming single-error correcting (N,K) code and encoder 2 uses the all zero word and two vectors from each of the $(2^{N-K}-1)$ cosets of this code.

It is easy to show from ordinary Shannon Theory that there exists a code to achieve the rate pair (1.,0.5). If one encoder sends at rate 1, the other encoder sees a binary erasure channel with erasure probability

0.5. The capacity for such a channel is 0.5 bits per channel use so that a code exists at a rate arbitrarily close to 0.5. Once the decoder decodes for that code, it can unambiguously determine the uncoded sequence from the other decoder.

All of the codes of Kasami and Lin have zero probability of error. It is not known whether all points in the capacity region can be achieved by codes with zero probability of error. Certainly a necessary condition to achieve zero probability of error is that the codes of encoder 1 and 2 have at most one word in common.

Noisy Erasure Channel

The noisy erasure channel is identical to the noiseless erasure channel except that all 12 transition probabilities are non-zero. Transitions which were not possible for the noiseless erasure channel but which are possible for the noisy erasure channel are referred to as "errors". One can consider a noisy erasure channel as composed of a noiseless erasure channel followed by a ternary input, ternary output channel with all transitions non-zero.

One method of correcting t or more errors in a block of length N has been proposed by Lin.[8] This procedure follows.

1. Encoder 1 is composed of an $(\frac{N}{2}, K_1)$ binary t error correcting code followed by a device which repeats every digit. (This device converts each 0 to (0 0) and each 1 to (1 1).) The output of this device is an (N, K_1) binary code.
2. Encoder 2 is composed of an $(\frac{N}{2}, K_2)$, ternary t error correcting code followed by a device which converts each 0 to (0 0), each 1 to

(0 1) and each 2 to (1 0). The output of this device is a (N, K_2) ternary code.

3. The decoder separates the block of N received digits into $\frac{N}{2}$ pairs of digits. It then tentatively decodes each pair of received digits using the following rules:

received pair	to binary decoder	to ternary decoder
0 0	0	0
0 e	0	1
0 1	erasure	erasure
e 0	0	2
e 1	1	1
e e	1	0
1 0	erasure	erasure
1 e	1	2
1 1	erasure	erasure

These symbols are then fed into a binary t error correcting decoder and a ternary t error correcting decoder respectively. The decoders are instrumented to correct both erasures and errors and usually more than t channel errors can be corrected. (A code of minimum distance d can correct any combination of t errors and f erasures where $d > 2t + f$.)

Modulo 2 Channel Without Errors

The next multiple access channel to be considered is the modulo 2 channel. Here all alphabets are binary, that is $X_1 = X_2 = Y = \{0,1\}$.

The conditional probabilities describing this channel are

$$1 = P_{Y|X_1X_2}(0|0,0) = P_{Y|X_1X_2}(1|0,1) = P_{Y|X_1X_2}(1|1,0) = P_{Y|X_1X_2}(0|1,1)$$

with all other conditional probabilities being zero. The capacity region for this channel[9] is given as the shaded region in Figure 3.

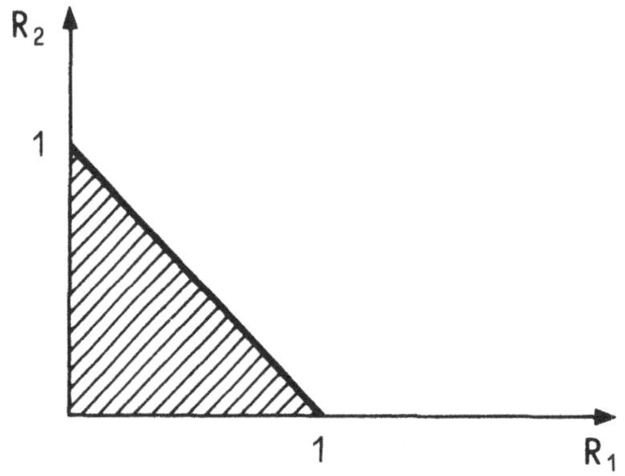

Figure 3. Capacity Region for Modulo 2 Channel

Note that any point on the line $R_1+R_2=1$ can be achieved by time sharing between two simple modes of operation where in each mode one encoder transmits uncoded data and the other encoder transmits all zeros.

An alternative scheme exists for achieving the rate pair $(R_1,R_2) = (\frac{K}{N}, 1 - \frac{K}{N})$. An (N,K) binary cyclic code is chosen as the code for encoder 1. This code has generator polynomial g(x) and parity check polynomial h(x). It is assumed that N is an odd integer so that g(x) and h(x) have no common factors.

Let encoder 1 transmit a code word from the (N,K) binary code and let encoder 2 transmit a code word from the (N,N-K) dual code with generator polynomial h(x). Let $I_1(x)$ be the idempotent for the (N,K) code and let $I_2(x) = 1 + I_1(x)$ be the idempotent for the dual code.

The decoder then receives a word of the form

$$a(x)\ g(x) + b(x)\ h(x).$$

To obtain the code word transmitted by encoder 1, it multiplies by $I_1(x)$, modulo x^N-1. To obtain the code word transmitted by encoder 2, it multiplies by $I_2(x)$, modulo x^N-1.

This scheme is a special case of the following. Encoder 1 transmits a word from an (N,K) group code. A coset table is formed with coset leaders forming an (N,N-K) group code. Encoder 2 transmits words from this code. The receiver receives a word in the coset table, say in the ith row and jth column. It then decodes to the jth code word used by encoder 1 and the ith code word used by encoder 2.

The advantage of this scheme over simple time sharing will be discussed when we consider the modulo 2 channel with errors.

Modulo 2 Channel with Errors

Let us consider a modulo 2 channel with errors as the cascade of the modulo 2 channel without errors and a binary symmetric channel with cross-over probability p. The channel capacity regions for this channel is given as the shaded region in Figure 4. Here $h(p) = -p \log_2 p - (1-p) \log_2 (1-p)$.

One approach to coding for such a channel is to time share between two modes of operation where in one mode one encoder uses a t error correcting code (say a BCH code) while the other encoder sends all zeros. In the other mode the encoders switch roles.

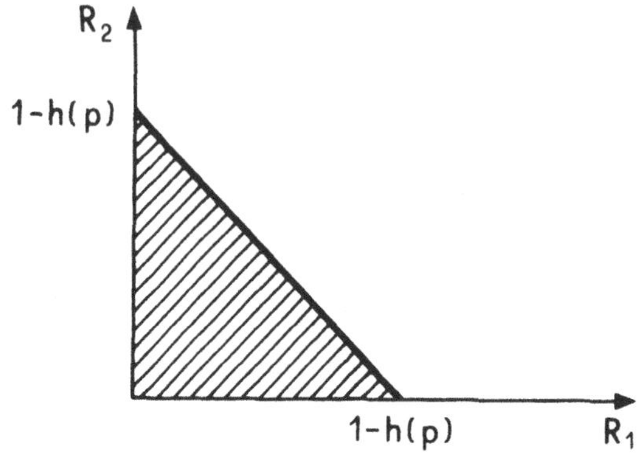

Figure 4. Capacity Region for Modulo 2 Channel with Errors.

Another approach is as follows. Let g(x) be the generator polynomial of a binary cyclic code which corrects t errors. Let $x^N-1 =$ $g(x)\ h_1(x)\ h_2(x)$ where N is odd so that g(x), $h_1(x)$ and $h_2(x)$ have no common factors. Let encoder 1 use code words from a cyclic code with generator polynomial $g(x)\ h_1(x)$ while encoder 2 uses code words from a cyclic code with generator polynomial $g(x)\ h_2(x)$.

The received word is of the form

$$a(x)g(x)h_1(x) \oplus b(x)g(x)h_2(x) \oplus n(x) = \alpha(x)g(x) \oplus n(x)$$

The received word can be decoded correctly to $\alpha(x)g(x)$ if no more than t errors occurred in n(x). Then one can find a(x) and b(x) by using the idempotents of the codes with generators $g(x)h_1(x)$ and $g(x)h_2(x)$.

The advantage of this scheme over time sharing is that if one source is not transmitting (i.e., the encoder is transmitting all zeros) the error correction capability of the code increases. For example, let N=63, $g(x)=m_1(x)m_3(x)m_5(x)m_7(x)$, $h_1(x)=m_9(x)m_{11}(x)m_{13}(x)$ and $h_2(x) =$ $m_{15}(x)m_{23}(x)m_{27}(x)m_{31}(x)$ where $m_i(x)$ is the minimum function of α^i and α

is a primitive element of GF(64). Then g(x) is the generator polynomial of a 4 error correcting code, $g(x)h_1(x)$ is the generator polynomial of a 7 error correcting code and $g(x)h_2(x)$ is the generator polynomial of an 8 error correcting code. Thus if both sources are transmitting, 4 errors can be corrected while if only one source is transmitting the code can correct 7 or 8 errors. It appears that the decoder must know when one source is not transmitting in order to achieve this added error correction capability.

Broadcast Channel (Gaussian Noise)

The broadcast channel was introduced by Cover[10] and has since been considered by others including Bergmans,[11] Wyner,[12] Gallager[13] and Cover.[14] Here we consider a special case of the broadcast channel where all interference is additive white Gaussian noise.

Consider the block diagram shown in Figure 5.

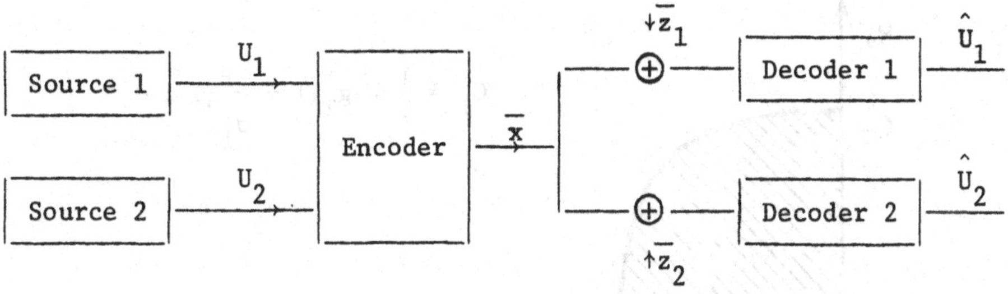

Figure 5. Broadcast Channel (Gaussian Noise).

Again U_i, i=1,2, are independent messages which are uniformly distributed over the sets $\{1,2,\ldots,M_i = 2^{NR_i}\}$. The encoder upon observing the pair of messages produces an N-tuple of real numbers $\bar{x}$. The average value (averaged over the message pairs) of the sum of the squares of the components of $\bar{x}$ is constrained to be less than or equal to NP. On the

way to decoder 1, each component of $\bar{x}$ is corrupted by additive Gaussian

noise of zero mean and variance σ_1^2. Similarly, the input to decoder 2

is the sum of $\bar{x}$ and a vector of Gaussian variates of zero mean and

variance σ_2^2, $\sigma_2^2 \geq \sigma_1^2$. All noise components are independent of each

other and the vector $\bar{x}$. Decoder 1 produces an estimate $\hat{U}_1$ and decoder 2

produces an estimate $\hat{U}_2$. The measure of goodness for the system is the

probability of error, P_e, given as

$$P_e = P_r\{\hat{U}_1 \neq U_1 \quad \text{or} \quad \hat{U}_2 \neq U_2\}.$$

As in the multiple access channel we are interested in ascertaining

those rate pairs (R_1, R_2) such that P_e can be made as small as desired

by choosing N large enough. This region in the (R_1, R_2) plane, called

the capacity region is given by the shaded region in Figure 6.

$$C_i = \frac{1}{2} \log_2(1 + \frac{P}{\sigma_i^2}) \quad i=1,2.$$

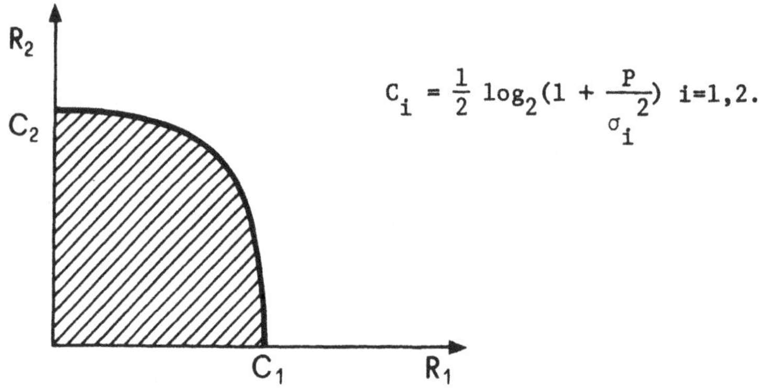

Figure 6. Capacity Region for Broadcast Channel (Gaussian Noise).

We are now interested in a constructive coding scheme for transmit-

ting information over the broadcast channel. The following scheme is an adaptation of the permutation codes of Slepian[15] to the clouds and cloud centers of Cover[11] and Bergmans.[12]

We will introduce this subject by a specific example. Let N=4 and consider the vector (-3,-3,-2,8). There are 12 distinct permutations of this vector which can be arranged in the following table. These vectors are the transmitted code words.

(-3,-3,-2,8)	(-3,-3,8,-2)	(-3,8,-2,-3)	(8,-3,-2,-3)
(-3,-2,-3,8)	(-3,-2,8,-3)	(-3,8,-3,-2)	(8,-2,-3,-3)
(-2,-3,-3,8)	(-2,-3,8,-3)	(-2,8,-3,-3)	(8,-3,-3,-2)

Then if M_1=3 and M_2=4, U_1 can dictate the row of the transmitted vector and M_2 can dictate its column. For example, if $(U_1,U_2) = (3,2)$, the encoder would produce the vector (-2,-3,8,-3). The vectors in the ith column will be said to comprise the ith cloud. Decoder 2, then must merely decide the cloud to which the transmitted vector belonged. Decoder 1, need only determine the row to which the transmitted vector belonged. However, since we have assumed $\sigma_1^2 \leq \sigma_2^2$, if decoder 2 can choose the correct cloud with high probability so can decoder 1. Thus decoder 1 can produce estimates for U_1 and U_2.

Slepian has shown that a simple instrumentation exists for a maximum likelihood decoder which is to choose from all permutations. Decoder 1 can be instrumented in this way. An easy instrumentation also exists for decoder 2 which must choose the most likely cloud. The performance of various codes are presently being investigated.

Acknowledgment

This work was partially supported by the Air Force Office of Scientific Research, Air Force Systems Command, USAF under Grant No. 74-2601 and partially by the National Science Foundation under Grant ENG 73-08235

References

1. Liao, H., "Multiple access channels" Ph.D. Dissertation, Dept. of Electrical Engrg., Univ. of Hawaii, Honolulu, Hawaii, 1972.

2. Slepian, D. and Wolf, J.K., "A coding theorem for multiple access channels with correlated sources," Bell Systems Technical Journal, vol. 52, 1037, September 1973.

3. Ahlswede, "Multi-way communications channels" presented at 2nd International Symposium on Information Transmissions, USSR, 1971.

4. Van der Meulen, E.C., "The discrete memoryless channel with two senders and one receiver," presented at 2nd International Symposium on Information Transmission, USSR, 1971.

5. Ulrey, M.L., "Sequential coding for channels with feedback and a coding theorem for a channel with several senders and receivers," Ph.D. Dissertation, Dept. of Mathematics, Ohio State Univ., 1973.

6. Gaarder, N.T. and Wolf, J.K., "The capacity region of a multiple-access discrete memoryless channel can increase with feedback," IEEE Transactions on Information Theory, vol. IT-21, 100, January 1975.

7. Kasami, T. and Lin, S., "Coding for a multiple access channel," submitted to IEEE Transactions on Information Theory.

8. Lin, S., private communication.

9. Wolf, J.K., "Multiple user communications," National Telemetry Conference, Atlanta, Georgia, 1973.

10. Cover, T., "Broadcast channels," IEEE Transactions on Information Theory, vol. IT-18, 2, January 1972.

11. Bergmans, P., "Random coding theorems for broadcast channels with degraded components," IEEE Transactions on Information Theory, vol. IT-19, 197, March 1973.

References (continued)

12. Wyner, A., "A theorem on the entropy of certain binary sequences and applications; Part II," IEEE Transactions on Information Theory, vol. IT-19, 772, November 1973.

13. Gallager, R.G., "Coding for degraded broadcast channels," to appear in Prob. Peradachi Informatsi.

14. Cover, T., "An achievable rate region for the broadcast channel," IEEE Transactions on Information Theory, vol. IT-21, 399, July 1975.

15. Slepian, D., "Permutation modulation," Proc. of the IEEE, 228, March 1965.

SOME METHODS IN MULTI-USER COMMUNICATION: A TUTORIAL SURVEY

János Körner
Mathematical Institute of the
Hungarian Academy of Sciences

INTRODUCTION

Just two years ago, in his survey paper on the Shannon Theory, Aaron Wyner[1] qualified multi-user communication as the most dynamic and exciting area in Shannon's Information Theory. I feel that recent progress in the field shows how right Wyner really was.

In this paper I will try to give an account of some of the recent results and provide a heuristic explanation of their meaning. Also, I will try to give some heuristic insight into the technique of the proofs.

No substantial new, unpublished results will be presented in this survey, however, it will be pointed out at several occasions, how seemingly new problems can be reduced to known ones. Far for being complete, our selection aims to provide the reader with a fairly broad view on the main problems of the theory.

Multi-user communication deals with the natural extension of classical Shannon-type coding theorems to the case of several channels and sources. No general theory of coding for networks of channels and sources is available as yet.

The fist work in the field, written by Shannon[2] in 1962 picked up quite an involved problem that up to this day has not been fully solved. A number of interesting papers emerged around 1971-1972. Ahlswede[3] and van der Meulen[4] introduced multi-access channels and,especially, Ahlswede[3] solved the coding problem for this channel model. Cover[5] published a very interesting paper on the broadcast channel. The first results on source coding were obtained by Slepian-Wolf[6] and Gâcs-Körner[7].

The main result of Slepian-Wolf[6] shows that in multi-user communication separation of channel and source coding becomes artificial. An other paper of great importance was written by Wyner and Ziv[8].

By means of a nice lemma (known as Mrs Gerber's lemma) they obtained results for special cases of several coding problems thus introducing a method which has influenced most of the later work.

For a better understanding of the central problems we prefer not to proceed chronologically. Some aspects of the theory will be neglected. These include results for infinite alphabets and the theory of constructive codes. More emphasis will be given to source coding, for it is our belief that source coding results are simpler to understand and thus are better for tutorial purposes. Furthermore, at several occasions, channel coding results have been obtained from source coding results, the two parts of the theory being strongly connected.

At several points results will be stated in a form which is slightly different from the original. These differences result from simplifications which, as I believe, serve better understanding.

Most of the ideas presented below without specific references came up in discussions with Rudy Ahlswede and Katalin Marton whom the author expresses his gratitude.

DEFINITION OF A STANDARD NETWORK

We will start with results in source coding. For avoiding merely technical difficulties we shall deal with random variables having finite range. Also, as it is usual in most of the papers in the field, we shall suppose independence in time.

A discrete memoryless stationary k-source is a sequence $\{\underline{X}_n\}$, of independent and identically distributed k-tuples of random variables where for each n $\underline{X}_n=(X_n^{(1)}, X_n^{(2)},\dots,X_n^{(k)})$.

The sequence $\{X_n^{(i)}\}_{n=1}^{\infty}$ is considered to be the *i-th marginal source*.

Most of the coding problems treated in this paper will have the following character:

Each marginal source i is observed by a separate encoder $E^{(i)}$. All the encoders are allowed to observe an output of the same length, n say, of their respective source, after which they have to produce a function $f_n^{(i)}(X_1^{(i)},\dots,X_n^{(i)})$ of this source. Also, there is a certain number $D_1,\dots,D_d$ of decoders. Decoder D_j has access only to a part of all the codes $f_n^{(i)}$. We shall denote by $\Lambda(j)\subseteq\{1,2,\dots,k\}$ that subset of the index set $\{1,2,\ldots,k\}$ which contains all the indices of the codes accessible to D_j. The j'th decoder has to construct a good reproduction (in some sense to be specified later) of one (!) of the marginal sources. We denote by $i(j)$ the index of the marginal source reproduced by D_j. The reproducing function ξ_j depends on the codes $\{f_n^{(i)}\}_{i\in\Delta(j)}$. We say that

ξ_j *(n,ε)-reproduces* $\{X_n^{i(j)}\}_{n=1}^{\infty}$ if

$$Pr(\xi_j \neq (X_1^{(i(j))} \ldots X_n^{(i(j))})) < \varepsilon$$

where $\xi_j = \xi_j(f_n^{(i)}(X_1^{(i)},\ldots, X_n^{(i)}));\ i\in\Delta(j))$.

We say that a *coding scheme* $\{f_n^{(i)},\xi_j\}$ *(n,ε)-reproduces the source* $\{\underline{X}_n\}_{n=1}^{\infty}$ if for every $1 \le j \le d$ ξ_j (n,ε)-reproduces $\{X_n^{i(j)}\}$. We emphasize that this does not necessarily involve the ε-reproduction of all the marginal sources.

The quality of a reproduction can be measured in part by how small ε can be, i.e. by the probability of an error. However, just as in the classical Shannon theory, we also want to control the "complexity" of realization of a coding scheme. Traditionally, this is done by measuring the cardinality of the range of the codes.

Denoting by $\|f\|$ the (finite) cardinality of the range of the function f, we shall be interested in how small these quantities can be. Clearly, as one of them gets smaller, an other might increase, and we have to establish their total tradeoff.

Now as an increase of n, i.e. the length of the encoded blocks results in more freedom for the choice of the codes, and in the Shannon theory we are looking for existence theorems about best-possible constructions, we shall be interested in deriving asymptotic results.

For a fixed ε $(0 < \varepsilon < 1)$ we shall say that a k-tuple $\underline{R} = (R^{(1)}, R^{(2)}, \dots, R^{(k)})$ of non-negative reals is an element of the *region of ε-achievable rates* $\mathsf{R}(\varepsilon)$ if for any $\delta > 0$ and large enough n there exists an (n,ε)-reproduction $\{f_n^{(i)}, \xi_j\}$ of the source satisfying

$$n^{-1} \log \| f_n^{(i)} \| \leq R^{(i)} + \delta \quad \text{for} \quad 1 \leq i \leq k .$$

We say that a k-tuple $\underline{R}$ of non-negative c.s. is achievable if it is an element of the region $\mathsf{R} = \bigcap_{\varepsilon > 0} \mathbf{R}(\varepsilon)$ i.e. if it is ε-achievable for every $0 < \varepsilon < 1$.

At this point two remarks have to be made. First of all we have to precise how the encoding-decoding procedure is conceived. Throughout the paper we suppose that all the encoders and decoders know the joint distribution of the source and that *they can cooperate in selecting the functions* $\{f_n^{(i)}, \xi_j\}$. This means that the non-cooperation constraints relate only to actual values of codes and reproductions (unless it is stated otherwise). (A different approach to similar problems was taken by Körner-Longo[9].)

Further we call the reader's attention to the fact that most of the writers in the field care only for the determination of R . More precisely, the usual approach is this: one finds a region G of non-negative k-tuples, and shows that $\mathsf{R} \subseteq G \subseteq \mathsf{R}(\varepsilon)$. Now, clearly, this implies $\mathsf{R} = G$, still leaving open the problem whether for some ε's $\mathsf{R}(\varepsilon)$ can be larger than G . Wolfowitz[10] was the first to fill up gaps of this kind in the single-user theory of channel coding. Adopting his terminology, we call a result like $G \supseteq R(\varepsilon)$ for every $0 < \varepsilon < 1$ *a strong converse.* A strong converse implies that $R(\varepsilon)=R$ for every ε. For all the source coding problems we shall treat, strong converses have been derived using a method of Ahlswede-Gâcs-Körner[11] which is based on a nice combinatorial result of Margulis[12].

Moreover, we do not know of any problem for source networks where for some ε $R(\varepsilon)$ would be larger than R. (The situation is more complicated in channel coding as it was pointed out by Ahlswede[13]. We shall return to this problem later.)

The theorems we shall treat are all so-called *single-letter characterizations of the rate regions,* i.e. expressions that do not involve limits over product spaces.

It is worth mentioning that a standard network can be represented by a bipartite graph. In fact, introducing two disjoint vertex sets; one, having k vertices that correspond to the k marginal sources of our network and an other with d vertices corresponding to the d decoders, vertices (i,j) $i\in\{1,2,\dots,k\}$, $j\in\{1,2,\dots,d\}$ are connected by an edge, if $i\in\Delta(j)$, i.e. if the code of the i'th source is accessible to the j'th decoder. This is the usual picture of a source network[16].

We denote vertices corresponding to sources with the index of the respective source, whereas the vertex corresponding to the j'th decoder is denoted by the index $i(j)$. The *short formal description of a standard network* consists in listing the sets $\{(\Delta(j),i(j));\ 1 \le j \le d\}$. If there are no more than 3 marginal sources, we shall denote them by the letters

X, Y and Z.

As an example, we describe the Slepian-Wolf[6] network as follows:

$\Delta(1) = \{X,Y\}; \quad i(1)=X$

$\Delta(2) = \{X,Y\}; \quad i(2)=Y.$

Preliminaries. Typical sequences and generated sets

The present approach to multi-user communication is based on a combinatorial tecnique introduced by Wolfowitz in his book[10]. In essence, he observed that in a source most of the output sequences behave "typically" inasmuch as their "information density" is close to the entropy of the source. Similar properties enabled him to count "typical" and "generated" sequences. Another important property of typical sequences is that every n-sequence is "typical" for some distribution over its elements. (Before giving a definition of typicality let us mention that in the present volume there is another paper which makes use of typical sequences, i.e. Wolf's work;applications of the AEP property[14]. However, typical sequences in Wolf's sense (which is also that of Cover[15]) form a larger set than ours. The Cover-Wolf definition is useful for obtaining results on sources with memory whereas ours is more suitable for deriving strong converse results.)

Definition. Typical sequences. Given a finite set X and a pr. d. P on it, we consider the set X^n (of n-sequences of elements from X), and the pr.d. $P^n = \prod_{i=1}^{n} P$. A sequence $x^n \in X^n$ will be called P-typical if the number of occurences $N(a|x^n)$ of any $a \in X$ in it will be close to $n\,P(a)$ in the following sense:

we fix a sequence of positive numbers r_n satisfying $r_n n^{-1} \to 0$, $r_n n^{-1/2} \to \infty$ (this sequence is coupled once for all with the set X) and call $x^n \in X^n$ typical if

$$|N(a|x^n)-nP(a)| < r_n \quad \text{for all} \quad a \in X \tag{1}$$

Remark: In reality, Wolfowitz used $\hat{r}_n = K n^{-1/2}$ which is not allowed here. The need for this slight modification will become transparent in the sequel. We denote by $T_n(P)$ the set of all n-typical sequences.

Notice that every sequence x^n is typical for the distribution $\{N(a|x^n) n^{-1};\ a \in X\}$.

$T_n(P)$ has the following useful elementary properties:

(i) $P^n(T_n(P)) \longrightarrow 1$ uniformly in P

(ii) $n^{-1} \log \| T_n(P) \| - H(P) \longrightarrow 0$ uniformly in P

(Here and in the sequel $\|A\|$ denotes the cardinality of the set A, $\|f\|$ that of the range of the function f .)

(iii) $n^{-1} \log P^n(x^n) + H(P) \longrightarrow 0$ uniformly for every $x^n \in T_n(P)$.

This latter convergence is not necessarily uniform in P .

Definition. Generated sequences. Given a sequence $x^n \in X^n$, a finite set Y and a transition probability matrix (i.e. a stochastic matrix) $F: X \longrightarrow Y$ we shall say that a sequence $y^n \in Y^n$ is generated by x^n if $N(a,b|x^n,y^n)$ will be close to $N(a|x^n) . F(b|a)$ for $a \in X$, $b \in Y$ in the following sense:

$$|N(a,b|x^n,y^n) - N(a|x^n) . F(b|a)| < s_n \quad \text{for} \quad (a,b) \in X \times Y$$

where s_n is a sequence coupled once for all with F and has the properties $s_n n^{-1} \to 0$, $s_n n^{-1/2} \to \infty$

We denote by $T_n(x^n,F)$ the set of all n-sequences in Y^n which are generated by x^n.

$T_n(x^n,F)$ has the following elementary properties:

(iv) $F^n(T_n(x^n,F)|x^n) \to 1$ uniformly in (x^n,F)

(v) $n^{-1}\log\|T_n(x^n,F)\|-H(Y|X) \to 0$ for $x^n \in T_n(\text{dist } X)$ uniformly in $\text{dist}(X,Y)$ where $(\text{dist } X)$ denotes the pr.d. of the r.v. X, and Y is the output r.v. of the channel F if the r.v. X is presented at the input. We shall use the notation $F_{Y|X}$ for the matrix of conditional distributions of a r.v. Y given the value of the r.v. X.

(vi) $n^{-1}\log F^n(y^n|x^n)+H(Y|X) \to 0$ uniformly in $x^n \in T_n(\text{dist } X)$

The last convergence need not be uniform in F and X.

Generated sets play a central role in Wolfowitz's proof of both the channel coding theorem[1] and the rate-distortion coding theorem[16]. In essence, decoding sets of an arbitrary channel code are "large subsets" of the set generated by the corresponding codeword. In Rate-Distortion Theory, the constant-value sets of the reproduction code are "large subsets" of a set which is generated by the corresponding codeword via a well-chosen channel. (In fact, Wolfowitz uses his proof of the channel coding theorem in order to obtain Shannon's rate distortion theorem. The merit of his proof technique is to yield the strong converse for the channel coding theorem.)

In multi-user communication we shall often use the following

Definition. Set η-generated by an other set. Given a transition probability matrix $F: X \to Y$ and a set $A \subseteq X^n$, we shall say that a set $B \subseteq Y^n$ is (pointwise) η-generated by A over the channel F if $F^n(B|x^n) \geq \eta$ for all $x^n \in A$.

We shall denote by $\Lambda_F(A,\eta)$ the minimum cardinality of a set which is η-generated by A over the channel F.

As an *example*, observe that if $x^n \in T_n(\mathrm{dist}\ X)$, $n^{-1} \log \Lambda_F(\{x^n\},\eta) - H(Y|X)$ converges to 0 uniformly in (X,F) for every $0 < \eta < 1$. Here Y is defined by the relation $F_{Y|X} = F$

We shall need the following somewhat more involved fact: given three r.v.'s U,X,Y such that U and Y are conditionally independent given X (this will be denoted by $U \to X \to Y$ in the sequel),

$$n^{-1} \log \Lambda_{F_{Y|X}}(T_n(u^n, F_{X|U}),\eta) - H(Y|U) \to 0 \tag{2}$$

uniformly in (U,X,Y) for every u^n which is typical in the distribution of U. The background for this fact is that a set which is η-generated by the set $T_n(u^n, F_{X|U})$, (i.e. the set consisting of sequences generated by a $(\mathrm{dist}\ U)$-typical sequence) is "almost" generated by the same sequence via the corresponding cascade channel, $F_{Y|U} = F_{Y|X} F_{X|U}$.

It was proved by Ahlswede-Gács-Körner[11] that asymptotically $n^{-1} \log \Lambda_F(A,\eta)$ is independent of η. This can be stated as follows (see Lemma 2 in Körner-Marton[17] for this form of the statement):

Strong converse Lemma. Let $\eta < \eta'$ be any two positive numbers in the open interval (0,1). We have

$$\lim_{n \to \infty} \max_{A \subseteq X^n} n^{-1} \log \frac{\Lambda_F(A,\eta')}{\Lambda_F(A,\eta)} = 0 \tag{3}$$

We shall see in the sequel how all the hitherto solved problems about standard networks can be reduced to the asymptotic characterization of the quantities $\{n^{-1}\log\|A\|,\ n^{-1}\log \Lambda_F(A,\eta)\}$ where in some cases one has to consider several channels with a common input and compute several quantities $\Lambda_F(.,.)$.

All the exp's and log's are to the base 2. Throughout the paper, we shall denote by N the set of the natural numbers. $H(Y|X)$ denotes the average conditional entropy of the r.v. Y given the value of the r.v. X . $I(Y\wedge X)=H(Y)-(Y|X)$ denotes the (average) mutual information between X and Y .

We abbreviate "random variable" by r.v., "discrete memoryless stationary source" by d.m.s. source, etc.

Rate regions for standard networks.

Both conceptually and historically, the first network to be considered is that of Slepian-Wolf[6]. Since it is already treated in this volume[14], we prefer to consider a generalized version[18] which we describe as follows:

Slepian-Wolf network with k *sources.* Short formal description:

$$\{\Delta(j)=\{1,2,\ldots,k\},\quad i(j)=j;\quad 1\le j\le k\}$$

In words, this means that we are given a discrete memoryless stationary k-source with k encoders and k decoders. Every encoder has access only to one of the marginal sources, and all the codes are available to each of the k-decoders. Every decoder reproduces one of the marginal sources. The rate region is given by the following

Theorem 1. [Slepian-Wolf[6], Wolf[18]]. For every $0 < \varepsilon < 1$

$$R(\varepsilon)=R=\{\underline{R};\ \sum_{i\in L} R_i \geq H(X^{(i)};i\in L|X^{(j)};j\in \bar{L})\ L\subseteq\{1,2,\ldots,k\}\}.$$

In words, R contains all the k-tuples satisfying all the inequalities $\sum_{i\in L} R_i \geq H(X^{(i)};i\in L|X^{(j)};j\in \bar{L})$ for all the subsets L of the index set.

The proof of this theorem consists of a simple reduction to the case $k=2$ which is the core of the problem. One can proceed by induction. We omit the details.

As we have already mentioned, the direct part of the present theorem is one of the main tools in obtaining existence results on codes for more involved networks. Another interest of the result is that channel codes are used for constructing a good source code.

The rate region R has finitely many extremal points. (In the case $k=2$ there are 2 extremal points.) These are connected by straight lines, i.e. the rate region for this problem is linear for every k. In fact, using the condition that every subset of the decoders ε-reproduces a corresponding subset of the sources, one obtains the obvious necessary conditions $\sum_{i\in L} R_i \geq H(X^{(i)} i\in L| X^{(j)} j\in \bar{L})$ on the sums of the corresponding rates, and the ensemble of these conditions proves to be sufficient. In general, we do not have a similar situation, and in general there is no "natural candidate" for a rate region.

This is the case of

Source Coding with Side Information. In short formal description,

$$\Delta(1) = \{X,Y\}\ ,\ i(1) = \{Y\}\ .$$

This problem was raised by Wyner and Ziv[8] as a generalization of the Slepian-Wolf problem[6] for 2-sources. In the special case of symmetrically correlated binary sources the first converse result goes back to Wyner--Ziv[8]. The complete solution, i.e. coding theorem and weak converse are due to Ahlswede-Körner[19] and Wyner[20]. The strong converse was proved by Ahlswede-Gâcs-Körner[11].

Before giving some information about the proofs, let us explain once more the intuitive content of the problem. We are given a 2-source $\{(X_n,Y_n)\}_{n=1}^{\infty}$. A decoder has the task to reproduce the $\{Y_n\}_{n=1}^{\infty}$ source within a prescribed probability of error ε. This decoder has access to the outputs of two encoders, one for each source. The encoders cannot cooperate. This is the classical data reduction problem for the source $\{Y\}_{n=1}^{\infty}$ with one additionalfeature. Namely, the decoder has access to a data stream which is correlated with $\{Y\}_{n=1}^{\infty}$ and thus provides him with some extra-information.

Theorem 2. [Ahlswede-Körner[19], Wyner[20]]

$$R=\{(R_x,R_y);\ R_x \geq I(X \wedge U),\ R_y \geq H(Y/U),\ U \to X \to Y,\ \|U\| \leq \|X\|+2\}\ .$$

Notice that in the definition of the right-hand side of the statement the pair (X,Y) is distributed according to the common distribution of the pairs (X_n,Y_n). U is arbitrary, and has arbitrary correlation with X.

We are going to reproduce the main ideas of the proof[19] in a rather heuristic manner. Technical details will be omitted. We will forget about the constraint $\|U\| \le \|X\|+2$. It was proved in Lemma 3 of the original proof[19] that dropping this condition does not increase the region R , Similar phenomena occur in conjunction with the other network problems.

First of all, it is intuitively clear that the no-cooperation restriction put on the encoder of $\{X_n\}$ and the encoder of $\{Y_n\}$ can be removed by means of the Slepian-Wolf theorem[6]. In fact their theorem assures that, in case the code $f_n(X^n)$ of X^n is itself an (n,ε)--code of the source $\{X_n\}$, it does not matter, asymptotically, whether this code is given to both the encoder and the decoder of the $\{Y_n\}$-source or to the sole decoder. Now, it is intuitively clear that this independence of the rate region of the existence of a link from the $\{X_n\}$-encoder to the $\{Y_n\}$-encoder carries over to the case of an arbitrary function $f_n(X^n)$ helping the coding-decoding procedure of the $\{Y_n\}$-source. This fact is reflected by the technical statement

Theorem 2A [Ahlswede-Körner[19]; Theorem 1]

$$R = C\{n^{-1}H(f_n(X^n)),\ n^{-1}H(Y^n | f_n(X^n));\ n\in N,\ f_n\} \tag{4}$$

Where C stands for closure (in the usual topology of the Euclidean plane).

Proof: Denoting the right-hand side of (4) by R^*, one immediately obtains the relation $R^* \subset R$ by applying the Slepian-Wolf theorem[6] to the "supersource" $\{(U_t, \tilde{Y}_t)\}_{t\in N}$, where $\{(U_t, \tilde{Y}_t)\}_{t\in N}$ are i.i.d. r.v.'s with the same distribution as $(f_n(X^n), Y^n)$, and noticing that R is a close set by definition. The relation $R^* \supset R$ is just Fano's lemma. For the details we refer the reader to the original paper[19]. Intuitively the statement of this theorem means that the only "degree of freedom" for the optimal construction is to choose the $\{X_n\}$-code.

Pursuing with the proof of Theorem 1 we try to give a single-letter description of R^*. Our task is to find those functions f_n for which $n^{-1}H(Y^n|f_n(X^n))$ is as small as possible, i.e. the constant-value sets of our functions f_n should be "compact". A typical example of "compact" sets are the "generated" sets. However, we need a whole partition of X^n into disjoint "compact" sets. Partitions into large subsets of generated sets are provided by partitions into decoding sets of the output of a discrete memoryless channel. This gives us the idea of using a so-called pre--channel, i.e. introducing a dummy variable U_ℓ having an arbitrary correlation with X^ℓ and satisfying $U_\ell \to X^\ell \to Y^\ell$. Doing so, we get the pre-channel $F_{X^\ell|U_\ell}$. Considering the n'th memoryless extension of this channel $F_{X^{\ell n}|U_\ell^n} = \prod_{i=1}^{n} F_{X^\ell|U_\ell}$ we can construct an $(n,\bar{\varepsilon})$-code for this channel such that all the codewords are U_ℓ-typical sequences of length n. If this is the case, tending with n to infinity the partition $F_{\ell n}(\cdot)$ of $X^{\ell n}$ that is defined by the decoding sets of our channel code will consist of nearly $\exp[nI(U_\ell \wedge X^\ell)]$ sets, and for every codeword $\underline{U}$ the entropy of the conditional distribution of $Y^{\ell n}$ given that codeword $(\underline{U}), n^{-1}H(Y^{\ell n}|f_{\ell n}(X^{\ell n})=\underline{U})$, will approximately equal $H(Y^\ell|U_\ell)$. Therefore, the same will hold for the expected value of this conditional entropy $n^{-1}H(Y^{\ell n}|f_{\ell n}(X^{\ell n}))$. (Details of the preceding deduction are given under (4.6)-(4.14) of the original paper.)

Thus we have constructed a function $f_{\ell n}$ such that

$$(n\ell)^{-1}H(f_{\ell n}(X^{\ell n})) = \ell^{-1}I(U_\ell \wedge X^\ell) \quad \text{and}$$

$$(n\ell)^{-1}H(Y^{\ell n}|f_{\ell n}(X^{\ell n}))= \ell^{-1}H(Y^{\ell}|U_{\ell}).$$

This shows that for the set

$$R^{***}=\{n^{-1}I(U_{\ell}\wedge X^{\ell}),\ n^{-1}H(Y^{\ell}|U_{\ell}):U_{\ell}\to X^{\ell}\to Y^{\ell},\ \ell\in N\}$$

we have $R^{***}\subseteq R^{*}$. On the other hand, we clearly have $R^{***}\supseteq R^{*}$, as U_{ℓ} can be a deterministic function of X^{ℓ} in which case $\ell^{-1}I(U_{\ell}\wedge X^{\ell})= =\ell^{-1}H(U_{\ell})$.

Hence we have proved that $R=R^{***}$.

The last step in our proof of Theorem 2 is the so-called single--letterization of R^{***}. In fact, it only remains to prove that R^{***} equals the right-hand side of the statement of Theorem 1. This is done in Lemma 2 of Ahlswede-Körner[19]. What is needed is to prove that the regions

$$R^{(\ell)}= \{(R_1,R_2):\ R_1 \geq I(X^{\ell}\wedge U_{\ell}),\ R_2\geq H(Y^{\ell}|U_{\ell});U_{\ell}\to X^{\ell}\to Y^{\ell}\}$$

do not get larger if ℓ increases. In fact, since $R=R^{***}=\bigcup_{\ell} R^{(\ell)}$, and the right-hand side of the statement of Theorem 1 equals $R^{(1)}$, the relation

$$R^{(\ell)}= R^{(1)} \tag{5}$$

will imply $R=R^{(1)}$. The proof of (5) consists in some computation with information quantities. As similar arguments enter all the other proofs, it is important to understand this step. We summarize the proof[19] as follows: given a Markov chain $U_{\ell} \to X^{\ell} \to Y^{\ell}$ and the corresponding information quantities $r_1=I(X^{\ell}\wedge U_{\ell})$, $r_2=H(Y^{\ell}|U_{\ell})$, we shall construct a Markov chain $U \to X \to Y$ such that $I(X\wedge U)\leq \ell^{-1}(X^{\ell}\wedge U_{\ell})$, and $H(Y|U)\leq \leq \ell^{-1}H(Y^{\ell}|U_{\ell})$. Clearly, this will assure that $(r_1,r_2)\in R^{(1)}$.

We consider a r.v. I which is uniformly distributed over the set $\{1,2,\dots,\ell\}$, and independent of the pair (X^ℓ,Y^ℓ). We claim that the choice $U \triangleq (I,U,X^{I-1})$, $X \triangleq X_I$, $Y \triangleq Y_I$, will be suitable for our purposes. In fact, we have $U \to X \to Y$, and $dist(X_I,Y_I)$ is equal to the common distribution of the (X_i,Y_i)'s because of the independence of I from the latter variables. Further, we have

$$\ell^{-1}H(Y^\ell|U_\ell)=\ell^{-1}\sum_{i=1}^{\ell}H(Y_i|U_\ell Y^{i-1})\geq \ell^{-1}\sum_{i=1}^{\ell}(Y_i|U_\ell Y^{i-1}X^{i-1}). \tag{6}$$

Now, $H(Y_i|U_\ell X^{i-1}Y^{i-1})=H(Y_i|U_\ell X^{i-1})$, i.e. $Y_i \to U_\ell X^{i-1} \to Y^{i-1}$. This Markov property necessitates some explanation. In fact, it is equivalent to say that for any given value of U_ℓ

$$\hat{Y}_i \to \hat{X}^{i-1} \to \hat{Y}^{i-1} \tag{7}$$

where $\hat{X}^i\hat{Y}^i$ denotes r.v.'s having as distribution the conditional distribution of X^iY^i given the fixed value of U_ℓ. In this case the $\hat{X}_i$'s need not be independent any more, but because of the original markovity their connection with the $\hat{Y}_i$'s remains the same, i.e. $F_{\hat{Y}^i|\hat{X}^i} = F_{Y^i|X^i}$. Now, (7) is a consequence of the memoryless character of this channel, i.e. of the fact that $F_{\hat{Y}^i|\hat{X}^i} = \prod_{j=1}^{i} F$. Indeed, if $\hat{X}^i$ is any sequence of r.v.'s ranging over X^i, and $F_{\hat{Y}^i|\hat{X}^i} = \prod_{j=1}^{i} F$, we have

$$\hat{Y}^{i-1} \to \hat{X}^{i-1} \to \hat{X}_i \to \hat{Y}_i \tag{8}$$

The relation (8) expresses that outputs of a DMC depend on each other only through the corresponding inputs. Obviously, (7) is a consequence of (8). Continuing with our proof, (6) becomes

$$\ell^{-1}H(Y^\ell|U_\ell)\geq \ell^{-1}\sum_{i=1}^{\ell} H(Y_i|U_\ell X^{i-1})=\sum_{i=1}^{\ell} Pr(I=i).H(Y_I|U_\ell X^{I-1},I=i)=H(Y|U) \quad (9)$$

where the last equality follows by definition.

Also

$$\ell^{-1}I(X^\ell\wedge U_\ell)=\ell^{-1}[H(X^\ell)-H(X^\ell|U_\ell)]=\ell^{-1}(\sum_{i=1}^{\ell} H(X_i)-\sum_{i=1}^{\ell} H(X_i|U_\ell X^{i-1})) =$$

$$= H(X_I)-H(X_I|U_\ell X^{I-1},I)=I(X\wedge U).$$

This and (9) complete the proof.

A more refined proof technique yields the strong converse:

Theorem 3 [Ahlswede-Gács-Körner[11]]. For every $0<\varepsilon<1$

$$R(\varepsilon)=R \; .$$

Though not reproducing the proof, we shall try to sketch some of the underlying ideas. Let us mention that the strong converse theorem[11] gives a different proof of the converse part of Theorem 2. Roughly speaking, the proof relies on the AEP-property and the strong converse lemma. The cornerstone of the proof is the following

Theorem 4. [Ahlswede-Gács-Körner[11]]. We write $F=F_{Y|X}$ and

$$s_n(c,\eta)\triangleq n^{-1}\log\min\{\mathbf{A}_F(A,\eta);\ A\subseteq T_n(\text{dist } X),\ Pr(X^n\in A)\geq 2^{nc}\}.$$

Then

$$\lim_{n\to\infty} s_n(c,\eta)=\min\{r_2;(r_1,r_2)\in R,\ r_1\leq -c\}. \quad (10)$$

It is highly important for proving the strong converse result that the limit in (10) does not depend on η. Before giving some information about the proof of this theorem, let us clarify its meaning which as I believe, is of some independent interest.

Considering for a moment to be "large" any set A in the range of X^n such that $Pr(X^n \in A) \geq 2^{nc}$, the quantity $s_n(c,\eta)$ is the smallest exponent of the cardinality of a set which is η-generated by a "large" set via channel F. In other words, if $B \subseteq T_n(dist\ X)$ is η-generated by a set the probability of which is at least $exp_2 nc$, then $\|B\| \geq$ $\geq exp_2[n s_n(c,\eta)]$ and this bound is tight. Therefore, $\lim_{n\to\infty} s_n(c,\eta)$ tells us about the asymptotical "spreading" of a set via channel F. More heuristically, if we observe a subset of the input of channel F, the noise will "fade" that set and what we can "observe" instead is a larger subset of the input space. The degree of this fading is controlled by $s_n(c,\eta)$, if we restrict ourselves to input sets consisting of typical sequences.

The direct part of Theorem 4 follows from the proof of Theorem 2. The converse part follows from the strong converse lemma and a deduction similar to that contained in the proof of Theorem 2. Details can be found in the original paper (Theorem 1[11]).

Let us explain how this result is used to yield Theorem 4.

We consider an arbitrary element of $(R_1,R_2) \in R$ and a sequence of (n,η)-codes (f_n,g_n,φ_n) achieving this rate, i.e. satisfying

$$n^{-1} log\|f_n\| \to R_1 \qquad n^{-1} log\|g_n\| \to R_2 \tag{11}$$

$$Pr(\varphi_n(f_n(X^n),g_n(Y^n))=Y^n) \geq 1-\varepsilon \tag{12}$$

For any given value $\underline{u}$ of the code f_n, we denote by $B_{\underline{u}}$ the ensemble of those sequences which are correctly decoded by φ_n given the value $\underline{u}$ of f_n. One easily realizes that because of (12) most of the sequences $x^n \in X^n$ satisfy

$$F^n(B_{fn(x^n)} | x^n) \geq 1-\varepsilon' \tag{13}$$

where ε' can be chosen as e.g. $\varepsilon' = \sqrt{\varepsilon}$. With this choice, the total probability of the sequences satisfying (13) will be at least $1-\varepsilon'$. Furthermore, as the probability of the $(dist\ X)$-typical sequences tends to 1, a large part of our sequences will be typical. We can suppose that for large enough n their probability is $1-\varepsilon''$ where say, $\varepsilon''=2\varepsilon'$. We denote the set of the typical sequences that satisfy (13) by A_n. If we consider those parts of the constant-value sets of f_n which are in A_n, and denote by A one of them that has largest probability, then

$$Pr(X^n \in A) . \| f_n \| \geq Pr(X^n \in A_n) \geq 1-\varepsilon''$$

implies that

$$\liminf_{n \to \infty} n^{-1} . \log Pr(X^n \in A) \geq - R_1 . \tag{14}$$

Furthermore, as f_n was constant on A by definition, (13) implies that A $(1-\varepsilon')$-generates one of the sets $B_{f_n(.)}$. Let us denote the latter by B, Theorem 4 implies (because of the obvious continuity of the lower boundary of $R=R^{(1)}$, that

$$\liminf_{n \to \infty} n^{-1} \log \| B \| \geq \min_{\substack{r_1 - R_1 \leq 0 \\ (r_1, r_2) \in R}} r_2 \tag{15}$$

It remains to observe that

$$\| g_n \| \geq \| B \| .$$

In fact, since $\|B\|$ consists of those sequences y^n which are correctly decoded provided that f_n has a certain fixed value, the decoder decides for one or an other element of B on the basis of his knowledge of g_n. This yields our last inequality. Comparing it with (15) and (11) we get

$$R_2 \geq \min r_2$$

$$r_1 \leq R_1$$

$$(r_1, r_2) \in R$$

Put in other words, this means that $(R_1, R_2) \in R$, i.e. $R(\varepsilon) \subseteq R$, what we wanted to prove.

Generalizing the coding scheme of source coding with side information, we first consider the case of several decoders having access to the same side information:

Side Information-Several Decoders. The short formal description is this:

$$\Delta(j) = \{1, j\},\ i(j) = j \quad \text{for} \quad 1 < j \leq k.$$

This problem grew out of the investigation of Wyner with Ziv and Gray, Wyner-Ziv[8], Gray-Wyner[21]; and was solved independently by Ahlswede-Körner[19,22] and Wyner[20]. Especially, the strong converse theorem was proved by Ahlswede and Körner[22].

It is important to understand that this problem does not present any genuinely new phenomenon for $k > 2$. Notice that $k=2$ is a case we have already treated.

Let us describe briefly in words what we are talking about. Given a discrete memoryless stationary k-source, each of the marginal sources encoded separately, $k-1$ non-cooperating decoders have the task to reproduce all but one of the marginal sources. Let us call "first source" the one which will not be reproduced. Then every decoder has available a code of the very source he has to reproduce plus a(common) code of the first source. Thus the latter serves as side information for all the decoders. This side information tells the decoders about the correlation of all the sources involved. (This is especially the case if the first source is equal to the $(k-1)$-source formed by all the remaining sources.) One has the following characterization of the rate region $R^{\langle k \rangle}$:

Theorem 5.

$$R^{\langle k \rangle} = \{(R_1,\dots,R_k);\ R_1 \geq I(X^{(1)} \wedge U),\ R_j \geq H(X^{(j)}|U)\ \ 1 < j \leq k,$$

$$U \to X^{(1)} \to (X^{(2)},\dots,X^{(k)}\}$$

where $(X^{(1)},\dots,X^{(k)})$ is distributed according to the common distribution of the $X_n^{(1)},\dots,X_n^{(k)}$'s.

Proving this result, one proceeds as in the case $k=2$, (i.e. Theorem 2). One obtains the technical result

Theorem 5 A. Put

$$\hat{R}=\{\underline{R};\ R_1 \geq n^{-1}H(f_n(X^{(1)n})),\ \ R_j \geq n^{-1}H(X^{(j)n}|f_n(X^{(1)n}))\ \ 2 \leq j \leq k$$

Then $R^{\langle k \rangle}$ equals the closure of $\hat{R}$.

As it was observed in Ahlswede-Körner[22], the present coding problem can be considered as a simultaneous source coding with side information for the 2-sources $\{X_n^{(1)},X_n^{(j)}\}_{n\in N}$ for $2 \leq j \leq k$, where in all cases

$\{x_n^{(1)}\}$ serves as side information with the additional constraint that the same code of $\{x_n^{(1)}\}$ has to be used for all the 2-sources. By this observation both the direct and converse part of Theorem 5A become obvious consequences of Theorem 2A.

Now the proof of Theorem 5 itself merely consists of a careful analysis of the proof for $k=2$. Let us start by the direct part. As it results from Theorem 5A, our only choice is to specify the function f_n, everything else being uniquely determined by this choice. Given a random variable U_ℓ (i.e. the joint distribution of $(U_\ell, X^{(1)\ell})$) such that $U_\ell \to X^{(1)\ell} \to \{X^{(j)\ell};\ 2 \le j \le k\}$, we can repeat the construction of the proof of Theorem 2 for any 2-source $\{x_n^{(1)}, x_n^{(j)}\}_{n\in N}$ $2 \le j \le k$. This yields - for each of the 2-sources - a function $f_{\ell n}(.)$ such that

$$(n\ell)^{-1} H(f_{\ell n}(X^{(1)\ell n})) = \ell^{-1}\, I(U_\ell \wedge X^{(1)\ell}) \quad \text{and} \qquad (16)$$

$$(n\ell)^{-1} H(X^{(j)\ell n} | f_{\ell n}(X^{(1)\ell n})) = \ell^{-1}\, H(X^{(j)\ell} | U_\ell).$$

However, the construction of the proof of Theorem 2 did not depend on the joint distribution of the two marginal sources involved. Therefore, the same $f_{\ell n}$ yields (16) for every $2 \le j \le k$. (In fact, we recall that the constant-value sets of $f_{\ell n}(.)$ were constructed as decoding sets of a channel code for the channel $F_{X^{(1)\ell}|U_\ell}$. More precisely, the construction was suitable only for large enough n, and it might well be that the threshold depended on the joint distribution. However, this dependence does not disturb us, since there are only finitely many 2--sources involved here, and thus one might take the largest threshold for the common one.)

The same holds true for what is left from the proof of the converse part, i.e. the "single-letterization" of the rate region. In fact, given a Markov chain $U_\ell \to X^{(1)\ell} \to \{X^{(j)\ell};\ 2 \le j \le k\}$, one constructs a chain $U \to X^{(1)} \to \{X^{(j)};\ 2 \le j \le k\}$ such that the single-letter information quantities lower-bound the corresponding product-space quantities by introducing a r.v. I uniformly distributed over $\{1,2,\dots,\ell\}$ and independent of $(U_\ell, X^{(1)\ell},\dots,X^{(j)\ell})$. Defining now $U \triangleq (I, U_\ell, X^{(1)I-1})$, $X^{(j)} \triangleq X_I^{(j)}$ for $1 \le j \le k$, we see by the inequalities (6)-(9) that in fact the single-letter information quantities $I(U \wedge X^{(1)})$, $H(X^{(j)}|U)$ for $2 \le j \le k$ lower-bound the product-space quantities $\ell^{-1} I(U_\ell \wedge X^{(1)\ell})$, $\ell^{-1} H(X^{(j)\ell}|U_\ell)$. This completes the proof of Theorem 5.

One can prove the strong converse

Theorem 6.

$$R^{\langle k\rangle}(\varepsilon) = R^{\langle k\rangle} \quad \text{for every} \quad 0 < \varepsilon < 1$$

where $R^{\langle k\rangle}(\varepsilon)$ denotes the ε-achievable rate region for the side information problem with many decoders.

Remark. We call the readers attention to the fact that the last problem did not depend on the total correlation of the k marginal sources. Instead, only the joint distributions $\{X_1^{(1)}, X_1^{(j)})\}$ played a role in the determination of the rate region.

Finally, there are many other possible generalizations of the source coding network with side information. Several others will be considered in subsequent sections.

Several side informators-one decoder

This section might disappoint the reader. It contains almost no result. Namely, the general problem

$$\Delta(1) = \{1,2,\dots,k\} \qquad i(1)=k$$

seems to be extremely difficult for $k > 2$. Already for $k=3$ the rate region is unknown though certain minimal rates have been determined. We shall restrict ourselves to this special case. Instead of enumerating all the known little partial results we prefer to present a very special case which seems to well illustrate what the difficulties are. Furthermore, our problem will have some features of independent interest.

In words, a discrete memoryless stationary 3-source is given. We denote the marginal sources by $\{X_n\}$, $\{Y_n\}$ and $\{Z_n\}$. There is a separate encoder for each of the sources which block-encode the sources they can observe. All the three codes are available to the sole decoder which constructs an (n,ε)-reproduction of the source $\{Z_n\}$. As we have mentioned before, the rate region is unknown. We restrict ourselves even more, and suppose that, for every n, X_n and Y_n are binary, i.e. $X_n \in \{0,1\}$ and $Y_n \in \{0,1\}$. Moreover, we suppose that Z_n is a deterministic function of the pair (X_n,Y_n), namely Z_n equals the (mod 2)-sum $X_n + Y_n$. This last problem sou-nds reasonably special to be attacked. Still, the solution is known only in the special case of $\{(X_n,Y_n)\}_{n=1}^{\infty}$ being a binary symmetric source.[23]

Definition. The d.m.s. 2-source $\{(X_n,Y_n)\}_{n=1}^{\infty}$ is binary symmetric if for every n $Pr(X_n=0,\ Y_n=0)=Pr(X_n=1,Y_n=1)=\frac{1}{2} - Pr(X_n=0,\ Y_n=1) =$

$= \frac{1}{2} - Pr(X_n = 1,\ Y_n = 0)$.

The following partial result which I believe is of very special interest was implicitly contained in Wyner's review paper[1] as a proof of the Slepian-Wolf theorem[6] in the binary symmetric case:

Theorem 7. Let $\{(X_n, Y_n, Z_n)\}_{n=1}^{\infty}$ be a d.m.s.3-source such that $\{(X_n, Y_n)\}$ is a binary symmetric source, and Z_n is the (mod 2)-sum of X_n and Y_n. Consider the standard network

$$\Delta(1) = \{X, Y, Z\} \quad i(1) = \{Z\}$$

Denoting the corresponding rate region by S we claim that

$$(R_X, R_Y, 0) \in S \text{ iff } R_X \geq H(X|Y) \text{ and } R_Y \geq H(Y|X). \tag{17}$$

Remark: Clearly, the essence of this statement is that the rate triple $(R_X = H(X|Y),\ R_Y = H(Y|X),\ R_Z = 0)$ is achievable, the rest being trivial. As we shall see, the proof of this statement, as we are going to outline it, is algebraic, and moreover, we do not know any purely combinatorial or probabilistic argument yielding the same result. This might suggest that the general solution of the problem $[\Delta(1) = \{1,2,3\},\ i(1) = 3]$ should be hard to get. In any case, one would like to have a non-algebraic proof of Theorem 7.

Proof [Wyner[1]]: It is a well-known result of Elias[24] that for binary symmetric channels there exist algebraic codes performing capacity. This can be expressed in the following way:

Lemma [Elias[24]]: Let us be given a sequence $\{Z_n\}$ of i.i.d. binary r.v.'s.

For any fixed $\delta > 0$ and sufficiently large n there exists a 0-1 matrix A_n of $m \times n$ entries such that $m < n[H(Z_1)+\delta]$, and a function $\varphi_n: \{0,1\}^m \to \{0,1\}^n$ such that denoting by $A_n(z^n)$ the matrix product over the (mod 2)-field of the matrix A with the column 0-1-vector z^n of length n we have

$$Pr(\varphi_n(A_n(z^n)) \neq z^n) \leq \delta.$$

This lemma immediately yields the direct part of our theorem. In fact, apply the lemma to the sequence $\{z_n\}$ of the statement of Theorem 7 and choose the resulting mapping $A_n(\cdot)$ for both the code of X^n and Y^n. Then, by the lemma we have

$n^{-1}\log\|A_n(X^n)\| = n^{-1}\log\|A_n(Y^n)\| \leq H(Z_1)+\delta$. Noticing that in case of binary symmetric correlation the (mod 2)-sum $Z_n = X_n + Y_n$ is independent of any of the summands, the last inequality results in

$$\begin{aligned} &n^{-1}\log\|A_n(X^n)\| \leq H(X_1+Y_1|Y_1)+\delta = H(X_1|Y_1)+\delta \quad \text{and} \\ &n^{-1}\log\|A_n(Y^n)\| \leq H(X_1+Y_1|X_1)+\delta = H(Y_1|X_1)+\delta \quad . \end{aligned} \tag{17}$$

The decoder can adopt the following strategy: he applies the function φ_n (assured by the lemma) to the (mod 2)-sum $A_n(X^n) + A_n(Y^n)$. Since $A_n(.)$ is a linear mapping, we have $A_n(X^n) + A_n(Y^n) = A_n(X^n + Y^n) = A_n(Z^n)$, and thus by the lemma

$$Pr(\varphi_n(A_n(X^n) + A_n(Y^n)) \neq Z^n) < \delta.$$

This and the relations (17) prove that the functions $A_n(X^n)$, $A_n(Y^n)$, $\varphi_n(.)$ yield an (n,δ)-reproduction of Z^n which has rate

$(H(X_1|Y_1)+\delta,\ H(Y_1|X_1)+\delta, 0)$. This proves the direct part. The converse is now easy. In fact, it is obvious that

$$R_X \geq H(Z_1|Y_1),\quad R_Y \geq H(Z_1|X_1)\ , \tag{18}$$

Since $H(Z_1|Y_1)$ is the remaining uncertainty about Z_1 once one knows Y_1 and in order to get an (n,δ)-code of Z^n one still needs a code of approximate rate $H(Z_1|Y_1)$ of Z^n even if one knows the whole sequence Y^n. Noticing that $H(Z_1|Y_1)=H(X_1|Y_1)$ and $H(Z_1|X_1)=H(Y_1|X_1)$ one gets the converse by (18).

One immediately sees that the converse statements $R_X \geq H(X|Y)$, $R_Y \geq H(Y|X)$ still hold true if one drops the condition of X_n and Y_n being symmetrically correlated. However, one easily sees[23], that the achievability of the rate triple $(H(X|Y), H(Y|X), 0)$ is equivalent to Z_n being independent from both X_n and Y_n. Now this property characterizes binary symmetric correlation. Hence our rate triple is not achievable in other cases.

The zigzag source network coding problem. In short description we define the zigzag source network by

$$\begin{aligned} \Delta(1) &= \{1\}\ ,\quad i(1)=1 \\ \Delta(j) &= \{j-1, j\}, i(j)=j \quad \text{for}\quad 2 \leq j \leq k. \end{aligned} \tag{19}$$

For $k=2$ this problem is a special case of the Slepian-Wolf network problem. For $k=3$ the problem has been solved by Körner and Marton[25]. For $k \geq 4$ the problem still seems to be open. It was noticed by I. Csiszár that the problem

$$\Delta(j)=\{j-1,j\}\quad i(j)=j \quad \text{for}\ 2\leq j\leq k \tag{20}$$

is a special case of the zigzag problem for $k+1$. This means in particular that the source coding problem with 1 side informator is a special case of the zigzag problem for 3-sources. To be more specific, we can state the following

Theorem [Csiszár[26]]. Let us be given a d.m.s. k-source $\{(X_n^{(1)},\ldots$ $\ldots,X_n^{(k)})\}_{n=1}^{\infty}$ and denote by $\hat{R}^{[k]}$ the rate region for the problem (20). - Define a d.m.s. $(k+1)$-source such that

$$\hat{X}_n^{(1)} = \hat{X}_n^{(2)} = (X_n^{(1)},$$

$$\hat{X}_n^{(j)} = X_n^{(j-1)} \quad \text{for} \quad j \geq 3,$$

and denote by $R^{[k+1]}$ the region of achievable rates for this problem. We claim that

$$(R_1,R_2,\ldots,R_k) \in \hat{R}^{[k]} \quad \text{iff} \quad (H(X^{(1)}),\ R_1,R_2,\ldots,R_k) \in R^{[k+1]}\ .$$

Heuristically, the theorem is true because the code of the second marginal source in problem (19) only serves as side-information for the third decoder in the case when the first and second marginal source coincide. In fact, since the second decoder has access to such a code of the first source which in itself suffices for the first decoder to decode on that source, therefore it is indifferent for the second decoder whatever code of the second source he has available.

Let us turn now to the zigzag problem for 3-sources in somewhat more detail.

Let us be given a 3-source $\{(X_n,Y_n,Z_n)\}$ which is discrete, memoryless and stationary. Three separate and non-cooperating encoders observe the three marginal sources and block-encode the first n outputs of them by means of some functions f_n, g_n and h_n. The code f_n is made available to a decoder who ε-reproduces $\{(X_n)\}$ by constructing a function $\varphi_n(f_n)$. The second decoder ε-reproduces $\{(Y_n)\}$ by means of a function $\psi_n(f_n, g_n)$, and the third decoder constructs an ε-reproduction $\xi_n(g_n, h_n)$ of Z^n. The difficulty of this problem results from the fact that the code of Y^n has to play two conflicting roles. This is best understood by examining a constant-value set of the code $g_n(Y^n)$. Say, $B \subseteq Y^n$ is such a set. Thus, the information given by the encoder of Y^n to the decoder of Z^n is that Y^n, which is correlated with Z^n, lies in B. By the help of this information, the decoder of Z^n has to locate Z^n in a set which has approximately $\Lambda_W(B, 1-\varepsilon)$ elements, (where $W = F_{Z|Y}$). Therefore, clearly, in order to please the Z-decoder, the Y-encoder has to pick up constant-value sets B which have a small $\Lambda_W(B, 1-\varepsilon)$, or in other words, which are "compact". (How large the B's themselves are, is determined in average by the rate of the Y-encoder). On the other hand, the information "Y^n is in B" is also meant for the Y-decoder who has to decide for the right Y^n in B by his knowledge of f_n. Since knowing f_n means knowing X^n with arbitrarily small probability of error, we can say that the Y-decoder decides for one or an other element of B by his knowledge of X^n. Since this decoder ε-reproduces Y^n, the conditional probability of his deciding well given the event $\{Y^n = y^n\}$ has to be large for most of the Y-sequences. This implies that this conditional probability is large for most of the elements of most of the constant-value sets of g_n. Hence for most of the B's a "large" subset $B'\subseteq B$ can be found such that B' is a channel code for $V \triangleq F_{X|Y}$, having small probability of error. However, a channel code is a "scarse" set, it generates "large" sets. Therefore, the two criteria of goodness of B conflict. This can be made particularly clear in the case of $F_{X|Y}=F_{Z|Y}$ where $\Lambda_V(B,1-\varepsilon)=\Lambda_W(B,1-\varepsilon)$, i.e. the same quantity should be large and small at the same time. We state this special case of the Körner-Marton result[25]: (In fact, the statement below can be proved without recurring to the general theorem.)

Corollary (to the future Theorem 9). Suppose that $F_{X|Y}=F_{Z|Y}$. Then the rate region $R^{[3]}$ for the corresponding zigzag problem is

$$R^{[3]}=\{(R_x,R_y,R_z): R_X \geq H(X),\quad R_Y \geq H(Y|X),\quad R_Y+R_Z \geq H(Z)+H(Y|X)=H(Y,Z)\}$$

Notice that this implies that e.g. the following rate triple is minimal: $(H(X), H(Y|X), H(Z))$. Why is this interesting? Well, this is the result of the Y-encoder "favouring" the Y-decoder. In fact, it shows that if the Y-encoder uses any functions having asymptotically minimal rate allowing an (n,ε)-reproduction of Y^n, then the resulting Y-code will give no information to the Z^n-decoder even though (Y_n,Z_n) are correlated.

Now we state

Theorem 9. Given a d.m.s. 3-source $\{(X_n,Y_n,Z_n)\}_{n=1}^{\infty}$, for every $0<\varepsilon<1$ we denote by $R^{[3]}(\varepsilon)$ the region of ε-achievable rates for the corresponding zigzag problem. Then

$$
\begin{aligned}
R^{[3]}(\varepsilon)=R^{[3]}=\{((R_x,R_y,R_z)\colon\ & R_x \geq H(X),\\
& R_y \geq H(Y|X)+I(X\wedge U)-r\\
& R_z \geq H(Z|U)+r\\
& U \rightarrow Y \rightarrow (X,Z)\\
& \|U\| \leq \|Y\|+2\\
& 0 \leq r \leq I(X\wedge U)\},
\end{aligned}
$$

where the joint distribution of (X,Y,Z) equals the (common) joint distribution of the (X_n,Y_n,Z_n)'s.

The proof[25] of this theorem is rather involved. The main tool is the technique we used for the side-information problem[19], and a new stronger version of Feinstein's lemma[27], also known as the maximal code lemma. Without detailing other parts of the proof, we devote some words to explain the new lemma (Theorem 1 in[25]) and its use. As we have seen from the discussion preceding the statement of Theorem 9, the constant-value sets of the source code $g_n(Y^n)$ are - roughly speaking-codeword sets for the channel $V=F_{X|Y}$. (This heuristics can be made precise.) On the other hand they have to have small Λ_W's. In order to keep the rate of the Y-encoder low, the constant-value sets of $g_n(Y^n)$, i.e. the channel codes have to be large.

One can suppose, as usual, that the constant-value sets consist of typical sequences of the distribution of Y_1. Therefore, the question one has to solve when dealing with the zigzag source can be stated as: how large a code for the channel V one can select from a set $B\subseteq Y^n$ of Y_1-typical sequences that has a given Λ_W. Now Theorem 1[25] implies that asymptotically this only depends on the Λ_V which is jointly achievable with Λ_W. Therefore our original problem can be reduced to an asymptotical characterization of (Λ_W, Λ_V). A particular feature of the above arguments is that the fixed error probabilities do not play any role in the asymptotical characterizations. This is a consequence of Margulis' result[12]. As we shall see later, Theorem 1[25] was also used for proving a converse result for non-degraded broadcast channels. The result itself says that it only depends on Λ_V how large a channel code for use on channel V one can select out of an arbitrary Q-typical subset of Y^n, where Q is an arbitrary fixed distribution over Y. The uniform exponential lower and upper bounds that we have given, asymptotically have the same exponent.

Let us denote for an arbitrary set B by $M_V(B,\varepsilon)$ the maximum number of codewords in an (n,ε)-code for the channel V such that all the codewords are chosen from B.

Theorem 10 [Körner-Marton[25], maximal code lemma]. Let a pair of numbers $0 < \varepsilon,\ \eta < 1$ be given. For sufficiently large n the number $M(B,\varepsilon)$ satisfies the relation

$$\max_{B \subseteq T_n(Q)} |n^{-1} \log M(B,\varepsilon) - (n^{-1} \log \Lambda_V(B,\eta) - H(Y|X))| \to 0$$

where $dist\ X = Q$ and $F_{X|Y} = V$.

In particular, this theorem says that restricting ourselves to sequences that are typical of the same type, $M(B,\varepsilon)$ is proportional to $\Lambda_V(B,\eta)$. (Since $\Lambda_V(B,\eta)$ is asymptotically independent of η, $M(B,\varepsilon)$ is asymptotically independent of ε.)

Remark: As we have already seen, seemingly different network problems often reduce to eachother. An interesting example of this is the problem

$$\begin{aligned} \Delta(1) &= \{1\} \quad i(1)=1 \\ \Delta(2) &= \{1,2,3\} \quad i(2)=2 \\ \Delta(3) &= \{2,3\} \quad i(3)=3. \end{aligned} \tag{21}$$

We can call the above a

Slepian-Wolf network with side information.

In words, we have a d.m.s. 2-source $\{(X_n^{(2)}, X_n^{(3)})\}_{n=1}^{\infty}$ and a corresponding Slepian-Wolf network, i.e. 2 separate encoders which do not cooperate and one decoder for each of the sources, so that the decoders have access to both of the codes. In addition, there is a third source, correlated with the two other, i.e. $\{(X_n^{(1)}\}_{n=1}^{\infty}$, and an (n,ε)-code of this latter source is the side information available to the $\{X_n^{(2)}\}$-decoder. However, this side information is inaccessible to the $\{X_n^{(3)}\}$-decoder. Now we claim that this problem can be reduced to the zigzag problem for 3-sources. (Moreover, the resulting zigzag problem is easier than the general problem. However, we shall not enter these details.)

Denote the rate region for problem (21) by T, and consider the zigzag problem for the following 3-source:

$$\hat{X}_n^{(1)} = (X_n^{(1)}, X_n^{(3)}); \quad \hat{X}_n^{(2)} = X_n^{(2)}; \quad \hat{X}_n^{(3)} = X_n^{(3)}$$

Denote the rate region for the latter problem by $\hat{T}$.

We claim that

Theorem 11

$(R^{(1)},R^{(2)},R^{(3)})\in T$ iff $R^{(1)}\geq H(X^{(1)})$; $(H(X^{(1)},X^{(3)}),R^{(2)},R^{(3)})\in\dot{T}$

Heuristically, the statement of the theorem can be proved as follows: suppose that for the Slepian-Wolf problem with side information (SW) f_n is the code of $X^{(1)n}$, g_n the code of $X^{(2)n}$, and h_n the code of $X^{(3)n}$. Then we claim that given any (n,ε)-code $\hat{f}_n$ of (X^n,Z^n), the functions $\hat{f}_n$, g_n,h_n provide a code for the zigzag source $(\hat{X}_n^{(1)},\hat{X}_n^{(2)},\hat{X}_n^{(3)})$. In fact, since the second decoder for the SW-problem was able to determine $X^{(2)n}$ from f_n,h_n and g_n within a small error probability, the second decoder for the zigzag problem will even more be able to do so, since, not considering the errors, he has available $X^{(1)n}$ and $X^{(3)n}$ rather than f_n and h_n. The third decoder can simply adopt the same decoding procedure for the two problems. It is sufficient to show that if $\hat{f}_n$, $\hat{g}_n$, $\hat{h}_n$ are the codes simultaneously used on the zigzag network, then there is an (n,ε)-code f_n of $X^{(1)n}$ such that one can reproduce $X^{(2)n}$ out of f_n,$\hat{g}_n$ and $\hat{h}_n$. Now $\hat{g}_n$ and $\hat{h}_n$ enable the second decoder for the SW-problem to reproduce $X^{(3)n}$ within small probability of error, if he adopts the decoding procedure of the third decoder of the zigzag problem. Doing so, he has now available - within small probability of error, the first and the second marginal source $(X^{(1)n},X^{(2)n})$, and the code g_n. Hence, adopting the decoding procedure used by the second zigzag decoder he is able to determine $X^{(2)n}$ within small probability of error. It is easy to make this argument precise. This is however not our aim at present. Finally, let us emphasize once more that we have omitted the rate-distortion aspects of the theory. The interested reader is referred to the IEEE-Transactions where several papers dealing with those generalizations of the present problems are being published.

PARTICULAR POINTS OF RATE REGIONS: NEW INFORMATION QUANTITIES

The interest in source networks is motivated in part by looking for coding interpretations of information quantities. While entropy and conditional entropy have obvious characterizations in terms of coding, no similar interpretation of mutual information is available as yet. Still, because of the many identities and inequalities they satisfy, all Shannon's information quantities do have a heuristic meaning which helps the expert in dealing with all those inequalities entering his often complicated arguments. Those identities do suggest certain networks, and then it happens that the quantities which there should correspond to certain Shannon-type information measures, fail to do so.

A network can always be considered as a particular way to encode and decode all the involved sources, so as to satisfy a certain amount of additional constraints. Now the constraints often prevent the whole construction from being a "lossless", i.e. optimal, code of the involved sources. (From this point of view, the Slepian-Wolf encoding of a 2-source is rather an exception to the rule.) Hence, those points of a given rate region which correspond to asymptotically lossless codes of some of the sources, create certain interest. (This aspect of multi-user communication might have some influence on other fields of probability theory, such as ergodic theory, etc. (cf. the work of R.M. Gray.))

We will not enumerate all the possible definitions. It is not clear at present whether any of these quantities can be of particular use. We cannot say as yet that one or the other has more meaning then the rest. Still, dealing with them might lead to a better understanding of information theory.

The simplest of the new quantities can be obtained as a particular point of the rate region of Theorem 2, the side information problem for 2-sources. Let us denote this rate region by R, as originally. We define for any pair of r.v.'s (X,Y)

Definition [Csiszár[26]]

$A(X:Y)$, the Y-part of X as

$$A(X:Y) \triangleq \min_{\mathsf{R}_X : (\mathsf{R}_X,\, H(Y|X)) \in \mathsf{R}} \mathsf{R}_X$$

Let us motivate this definition. Let us be given a d.m.s. 2-source $\{(X_n,Y_n)\}_{n=1}^{\infty}$ such that for every n the pair (X_n,Y_n) is distributed as (X,Y), and consider the source $\{X_n\}$ as side information for a decoder who wants to reproduce $\{Y_n\}$. If this decoder has access to an (n,ε)-code of the $\{X_n\}$-source, he will be contented with a code of $\{Y_n\}$ that has approximate rate $H(Y|X)$ and still able to reproduce Y^n within small error probability. Now, is an (n,ε)-reproduction of X^n necessary to performing a good reproduction of Y^n while keeping the Y-encoder at rate $H(Y|X)$? The answer is: not necessarily. In fact, consider the following example. Let us be given three r.v.'s C,D,E forming a Markov chain $C \rightarrow D \rightarrow E$. Let X_n be distributed according to the joint distribution of (C,D) and Y_n according to the distribution of the r.v. E. Then clearly, $H(Y_1|X_1)=H(E|C,D)=H(E|D)$, and the pair $(H(D), H(E|D))$ is an achievable rate pair even though generally we have $H(D) < < H(C,D)$. Therefore $A(X:Y)$, that minimal rate of the X-encoder which is needed in order to keep the Y-encoder at his lowest possible rate $H(Y|X)$, is not necessarily equal to $H(X)$. In general, we have

$$I(X \wedge Y) \leq A(X:Y) \leq H(X).$$

The first paper in the present direction[7], by Gâcs and Körner, can now be related to the side information problem with 2 decoders in the special case of the side information-source equaling the pair formed by the two to-be-decoded sources. For the sake of convenience we recall this network.

Suppose we are given the d.m.s. 2-source $\{(X_n,Y_n)\}_{n=1}^{\infty}$. There is one encoder for each of the sources plus a joint encoder which observes the pairs. There is a separate decoder for each of the two marginal sources having access to the outputs of the joint encoder plus the separate encoder of that particular source he has to reproduce. Let us denote by R_X and R_Y the rates of the separate encoders, and by R_{XY} the rate of the joint encoder. We denote by Q the rate region itself and by $Q(\varepsilon)$ the region of ε-achievable rates. (It results from the foregoing that $Q(\varepsilon)=Q$ for $0 < \varepsilon < 1$.) Now, generalizing the earlier result of Gâcs--Körner[7], Ahlswede and Körner[22] introduced the following

Definition: (Common information of two random variables)

$$A_1(X,Y) \overset{\Delta}{=} \max_{\substack{R_x+R_{xy}=H(X)\\ R_y+R_{xy}=H(Y)\\ (R_x,R_{xy},R_n)\in Q}} R_{XY}$$

and showed that $A_1(X,Y)$ in fact equals the common information introduced by Gâcs-Körner[7]. Since by the results of Ahlswede-Gâcs-Körner[11] $Q(\varepsilon)=Q$, the present result[22] generalizes those of[7].

Let us spend some words on explaining why $A_1(X,Y)$ can be considered as common information, though, in most cases it equals zero, (In fact, it only differs from zero if there exists a common function of X and Y that has non-zero entropy.) Observe that $A_1(X,Y)$ is the largest possible rate of a code which can at the same time be part of a lossless code of both of the sources $\{X_n\}$ and $\{Y_n\}$. Well, common information of the sources can only be what is *separately contained in them*. How could it be otherwise? (More arguments on this can be found in the original paper[22].) If this quantity turns out to be vanishing in most cases, then this is a property of *the* common information. Other quantities can be defined and they might be less trivial, but they cannot be common information. (This argument relates to the original definition[7]. Here the common code is allowed to be a function of the pair.)

Let us add that recently Ahlswede and Gâcs[28] obtained a result showing that if $\{(X_n,Y_n)\}_{n=1}^{\infty}$ is a d.m.s. 2-source, $f_n(X^n)$ and $g_n(Y^n)$ are functions satisfying

$$n^{-1}H(f_n(X^n)) \le H(X_1), \quad n^{-1}H(g_n(Y^n)) \le H(Y_1)$$

and F_n and G_n are such functions that $F_n(f_n(X^n))$ and $G_n(g_n(Y^n))$ almost coincide in the following sense:

$$Pr\{F_n(f_n(X^n))=G_n(g_n(Y^n))\} \geq 1-\varepsilon,$$

then the range of $F_n(f_n(X^n))$ is finite. This is another type of generalization of the original result[7] which - at the same time - generalizes an "almost-generalization" of it due to Witsenhausen[29].

In two subsequent papers[21,30] Gray and Wyner introduced an interesting quantity that - in virtue of the later results[22,20] we now define as

Definition (Wyner's common information[20], indecomposable entropy[22])

$$A_2(X,Y) \triangleq \min_{\substack{(R_X,R_{XY},R_Y)\in Q \\ R_X+R_{XY}+R_Y = H(X,Y)}} R_{XY}$$

Notice that $I(X\wedge Y) \leq A_2(X,Y) \leq \min[H(X),H(Y)]$

The heuristics behind this definition (and especially the name indecomposable entropy) is that $A_2(X,Y)$ is the minimum rate of a joint code (i.e. a code providing information about the *correlation* of the two marginal sources) which must enter any coding scheme altogether achieving a lossless reproduction of the 2-source $\{(X_n,Y_n)\}_{n=1}^{\infty}$. A result relating $A_1(X,Y)$ and $A_2(X,Y)$ to eachother and mutual information is the following:

Theorem 12 [Ahlswede-Körner[22]]

$$A_2(X,Y)=I(X\wedge Y) \text{ iff } A_1(X,Y)=I(X\wedge Y) \text{ iff}$$

all the correlation of X and Y is deterministic.

For the proof we refer the reader to the original paper[22]. The above is the only case where A_2 equals A_1 , since the one is above, the other below mutual information. For the above quantities one obtains a more explicit characterization in terms of Shannon-type information measures by recurring to the characterizations of the corresponding rate regions.

CHANNEL CODING

There are rather strong connections between channel and source coding results in multi-user communication. We have already seen how channel codes are used in constructing good source codes. The sequences of entropy inequalities used in the "single-letterizations" are often the same. In case of binary symmetric sources and channels converse results were obtained from the same starting point - the so-called Mrs Gerber's lemma by Wyner-Ziv[8]. Their basic inequality was generalized independently by Ahlswede-Körner[31] and Witsenhausen[32]. However, as we have already mentioned, investigations in multi-user communication started with multi-way channels, and,of course, with Shannon. The first model that has been studied successfully is the multiple-access channel. The determination of the rate region for the two-sender one-receiver case for independent message sets and average error probability is due to Ahlswede[3]. For a simpler proof of the same result, and a generalization to two receivers, see Ahlswede[33]. This result was generalized by Ulrey[34] to an arbitrary but finite number of senders and receivers in case of independent message sets and average error probability. The essential feature of multiple--access channels consists in all the senders sending to all the receivers. Ahlswede[13] called the attention to the fact that unlike for single-user communication channels, in case of multi-access channels the rate regions for average and maximal error probability might be different. The only available result for dependent message sets is an interesting though rather special theorem of Slepian and Wolf[35]. Gaarder and Wolf[36] showed that - again unlike in the classical case of one discrete memoryless channel - feedback does increase the capacity region. Arutjunjan[36] gave exponential error bounds for rates lying in the capacity region for Slepian-Wolf type multiple-access channels[35]. Bergmans[37] was the first to insist on the fact that, unlike for the d.m. channel with one sender and one receiver, separation of source and channel coding cannot be carried out for multi-access channels. For more details on this channel model see Wolf's paper[14].

Boradcast channels are - in some vague sense - dual to the multi--access channel. Cover[5] defined the two-receiver broadcast channel as a channel with three senders and two receivers. All the three senders present their messages (the three message sets being supposed to be independent) to an encoder who assigns to any message triple a single codeword which is a fixed length sequence of the input alphabet Y of the channel. The length of the input sequence defines the length of transmission. The output factorizes into two marginal alphabets X and $\mathbf{Z}$, since the two receivers are located at different terminals and cannot cooperate. One message set - call it the common message - is meant for both receivers, and there is a separate (private) message for each of them. The problem consists in determining all the possible rate triples, say, for maximal error. Here again, it is not clear whether rate regions for maximal and average error coincide. Putting the foregoing into mathematical language, we have a transition probability matrix $S: Y \to X \times Z$ and its n'th memoryless extension $S^n: Y^n \to X^n \times Z^n$, i.e. $S^n(x^n, z^n | y^n) = \prod_{i=1}^{n} S^n(x_i, z_i | y_i)$ where e.g. $y^n = y_1 \ldots y_n$. An (n,ε)-code $(0 < \varepsilon < 1)$ for this channel is a family of triples $\{(y^n_{jk\ell}, A_{j\ell}, C_{k\ell});\ 1 \le j \le M_1,\ 1 \le k \le M_2,\ 1 \le \ell \le M_o\}$ such that $y^n_{jk\ell} \in Y^n$, $A_{j\ell} \subseteq X^n$, $C_{k\ell} \subseteq Z^n$, the $\{A_{j\ell}\}$'s and $\{C_{k\ell}\}$'s form disjoint families, and satisfy

$$S^n(A_{j\ell}, C_{k\ell} | y^n_{jk\ell}) \ge 1-\varepsilon \quad \text{for all } j,k,\ell. \tag{22}$$

A triple of non-negative numbers (R_1, R_2, R_o) is called an ε-achievable rate triple for the channel, if for any $\delta > 0$ and large enough n there exists an (n,ε)-code satisfying

$$n^{-1} \log M_i \ge R_i + \delta \quad i=1,2,o.$$

(R_1, R_2, R_o) is achievable, if it is ε-achievable for every positive ε. Denote by $C(\varepsilon)$ the region of ε-achievable rates, and put $C = \bigcap_{\varepsilon>0} C(\varepsilon)$.

It is easy to check that the above problem does not really depend on the transition probability matrix S. Instead, it only depends on the so-called marginal channels

$$V(x|y) \triangleq S(x, Z|y), \quad W(z|y) \triangleq S(X, z|y).$$

In fact, substituting condition (22) by

$$V^n(A_{j\ell} | Y^n_{jk\ell}) \ge 1 - \tfrac{1}{2}\varepsilon, \quad W^n(C_{k\ell} | Y^n_{jk\ell}) \ge 1 - \tfrac{1}{2}\varepsilon \tag{23}$$

one sees that if ε tends to 0, (22) implies (23) and vice versa. This shows that the region of achievable rates does not depend on the joint conditional probabilities.

The problem is unsolved, and it has quite a literature. Bergmans and Cover[5] realized that the problem might be easier to solve in the case where one of the channels is a "noisy version" of the other, i.e. there exists a stochastic matrix D such that $W(z|y)=\sum_x D(z|x)V(x|y)$. This has been called the degraded case[5]. One immediately sees that if this condition holds, the receiver which is at the output of V can decode any message meant for the W-receiver. Bergmans[38] gave a conjecture for the degraded case and proved the corresponding direct theorem for the rates he had proposed. His conjecture was proved by Wyner and Ziv[8] under the assumption that both V and W are binary symmetric. Then Gallager[39] proved the converse for the convex hull of Bergmans' rate region, and finally Ahlswede-Körner[19] showed that Bergmans' rate region is convex, thus proving the original conjecture[38]. The strong converse was proved by Ahlswede, Gâcs and Körner[11] for the degraded case. As we have already mentioned, degradedness implies that every code for the worse channel can be decoded at the output of the better one. It was shown by Körner and Marton[40] that this situation is not restricted to the degraded case, by extending the degraded broadcast channel theorem to a larger class of channels. Van der Meulen[41] and Cover[42] independently suggested that a certain rate region was achievable and Cover[42] proved this statement. (Here we state it in a slightly modified form):

Theorem 13 [Cover[42], Van der Meulen[41]]. Rates (R_1, R_2, R_0) satisfying the following conditions are achievable for the broadcast channel:

there exists a sextuple of r.v.'s (X_1,X_2,X_o,Y,X,Z) such that X_1,X_2,X_o are independent, $(X_1,X_2,X_o) \to Y \to (X,Z)$, $F_{X|Y}=V$, $F_{Z|Y}=W$, and the following inequalities are satisfied:

$$R_1 < I(X_1 \wedge X_o, X)$$

$$R_2 < I(X_2 \wedge X_o, Z)$$

$$R_o < I(X_o \wedge X_1, X)$$

$$R_o < I(X_o \wedge X_2, Z)$$

$$R_1+R_o < I(X_1, X_o \wedge X)$$

$$R_2+R_o < I(X_2, X_o \wedge Z).$$

Further, every rate triple that is a convex combination of the above ones, is also achievable.

We omit the proof. It is not clear at all whether this is the whole rate region. However, recently, Körner and Marton[43] proved that all the triples (R_1,R_2,R_o) sucht that one of the private rates (i.e. R_1 or R_2) is zero, are contained in the region suggested by Cover[42] and Van der Meulen[41], and even the strong converse is true. This new theorem contains the previous converse results of Wyner-Ziv[8], Gallager[39], Ahlswede-Gács-Körner[11], and Körner-Marton[40] as a special case and restates the direct theorem of Cover[42] in a simplified form:

Theorem 14 [Körner-Marton[43]] Denote

$$C = \{(r_1,r_o);\ r_1 \le I(Y \wedge X|U),\quad r_2 \le I(U \wedge Z),\ r_1+r_2 \le I(Y \wedge X)$$

$$U \to Y \to (X,Z),\ F_{X|Y}=V,\ F_{Z|Y}=W,\ \|U\| \le 3\}$$

For any $0 < \varepsilon < 1$

$$(R_1, O, R_o) \in C(\varepsilon) \quad \text{iff} \quad (R_1, R_o) \in \tilde{C}$$

It is worthwile mentioning that the proof of this theorem is intimately connected with that of Theorem 9. For the proof we refer the reader to the original paper[43]. Nevertheless we make some observations.

First of all, one easily shows that

$$\tilde{C} = \{(r_1, r_o);\ r_1 = I(Y \wedge X|U),\ r_2 = I(U \wedge Z),\ r_1 + r_2 \leq I(Y \wedge X),$$
$$U \to Y \to (X,Z),\ F_{X|Y} = V_1 F_{Z|Y} = W\}.$$

Now the condition $I(Y \wedge X|U) + I(U \wedge Z) \leq I(Y \wedge X)$ implies that $I(U \wedge X) \geq$ $\geq I(U \wedge Z)$. By this observation one easily reduces the direct part of Theorem 14 to Bergmans' coding theorem[38] for the degraded case. Namely, one considers the channels $F_{Z|U}$ and $F_{X|U}$ constructs a code of rate $\approx I(Z \wedge U)$ consisting of $(\text{dist } U)$-typical codewords such that it be an ε-code for both channels $F_{X|U}$ and $F_{Z|U}$. This is possible because $I(Z \wedge U) \leq$ $\leq I(X \wedge U)$. Now what one does can *heuristically* be described like this: The above code can be decoded by a decoder located at the output of the channel $F_{Y|U}$. Consider the decoding sets this decoder would use, and select from each of them a channel code for $F_{X|Y}$. Since the decoding sets at the output of $F_{Y|U}$ will consist of $(\text{dist } Y)$-typical sequences, one can apply the maximal code lemma[25] and gets out of each decoding set a code of rate $I(Y \wedge X|U)$ for the channel $F_{X|Y}$. (See the preliminaries for the Λ_V of a decoding set.)

The converse part is strongly connected with the proof of theorem 9. Namely, we reduce the problem to simultaneous estimates of $\Lambda_V(.,.)$ and

$\Lambda_w(.,.)$ for the same subset of Y^n. We prefer to avoid more heuristic arguments, and simply refer to the original papers[25,43].

ACKNOWLEDGEMENT

The author is indebted to Rudy Ahlswede, Imre Csiszár, Giuseppe Longo and Katalin Marton for many valuable discussions, during the preparation of this manuscript.

REFERENCES:

1. Wyner, A.D.: Recent results in the Shannon theory. IEEE-IT vol. 20.No. 1, Jan 74, pp. 2 - 10
2. Shannon, C.E.: Two-way communication channels. Proc. 4th Berkeley Symposium on Math. Statistics and Probability, vol.I. pp. 611-644.
3. Ahlswede, R.: Multi-way communication channels Transactions of the 2nd International Symposium on Information Theory held in Tsahkadsor, 1971, pp.23-52.
4. Van der Meulen, E.: The discrete memoryless channel with two senders and one receiver. Presented at the 2nd Intern. Symp. Info.Th., Tsahkadsor, Armenian SSR, 1971.
5. Cover, T.: Broadcast Channels. IEEE-IT vol. IT-18, January 1972, pp. 2-14.
6. Slepian, D. and Wolf, J.K.: Noiseless Coding of Correlated Information Sources. IEEE-IT vo. 19 No.4, July 1973, pp.471-480
7. Gâcs, P. and Körner, J.: Common information is far less than mutual information. Problems of Control and Information Theory vol. 2. No.2, pp. 149-162. 1973.
8. Wyner, A.D. and Ziv, J.: A theorem on the entropy of certain binary sequences and applications I-II. IEEE-IT vol. 19. No. 6. November 1973 pp. 769-778.
9. Körner, J. and Longo, G.: Two-step encoding for finite sources. IEEE-IT vol. 19 No.6. November 1973 pp. 778-782.
10. Wolfowitz, J.: Coding theorems of information theory. 2nd edition. Springer-Verlag. Berlin 1964.
11. Ahlswede, R.-Gâcs, P.-Körner, J.: Bounds on conditional probabilties with applications in multi-user communication. To appear in Z.f. Wahrscheinlichkeitstheorie verw.Geb.

12. Margulis, G.A.: Verojatnostnije charakteristiki grafov s bolsoj svjaznostju.
Probl. Peredaci Inform. Vol.X. No.2, pp. 101-108.

13. Ahlswede, R.: On two-way communication channels and a problem by Zarankiewicz.
Transactions 6th Prague Conference on Info. Theory etc. held in 1971. Academia. Prague 1973.

14. Wolf, J.K.: The AEP property of random sequences and applications to information theory.
This volume, pp. 125 - 156 .

15. Cover, T.M.: A proof of the data-compression theorem of Slepian and Wolf for ergodic sources.
IEEE Transactions on Inform. Theory vol.21. No.2, March 1975 pp. 226-228.

16. Wolfovitz, J.: Approximation with a fidelity criterion.
Proc. Fifth Berkeley Symp. on Math. Stat. etc.
University of California Press, Berkeley 1967 vol.I. pp.565-575.

17. Körner, J.-Marton, K.: A source network problem involving the comparison of two channels I.
Submitted to IEEE Trans. on Inform. Theory

18. Wolf, J.K.: Data reduction for multiple correlated sources.
Proceedings of the Fifth Colloquium on Microvawe Communication, Budapest, June 24-30, 1974, pp.287-295.

19. Ahlswede, R.-Körner, J.: Source coding with side information and a converse for degraded broadcast channels
IEEE Transactions on Inform. Theory, vol.21, No.6, Nov. 1975.

20. Wyner, A.D.: On source coding with side information at the decoder.
IEEE Transactions on Inform. Theory, vol. 21, no.3, May 1975.

21. Gray, R.M.-Wyner, A.D.: Source Coding for a Simple Network. Bell System Technical Journal, vol.58, pp.1681-1721, November 1974

22. Ahlswede,R.-Körner,J.: On common information and related characteristics of correlated information sources. Presented at the 7th Prague Conference on Information Theory, Sept. 1974. To appear in IEEE Transactions on Inform. Theory.

23. Körner, J.-Marton, K.: paper in preparation

24. Gallager, R.G.: Information Theory and Reliable Communication. §.6.2. Wiley New York. 1968.

25. Körner, J.-Marton, K.: A source network problem involving the comparison of two channels. Presented at the Keszthely Colloquium on Information Theory, August 1975, Hungary. Submitted to IEEE Transactions on Inform. Theory.

26. Csiszár, I.: oral communication

27. Feinstein, A.: A new basic theorem of information theory. IRE Trans. PGIT pp. 2-22 Sept. 1954.

28. Ahlswede, R.-Gács, P.: Spreading of sets in product spaces and exponent contraction of the Markov operator. To appear in Ann. Probability.

29. Witsenhausen, H.S.: On sequences of pairs of dependent random variables SIAM J. on Appl. Math., 28, pp.100-113 Jan. 1975.

30. Wyner, A.D.: The common information of two dependent random variables. IEEE Transactions on Inform. Theory vol. 21., pp. 163-179. March. 1975.

31. Ahlswede, R.-Körner, J.: On the connections between the entropies of input and output distributions of discrete memoryless

31. channels.
Transactions of the Brasov Conference on Probability Theory, 1974.

32. Witsenhausen, H.S.: Entropy Inequalities for discrete channels
IEEE-IT vol.20, No.5, Sept.1974 pp. 610-616.

33. Ahlswede, R.: The capacity region of a channel with 2 senders and 2 receivers.
Ann. of Probability, Vol.2. No.5, Oct. 1974. pp.805-814.

34. Ulrey, M.: A coding theorem for a channel with s senders and r receivers.
Inform. and Control, to appear.

35. Slepian, D.-Wolf, J.K.: A coding theorem for multiple access channels with correlated sources.
Bell Syst. Technical Journ. vol.52, pp.1037-1076, September 1973.

36. Arutjunjan, E.A.: Lower bound on error probability for multiple access channels
Probl. Peredaci Informacii vol.XI.No.2, pp.23-37.

37. Bergmans, P.P.: Degraded Broadcast Channels
Ph.D. dissertation. Stanford. June 1972.

38. Bergmans, P.P.: Coding theorem for broadcast channels with degraded components.
IEEE Transactions on Inform. Theory, vol. 19, No.2, pp.197-207. March 1973.

39. Gallager, R.G.: Capacity and coding for degraded broadcast channels.
Probl. Peredaci Informacii vol. 10, No.3, pp.3-14. July-Sept. 1974.

40. Körner, J.-Marton,K.: A source network problem involving the comparison of two channels II.
Presented at the Keszthely Coll. on Inf. Theory, August 1975.Hungary.Submitted to the Transactions of the Colloquium

41. Van der Meulen, E.C.: Random coding theorems for the general discrete memoryless broadcast channel
IEEE Trans. Inform. Theory vol. 21, No.2., March 1975. pp. 180-190.

42. Cover, T.M.: An achievable rate region for the broadcast channel.
IEEE Trans. Inform. Theory, vol. 21, No.4., July 1975. pp. 399-404.

43. Körner, J. and Marton, K.: General broadcast channels with degraded message sets. Preprint.
Submitted to IEEE Trans. Inform. Theory.

Part Three

CODING THEORY

Combinatorial designs constructed from or with coding theory

J.H. van Lint
Department of Mathematics
Eindhoven University of Technology

Most of the lecturers in this session on information theory are interested mainly in the probabilistic side of the subject. However, the participents are undoubtedly aware of the fact that much of what has been promised by probabilistic methods, e.g. by Shannon's Theorems, has not been realized constructively because constructions (of codes, etc.) have all been extremely regular. Very likely, this regularity limits the class from which one can choose so much that the results are not as good as one knows should be possible. Nevertheless, we have to manage with what we have. Thus it is not surprising that coding theorists have either rediscovered a number of concepts from the mathematical discipline known as *combinatorics* or that they have studied parts of that theory so as to apply the results to their own problems. Since the theme of this session is recent trends in information theory it seems proper to give a survey of a development of the past few years, to wit the use of methods of coding theory to expand the mathematical theory! At present the area known as theory of designs and coding theory are influencing each other. It looks like this will become a very fruitful cooperation. It is the purpose of these lectures to explain some of the connections between these subjects to an audience familiar with algebraic coding theory. We shall assume that the reader is familiar with the standard topics from the theory as presented in E.R. Berlekamp's Algebraic Coding Theory [1] (or e.g. the author's lectures on Coding Theory [2]. A summary of what one is expected to know is given in section 2. A few years ago the author gave a similar series of lectures to an audience of experts in the theory of combinatorial designs, stressing the coding theory background. Nevertheless, much of the material for these lectures will be the same. For a complete treatment of these parts and also an extensive treatment of connections between graph theory, coding and designs we refer the reader to the published notes of these lectures [3]. Since we do not assume the reader to be more than slightly familiar with combinatorial theory we shall introduce a number of combinatorial designs in section 1. For the general theory of these topics we refer the reader to M. Hall's Combinatorial Theory [4].

The main topics, i.e. the Assmus-Mattson theorem, codes generated by designs and projective planes, and uniformly packed codes have been organized in such a way that knowledge of sections 1 and 2 is sufficient to understand the remainder of the lectures.

I. INTRODUCTION TO COMBINATORIAL DESIGNS

A) q-ary t-designs (cf. Goethals [5])

Let $R^{(n)}$ denote the set of all n-tuples from a q-symbol alphabet, e.g. $\mathbb{Z}_q$ (as usual we take this to be GF(q) if q is a prime; if q is a prime power we take GF(q) instead of $\mathbb{Z}_q$ in most applications).
For any two n-tuples $\underline{u} = (u_1,\ldots,u_n)$, $\underline{v} = (v_1,\ldots,v_n)$ of $R^{(n)}$ we say that $\underline{u}$ is *covered* by $\underline{v}$ if for all i $u_i(u_i - v_i) = 0$. Let $1 \le t \le k \le n$.

Definition 1.1. A q-ary t-design t-(n,k,λ) is a collection $\mathcal{D}$ of words of weight k from $R^{(n)}$ such that every word of weight t is covered by exactly λ words of $\mathcal{D}$. The words of $\mathcal{D}$ are usually called the *blocks* of the design.

Example 1.1. The 8 non-zero words of the ternary (4,2) Hamming code (cf. Section 2) are

0 1 1 2
0 2 2 1
1 0 1 1
1 1 2 0
1 2 0 2
2 0 2 2
2 1 0 1
2 2 1 0 .

These words all have weight 3.
The reader can easily check that each of the 24 possible words of weight 2 is covered by exactly one of the above words of weight 3. Hence we have found a ternary design 2-(4,3,1).

Example 1.2. The ternary Golay code (cf. *Example* 3.2 or Van Lint [2]) has word length 11 and minimum distance 5. The code contains 132 words of weight 5. We observe two facts:

a) two different code words of weight 5 cannot cover the same triple because if they did, then their difference would have weight at most 4. This is impossible since the code is linear;

b) each code word of weight 5 covers 10 triples.

By a) and b) the code words of weight 5 cover 1320 distinct triples. Since $1320 = \binom{11}{3} 2^3$, i.e. the total number of distinct words of weight 3, we have shown that the set of words of weight 5 in the ternary Golay code is a ternary 3-design 3-(11,5,1).

Exercise. As a preparation for a method to be used later the reader should prove that if one takes the design of the previous example, and in each block replaces all non-zero entries by ones, the result is a binary design 4-(11,5,8). In this design each block occurs 8 times. Therefore, if we take only one copy of each block we find a 4-(11,5,1).

By a straightforward counting argument one finds

Lemma 1.1. If $\mathcal{D}$ is a t-(n,k,λ) and $i \le t$, then $\mathcal{D}$ is also an i-(n,k,λ_i), where

$$\lambda_i := \lambda \binom{n-i}{t-i} (q-1)^{t-i} / \binom{k-i}{t-i} .$$

The fact that each λ_i must be an integer provides a necessary condition for the existence of a t-design.

In the following a t-design will mean a *binary* t-design (i.e. a t-design in the usual sense). Of course a q-ary t-design t-(n,k,λ) can be mapped in a natural way onto a t-design t-(n,k,μ) by changing all non-zero coordinates into ones. Then $\mu = \lambda(q-1)^t$. However, this has the effect that the new t-design could have several repeated blocks. This is the case in the exercise above.

Usually one requires the blocks to be distinct. With that restriction there is no non-trivial 6-design known today. Until recently very few 5-designs were known. However, many have been found in the past 10 years using coding theory.

A t-design with $\lambda = 1$ is called a *Steiner system*. A 2-(n,3,1) is called a *Steiner Triple System* (STS(n)).

B) Block designs (cf. Hall [4])

A 2-(v,k,λ) is usually called a *(balanced incomplete) block design*. For the number of blocks (i.e. λ_0) one usually uses the letter b. For the number of blocks through a point (i.e. λ_1) the letter r. By counting in two ways the sum of the numbers of points in blocks, resp. the total number of pairs of points in all the blocks one finds

$$bk = vr \ , \tag{1.1}$$

$$\lambda(v-1) = r(k-1) \ . \tag{1.2}$$

One way of describing a q-ary t-design is to list all the blocks as the rows of a matrix A. If $q = 2$ this is called the *incidence matrix* of the design. The definition implies that A, a (0,1)-matrix, is the incidence matrix of a 2-(v,k,λ) iff

$$A^T A = (r-\lambda)I + \lambda J \ , \tag{1.3}$$

where J is the matrix with all entries 1.

C) Projective planes (cf. Hall [4], Hughes and Piper [6])

A *projective plane of order* n, which we shall indicate by PG(2,n), is a system of *points* and *lines* with an incidence relation such that

i) any two points are incident with a unique line,

ii) any two lines are incident with a unique point,

iii) there are 4 points, no three on a line,

iv) there are n+1 points on each line, n+1 lines through each point and the total number of points (resp. lines) is n^2+n+1.

It is easy to show that (i), (ii), (iii) imply that the number of points on a line is a constant. If we call this constant n+1, then (iv) is a consequence of (i) to (iii). If we consider the lines as (n+1)-subsets of the set of n^2+n+1 points of the plane and call the lines blocks, we see that PG(2,n) is a $2\text{-}(n^2+n+1, n+1, 1)$. Here $b = v$.

The smallest example of a projective plane is PG(2,2) known as the Fano plane:

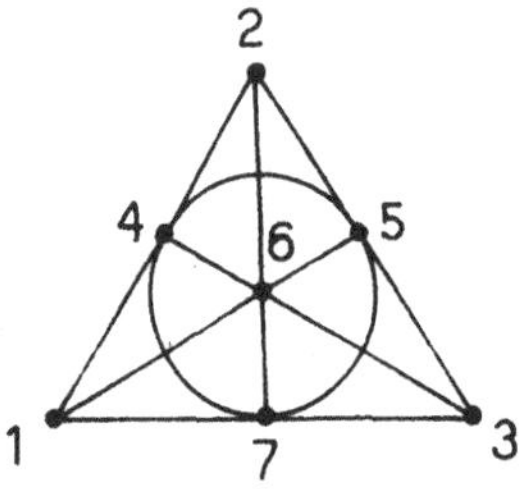

(This is an STS(7).)

$$\begin{array}{l} \quad\ \ 1\ 2\ 3\ 4\ 5\ 6\ 7 \leftarrow \text{points} \\ \text{i.e. } A = \begin{bmatrix} 1&1&0&1&0&0&0 \\ 0&1&1&0&1&0&0 \\ 0&0&1&1&0&1&0 \\ 0&0&0&1&1&0&1 \\ 1&0&0&0&1&1&0 \\ 0&1&0&0&0&1&1 \\ 1&0&1&0&0&0&1 \end{bmatrix} \left.\vphantom{\begin{bmatrix}1\\1\\1\\1\\1\\1\\1\end{bmatrix}}\right\} \text{blocks} = \text{lines} \end{array} \qquad (1.4)$$

The plane PG(2,4) is a configuration of 21 points and 21 lines, with 5 points on each line and 5 lines through each point.

Observe that the 7 rows of A for PG(2,2) are exactly the 7 words of weight 3 in the (7,4) binary Hamming code.

Exercise. Consider PG(2,4). Let ℓ be a line in the plane. Let S be the set of 16 points, not on ℓ. If 3 points of S are on a line, then there is a unique fourth point on this line, not on ℓ. If 3 points of S are not on one line, then they determine 3 lines, which intersect ℓ in 3 different points. These 3 points with the original 3 points, determine a unique 7th point such that together they form the configuration of (1.4), i.e. PG(2,2). Prove this and show that we have thus constructed a 3-design on 16 points with blocks of size 4, i.e. a 3-(16,4,1).

D) Geometries (cf. Hughes and Piper [6])

The n-dimensional space $R^{(n)}$ over GF(q) can be interpreted in the usual way as an n-dimensional geometry called *affine* or *euclidean* space of dimension n, written as AG(n,q). Now we call a line through $\underline{0}$ a *projective point* and a 2-dimensional linear subspace a *projective line*, etc. We thus obtain a combinatorial configuration called (n-1)-dimensional *projective geometry* of order q, written as PG(n-1,q). The case n = 3, q a prime power gives us a system of coordinates for the projective plane PG(2,q).

Observe that AG(2,q) is a block design, namely a 2-(q^2,q,1). The example q = 3 yields an STS(9), namely

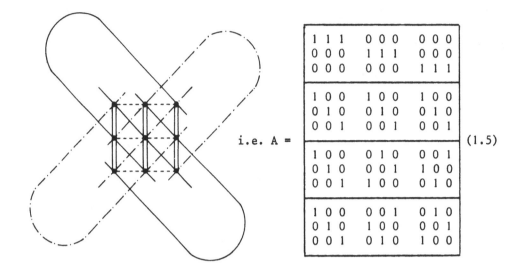

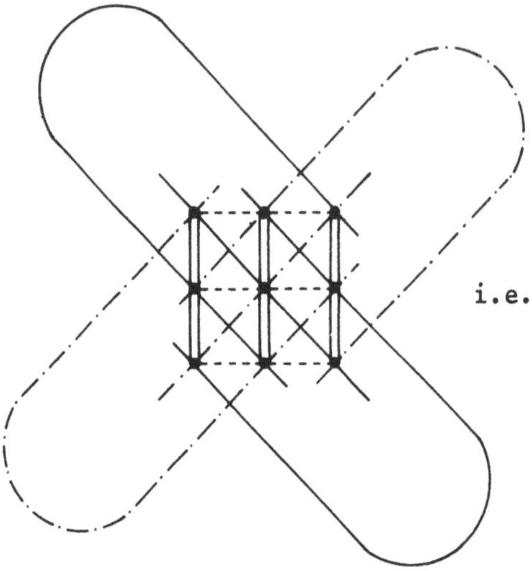

$$\text{i.e. } A = \left[\begin{array}{ccc ccc ccc}
1&1&1&0&0&0&0&0&0\\
0&0&0&1&1&1&0&0&0\\
0&0&0&0&0&0&1&1&1\\ \hline
1&0&0&1&0&0&1&0&0\\
0&1&0&0&1&0&0&1&0\\
0&0&1&0&0&1&0&0&1\\ \hline
1&0&0&0&1&0&0&0&1\\
0&1&0&0&0&1&1&0&0\\
0&0&1&1&0&0&0&1&0\\ \hline
1&0&0&0&0&1&0&1&0\\
0&1&0&1&0&0&0&0&1\\
0&0&1&0&1&0&1&0&0
\end{array}\right] \tag{1.5}$$

In this design the fourth to twelfth block can be described by letting (i,j,k) denote the position of the one underneath the first, second and third block, respectively. Then the blocks are characterized by $i+j+k \equiv 0 \pmod 3$.

Consider the affine geometry AG(2m,2). Later on we shall be interested in the surface Q, called a *quadric*, described by the equation

$$X_1X_2 + X_3X_4 + \ldots + X_{2m-1}X_{2m} = 0 \ . \tag{1.6}$$

One easily sees that $|Q| = 2^{2m-1} + 2^{m-1}$. (The reader should check this as an exercise.)

E) Hadamard matrices and C-matrices (cf. Hall [4], Goethals and Seidel [7])

A Hadamard matrix H is a matrix with all its entries +1 or -1 such that

$$HH^T = nI \ , \tag{1.7}$$

where n is the order of H.

For the existence of H it is necessary that $n = 1$ or $n = 2$ or $n \equiv 0 \pmod 4$. It is not known whether this is sufficient.

A C-matrix is a matrix with entries 0 on the diagonal, +1 or −1 elsewhere such that

$$CC^T = (n-1)I , \tag{1.8}$$

where n is the order of C.

If C is a skew C-matrix, then I + C is a Hadamard matrix. (The reader should also check this!) This idea was used in Paley's well-known construction of Hadamard matrices of order n, where n−1 is a prime power. E.g. a H_{12} is constructed as follows. Let $\underline{c} := (c_0, c_1, \ldots, c_{10})$, where $c_i = -1$ if i is a square mod 11 and $c_i = +1$ otherwise. Let S be a circulant matrix with $\underline{c}$ as its first row. Border S on the left by a column of −1's and border the new matrix by a row of +1's at the top. We find

$$H_{12} = \begin{bmatrix} + & + & + & + & + & + & + & + & + & + & + & + \\ - & + & - & + & - & - & - & + & + & + & - & + \\ - & + & + & - & + & - & - & - & + & + & + & - \\ - & - & + & + & - & + & - & - & - & + & + & + \\ - & + & - & + & + & - & + & - & - & - & + & + \\ - & + & + & - & + & + & - & + & - & - & - & + \\ - & + & + & + & - & + & + & - & + & - & - & - \\ - & - & + & + & + & - & + & + & - & + & - & - \\ - & - & - & + & + & + & - & + & + & - & + & - \\ - & - & - & - & + & + & + & - & + & + & - & + \\ - & + & - & - & - & + & + & + & - & + & + & - \\ - & - & + & - & - & - & + & + & + & - & + & + \end{bmatrix} \tag{1.9}$$

(cf. Hall [4], p. 209).

II. CODING THEORY PREREQUISITES (cf. Van Lint [2])

As before, $R^{(n)}$ denotes the space of all n-tuples from an alphabet of q symbols for which we take GF(q) if q is a prime power.
For $\underline{x} \in R^{(n)}$ and $\underline{y} \in R^{(n)}$ we denote by $d(\underline{x},\underline{y})$ their Hamming distance.
For $\rho > 0$ and $\underline{x} \in R^{(n)}$ we define the sphere $S_\rho(\underline{x})$ by

$$S_\rho(\underline{x}) := \{\underline{y} \in R^{(n)} \mid d(\underline{x},\underline{y}) \le \rho\} . \tag{2.1}$$

For $S_\rho(\underline{0})$ we write S_ρ.

A k-dimensional linear subspace C of $R^{(n)}$ is called a *linear code* or (n,k)-code. The code is described by a *generator matrix* G which has as its rows a basis of C.

The dual code $C^\perp$ is defined by

$$C^\perp := \{\underline{x} \in R^{(n)} \mid \forall_{\underline{y} \in C} [(\underline{x},\underline{y}) = 0]\} , \tag{2.2}$$

where $(\underline{x},\underline{y})$ denotes the usual inner product. A matrix H with a basis of $C^\perp$ as its rows is called a *parity check* matrix of C. Clearly

$$C = \{\underline{x} \in R^{(n)} \mid \underline{x}H^T = \underline{0}\} . \tag{2.3}$$

As usual $\bar{C}$ denotes the code C, extended by an extra parity check bit, such that for every word in the extended code the sum of the coordinates is 0. An e-error-correcting code is a code C with $d(\underline{x},\underline{y}) \ge 2e+1$ for all distinct pairs $(\underline{x},\underline{y})$ in C.

A cyclic code C is a code with

$$\forall_{(c_0,c_1,\ldots,c_{n-1}) \in C} [(c_{n-1},c_0,c_1,\ldots,c_{n-2}) \in C] . \tag{2.4}$$

By the identification $(c_0,c_1,\ldots,c_{n-1}) \leftrightarrow c_0 + c_1x + \ldots + c_{n-1}x^{n-1}$ the code is mapped into a subset of $GF(q)[x] \bmod (x^n - 1)$. It is easy to show that a code is cyclic iff the image is an ideal in this polynomial ring. Hence every cyclic code is described by a generator polynomial $g(x)$, where $g(x) \mid (x^n - 1)$. One often characterizes $g(x)$ by giving sufficiently many zeros of $g(x)$ in some extension field of $GF(q)$.

We shall use the following codes in our examples:

(i) If α is a primitive element of $GF(2^m)$, $n = 2^m - 1$, and $m_1(x)$ is the minimal polynomial for α, then the cyclic code generated by $m_1(x)$ is the $(n,n-m)$-*Hamming code*.

(ii) If α is a primitive n-th root of unity in an extension field of $GF(q)$ and the polynomial $g(x)$ is the polynomial of lowest degree for which $g(\alpha) = g(\alpha^2) = \ldots = g(\alpha^{d-1}) = 0$, then the corresponding cyclic code is the *BCH-code* of designed distance d. Its minimum distance is at least d.

(iii) If q is a prime, $q^{\frac{n-1}{2}} \equiv 1 \pmod n$ and $g(x)$ is the polynomial for which α^r is a zero iff r is a quadratic residue (mod n), (α is a primitive n-th root of unity in $GF(q^m)$), then the corresponding code is called a *quadratic residue code* (QR-code). Its minimum distance d satisfies $d(d-1) \geq n-1$. (This is known as the square root bound.)

(iv) Consider $AG(m,2)$. Let $n = 2^m$. For $k = 0,1,\ldots,r$ we consider the (0,1)-vector of length n which is the characteristic function of a subspace $\{\underline{x} \in AG(m,2) \mid x_{i_1} = 0 \wedge \ldots \wedge x_{i_k} = 0\}$. These vectors generate a binary code known as the r-*th order Reed-Muller code* of length 2^m.

(v) The reader is also assumed to be familiar with the *Preparata codes* (cf. e.g. Cameron and Van Lint [3]). These are nonlinear codes C_m with $|C_m| = 2^{2n-2m}$ where $n = 2^m-1$, m odd. They have minimum distance 5 and word length 2n+1.

In the following we shall frequently use the *MacWilliams relations* for the *weight-enumerator* of a code and its dual. They are the basis for most of the results treated in these lectures.

If C is a code in $R^{(n)}$, then the polynomial

$$A(\xi,\eta) := \sum_{i=0}^{n} A_i \xi^i \eta^{n-i} , \qquad (2.5)$$

where A_i is the number of code words of weight i, is called the weight-enumerator of the code.

The reader is assumed to be familiar with the following theorem (but we give the proof anyway).

Theorem 2.1. Let $A(\xi,\eta)$ be the weight enumerator of an (n,k)-code over GF(q) and let $A^{\perp}(\xi,\eta)$ be the weight enumerator of the dual code. Then

$$A^{\perp}(\xi,\eta) = q^{-k} A(\eta - \xi, \quad \eta + (q-1)\xi) .$$

The proof of this theorem depends on the following lemma. (We write R instead of $R^{(n)}$.)

Lemma 2.1. Let χ be a non-trivial character on the group $(GF(q),+)$ and for any $\underline{v} \in R$ define $\chi_{\underline{v}} : R \to \mathbb{C}$ by

$$\forall_{\underline{u}\in R}\ [\chi_{\underline{v}}(u) := \chi((\underline{u},\underline{v}))] .$$

If A is a vector space over $\mathbb{C}$, $f : R \to A$, and if $g : R \to A$ is defined by

$$\forall_{\underline{u}\in R}\ [g(\underline{u}) := \sum_{\underline{v}\in R} f(\underline{v})\chi_{\underline{v}}(\underline{u})] ,$$

then for any linear subspace $V \subset R$ and the dual subspace $V^{\perp}$ we have

$$\sum_{\underline{u}\in V} g(\underline{u}) = |V| \sum_{\underline{v}\in V^{\perp}} f(\underline{v}) .$$

Proof. $\sum_{\underline{u}\in V} g(\underline{u}) = \sum_{\underline{u}\in V}\sum_{\underline{v}\in R} f(\underline{v})\chi_{\underline{v}}(\underline{u}) = \sum_{\underline{v}\in R} f(\underline{v}) \sum_{\underline{u}\in V} \chi((\underline{u},\underline{v})) =$

$$= |V| \sum_{\underline{v}\in V^{\perp}} f(\underline{v}) + \sum_{\underline{v}\notin V^{\perp}} f(\underline{v}) \sum_{\underline{u}\in V} \chi((\underline{u},\underline{v})) .$$

In the inner sum of the second term $(\underline{u},\underline{v})$ takes on every value in $GF(q)$ the same number of times and since $\sum_{\alpha\in GF(q)} \chi(\alpha) = 0$ for every non-trivial character, this proves the lemma. □

Proof of Theorem 2.1. In Lemma 2.1 let A be the space of all polynomials in 2 variables ξ, η with coefficients in $\mathbb{C}$ and let $f(\underline{v}) := \xi^{w(\underline{v})}\eta^{n-w(\underline{v})}$. If $a \in GF(q)$ write $w(a) := 1$ if $a \neq 0$, $w(0) := 0$.

Then we have

$$g(\underline{u}) = \sum_{v_1 \in GF(q)} \cdots \sum_{v_n \in GF(q)}$$

$$\xi^{w(v_1)+\dots+w(v_n)} \eta^{(1-w(v_1))+\dots+(1-w(v_n))} \chi(u_1v_1+\dots+u_nv_n) =$$

$$= \prod_{i=1}^{n} \{ \sum_{v \in GF(q)} \xi^{w(v)} \eta^{1-w(v)} \chi(u_i v) \} .$$

Since the inner sum is $\eta + (q-1)\xi$ if $u_i = 0$ and $\eta + \xi(\sum_{\alpha \in GF(q)\setminus\{0\}} \chi(\alpha)) = \eta - \xi$ if $u_i \neq 0$, we find

$$g(\underline{u}) = (\eta + (q-1)\xi)^{n-w(\underline{u})} (\eta - \xi)^{w(\underline{u})} .$$

Now by the result of Lemma 2.1 we have (taking $V = C$) :

$$\sum_{\underline{v} \in C^{\perp}} f(\underline{v}) = A^{\perp}(\xi,\eta) = q^{-k} \sum_{\underline{u} \in C} g(\underline{u}) = q^{-k} A(\eta - \xi, \eta + (q-1)\xi) . \quad \square$$

Later we shall show how this equation played a role in recent investigations on the existence of a projective plane of order 10.

For the sake of completeness we mention that generalisations of Theorem 2.1 to nonlinear codes are known.

III. THE ASSMUS-MATTSON THEOREM

Many of the most interesting t-designs with $t > 2$ which are known today were either found by applying a theorem due to E.F. Assmus, Jr. and H.F.Mattson, Jr. [8] or they could have been found in this way. This theorem is one of the really important links between combinatorial theory and coding theory.

We first prove a lemma on t-designs.

Lemma 3.1. Let $\mathcal{D}$ be a t-design on the points of S. Then the complements of the blocks of $\mathcal{D}$ also form a t-design.

Proof. Let T be a t-subset of S. Denote by α_k the number of blocks D of $\mathcal{D}$ with $|D \cap T| = k$. Then by Lemma 1.1 we have

$$\sum_{k=0}^{t} \binom{k}{j}\alpha_k = \binom{t}{j}\lambda_j \qquad (j = 0,1,\ldots,t) .$$

By solving these equations we find that α_k does not depend on the choice of the set T. The statement for k = 0 implies that the complements of the blocks of $\mathcal{D}$ also form a t-design. □

In the following, if A is a linear code with minimum weight d, we shall consider words of weight v determined except for a scalar factor by their supports. We claim this is true if $v - \lceil \frac{v}{q-1} \rceil < d$. Indeed, if two words of weight v have the same support we consider the quotients of entries in corresponding places. These take q-1 nonzero values. So at least one of them occurs $\lceil \frac{v}{q-1} \rceil$ times. Hence there is a linear combination of the two words with weight $\le v - \lceil \frac{v}{q-1} \rceil$. Since this weight is less than d, the linear combination is $\underline{0}$.

Theorem 3.1. Let A be an (n,k)-code over GF(q) and let $A^{\perp}$ be the (n,n-k) dual code. Let the minimum weights of these codes be d and e. Let t be an integer less than d. Let v_0 be the largest integer satisfying $v_0 - \lceil \frac{v_0}{q-1} \rceil < d$ and w_0 the largest integer satisfying $w_0 - \lceil \frac{w_0}{q-1} \rceil < e$, where if $q = 2$, we take $v_0 = w_0 = n$. Suppose the number of non-0 weights of $A^{\perp}$ which are less than or equal to n-t is itself less than or equal to d-t. Then, for each weight v with $d \le v \le v_0$, the subsets of $S := \{1,2,\dots,n\}$ which support code words of weight d in A form a t-design. Furthermore, for each weight w with $e \le w \le \min\{n-t, w_0\}$, the subsets of S which support code words of weight w in $A^{\perp}$ form a t-design.

Proof. In the proof we shall use the following notation. For $A^{\perp}$ we write B. If t is a fixed t-subset of S and C is any code then we denote by C' the code obtained by deleting the coordinates in T from the code words of C which have zeros at all the positions of T.

(i) Consider any d-1 columns of the generator matrix of A and delete these. From the definition of d it follows that the resulting matrix still has rank k.

(ii) Consider any t-subset T of S. By (i) A' is an (n-t,k)-code. Clearly $(B_0)' \subset (A')^{\perp}$. The dimension of B_0' is at least n-k-t. Hence $B_0' = (A')^{\perp}$. Let $0 < v_1 < v_2 < \dots < v_r \le n-t$ (where $r \le d-t$) be the possible nonzero weights less than or equal to n-t in the code B. Then these are also the only possible nonzero weights for B_0'. Since the minimum weight of A' is at least d-t we know d-t coefficients of the weight enumerator of A'. This is $\ge$ the number of coefficients of the weight enumerator of B_0' which we do not know yet. The MacWilliams relations, i.e. Theorem 2.1, yield a system of linearly independent equations which we can solve in principle. The important observation, however, is that the solution, i.e. the weight enumerator of B_0', does not depend on the choice of T. Since $A' = (B_0')^{\perp}$ the same holds for A', again by Theorem 2.1.

(iii) We first prove the second assertion of the theorem. Let $w \le \min\{n-t, w_0\}$. Let $\mathcal{E}$ be the collection of w-subsets of S which support words of weight w in B. Consider the set $\mathcal{E}'$ of complements of sets in $\mathcal{E}$. For any t-subset T of s, $w \le w_0$ implies that the number of sets of $\mathcal{E}'$ containing T is $\frac{1}{q-1}$ times the number of words of weight w in B_0'. By (ii) this number does not depend on T. Hence $\mathcal{E}'$ is a t-design. By Lemma 3.1 $\mathcal{E}$ is also a t-design.

(iv) To prove the first assertion of the theorem we start with v = d. Let $\mathcal{D}$ be the collection of v-subsets of S which support words of weight v in A. In the same way as in (iii) we see that the number of sets in $\mathcal{D}$ containing a given t-subset T of S is $\frac{1}{q-1}$ times the number of words of weight d-t in A'. By (ii) this number does not depend on T. We now proceed by induction. Let $d \le v \le v_0$ and assume that the assertion of the theorem is true for all v' with $d \le v' < v$. Let $\mathcal{D}$ be as before. The number of subsets of $\mathcal{D}$ containing a given t-subset T of S is $\frac{1}{q-1}$ times the number of words of weight v-t in A' corresponding to words of weight v in A. By (ii) the total number of words of weight v-t in A' does not depend on T. By the induction hypothesis and Lemma 3.1 the number of words of weight v-t in A' corresponding to words of weight < v in A is also independent of T. Hence $\mathcal{D}$ is a t-design. □

We consider several examples.

Example 3.1. Take n = 8, k = 4, q = 2 and let $A = A^{\perp}$ be the extended (8,4)-Hamming code. Then d = e = 4. Take t = 3. The condition of Theorem 3.1 is satisfied. Taking v = 4, we find a 3-design with 14 blocks of size 4. This design is also known as a Hadamard-design. Consider a H_8 with a first row of +'s only. For the remaining 7 rows replace + by 1 and - by 0. Then take the complements of these rows. We find the same design as above.

Example 3.2. Take n = 12, k = 6, q = 3 and let $A = A^{\perp}$ be the extended ternary Golay code *). Then d = e = 6. The condition of Theorem 3.1 is satisfied for t = 5. We now find a 5-design!

Example 3.3. Let A be a $(12\ell, 6\ell)$-self-dual code over GF(3). Suppose $d > 3\ell$. Take t = 5. Since all weights in A are divisible by 3 the condition of the theorem is satisfied. Taking v = d we find that the supports of the minimum weight words of A form a 5-design.

---

*) Besides trivial examples there are only 2 *perfect codes* with e > 1. (A perfect e-error-correcting code is a code for which the set $\bigcup_{\underline{x} \in C} S_e(\underline{x})$ is the whole space $R^{(n)}$.) These codes are the so called *Golay codes*. Both are examples of Q.R. codes. E.g. the binary Golay code has n = 23 and hence by the square root bound it has d ≥ 6. Since d must be odd d ≥ 7. It follows by a counting argument that the code is perfect. From the definition of perfect codes it is immediately clear that the words of weight 7 in the code form a 4-(23,7,1). This is a design which can then be *extended* to the design of Example 3.4 (cf. Cameron and Van Lint [3]),

Example 3.4. Take $n = 24$, $k = 12$, $q = 2$ and let $A = A^{\perp}$ be the extended binary Golay code $\bar{C}$ (see * on p.18). Then $d = e = 8$. Since C is perfect the weight enumerator is determined. It is easy to check that 0, 8, 12, 16 and 24 are the only weights which occur. Therefore we can again apply the theorem with $t = 5$. The supports of the code words of weight 8 in A form the well-known 5-(24,8,1) Steiner system.

We consider another interesting application.

Definition 3.1. Let $q \equiv -1 \pmod 6$. We define a *symmetry code* of dimension $q+1$ as a $(2q+2,q+1)$-code Sym_{2q+2} over GF(3) with generator

$$G_{2q+2} := (I_{q+1} C_{q+1})$$

where C_{q+1} is a C-matrix of order q+1. If q is a power of an odd prime we take C_{q+1} to be defined by the Paley construction (cf. Hall [4]).

The symmetry codes (defined by V. Pless [9]) have the following properties (for proofs cf. Cameron and Van Lint [3]).

(i) A Sym_{2q+2} is self-dual (and therefore all weights are $\equiv 0 \pmod 3$)),

(ii) for q a power of an odd prime we have a C-matrix with $C^T_{q+1} = (-1)^{\frac{q-1}{2}} C_{q+1}$. Then

$$G^{*}_{2q+2} := \left((-1)^{\frac{q+1}{2}} C_{q+1} I_{q+1}\right)$$

is also a generator for Sym_{2q+2},

(iii) if $w_\ell(\underline{x})$ and $w_r(\underline{x})$ respectively denote the weight of the first half of $\underline{x}$, resp. the second half then

(a) $w_\ell(\underline{x}) = 1 \Rightarrow w_r(\underline{x}) = q$,

(b) $w_\ell(\underline{x}) = 2 \Rightarrow w_r(\underline{x}) = (q+3)/2$,

(c) $w_\ell(\underline{x}) = 3 \Rightarrow w_r(\underline{x}) \geq \lceil 3(q-3)/4 \rceil$,

(d) if there is a code word $\underline{x}$ with $w_\ell(\underline{x}) = w_1$, $w_r(\underline{x}) = w_2$, then there is a code word $\underline{y}$ with $w_\ell(\underline{y}) = w_2$, $w_r(\underline{y}) = w_1$,

(e) all code words $\underline{x}$ have $w_r(\underline{x}) > 0$.

Example 3.5. Consider the example $q = 17$. It is now easy to show that Sym_{36} has minimum weight 12. From the properties stated above we see that only the possibility $w_\ell = 4$, $w_r = 5$ must be ruled out. Using the circulant structure of C_{18} one can limit the amount of computation enough to make the problem feasible for hand computation. For a computer it is a trivial problem. Applying Theorem 3.1 we therefore find 5-designs on 36 points with blocks of size 12, 15, 18 or 21. These designs were discovered in this way.

We mention one more example of an application of Theorem 3.1. This example will turn up later in a different way.

Example 3.6. Consider a $(2^{2\ell-1} - 1,\ 2^{2\ell-1} - 1 - 2\ell)$-2-error-correcting primitive binary BCH-code C. Using Theorem 2.1 one can show that in $C^\perp$ the only weights which occur are $2^{2\ell-2}$, $2^{2\ell-2} \pm 2^{\ell-1}$. Now take $n = 2^{2\ell-1}$,

$k = 2^{2\ell-1} - 1 - 2\ell$, $q = 2$ and let A be $\bar{C}$. In $A^{\perp}$ only 3 weights occur. Hence if we take $t = 3$ the condition of Theorem 3.1 is satisfied. It follows that for each v the subsets which support code words of weight v form a 3-design.

IV. LINEAR CODES SUPPORTED BY STEINER TRIPLE SYSTEMS

A number of known codes, e.g. examples 3.1, 3.2, 3.4 have the property that the words of minimum weight form a t-design with $\lambda = 1$, i.e. a Steiner system.

In 1971 Assmus and Mattson [10] proposed a search for single-error-correcting linear codes for which the supports of the words of weight 3 are a STS. If the word length of C is n, then $n \equiv 1$ or 3 (mod 6) and the STS is a 2-(n,3,1). If we look at the 0's of any word in $C^{\perp}$ it is clear that the STS must have a subsystem on these positions. Hence, if we assume that the STS has *no* non-trivial subsystem, then the minimum weight in $C^{\perp}$ must be $\geq n-3$. Also the weight n-2 cannot occur. By Theorem 3.1 we see that this indeed yields a STS.

A few months ago L.M.H.E. Driessen, G.H.M. Frederix and the author found an infinite class of codes supported by AG(2,3) (cf. (1.5)).

Let

$$H := \begin{pmatrix} 0 & 0 & 0 & -1 & -\alpha & -\alpha^2 & 1 & 1 & 1 \\ 1 & 1 & 1 & 0 & 0 & 0 & -1 & -\alpha & -\alpha^2 \\ -1 & -\alpha & -\alpha^2 & 1 & 1 & 1 & 0 & 0 & 0 \end{pmatrix}$$

where α is a primitive 3rd root of 1 in GF(q), $q \equiv 1 \pmod 3$. Then H is the parity check matrix of the required code C. Clearly $(1,\alpha,\alpha^2,0,0,0,0,0,0)$ and cyclic shifts over 3 or 6 places are code words of C yielding the first 3 blocks of (1.5). To find other code words we must find a linear combination of

$$\begin{pmatrix} 0 \\ 1 \\ -\alpha^i \end{pmatrix}, \begin{pmatrix} -\alpha^j \\ 0 \\ 1 \end{pmatrix}, \begin{pmatrix} 1 \\ -\alpha^\ell \\ 0 \end{pmatrix}$$

which is $\underline{0}$. The reader should have no difficulty checking that this implies $i + j + k \equiv 0 \pmod 3$ as in (1.5).

One can show that a STS on 13 points cannot support a code. PG(2,2), as we know, supports the (7,4) Hamming code. In fact it supports a linear code over GF(q) iff $q = 2^\alpha$. This research is being continued.

V. PROJECTIVE PLANES AND CODES

We now consider another way to relate designs and codes. Consider the incidence matrix A of a projective plane PG(2,n). We consider the subspace C of $R^{(n^2+n+1)}$ over GF(2) which is generated by the rows of A. If n is odd it is easy to see what the code C is. If we take the sum of the rows of A which have a 1 in a fixed position the result is a row with a 0 in that position and 1's elsewhere. These vectors generate the subspace of $R^{(n^2+n+1)}$ consisting of all words of even weight and this is C (because C obviously has no words of odd weight). The case of even n is more difficult.

Theorem 5.1. If $n \equiv 2 \pmod 4$ then the rows of the incidence matrix A of PG(2,n) generate a code C with dimension $\frac{1}{2}(n^2+n+2)$.

<u>Proof</u>. (i) Since n is even the code $\bar{C}$ is self-orthogonal, i.e. $\bar{C} \subset (\bar{C})^{\perp}$. Therefore $\dim C \le \frac{1}{2}(n^2+n+2)$.

(ii) Let $\dim C = r$ and let $k := n^2+n+1-r = \dim C^{\perp}$. Let H be a parity check matrix of rank k for C and assume the coordinate places have been permuted in such a way that H has the form $(I_k \;\; P)$.

Define $N := \begin{pmatrix} I_k & P \\ 0 & I_r \end{pmatrix}$. Interpret A and N as rational matrices. Then $\det AN^T = \det A = (n+1)n^{\frac{1}{2}(n^2+n)}$. Since all entries in the first k columns of AN^T are even we find that $2^k | \det A$. It then follows that $r \ge \frac{1}{2}(n^2+n+2)$. Form (i) and (ii) the theorem follows. □

From Theorem 5.1 we immediately have:

Theorem 5.2. If $n \equiv 2 \pmod 4$ then the rows of the incidence matrix A of PG(2,n) generate a code C, for which $\bar{C}$ is self-dual.

We continue with a few other properties of the plane PG(2,n), where $n \equiv 2 \pmod 4$, interpreted in coding terms.

Theorem 5.3. The code C of Theorem 5.1 has minimum weight n+1 and every vector of minimum weight is a line in PG(2,n).

Proof. Let $\underline{v} \neq 0$ be a code word with $w(\underline{v}) = d$. Since every line has a 1 as overall parity check we see that:

(i) if d is odd then $\underline{v}$ meets every line at least once and

(ii) if d is even then every line through a fixed point of $\underline{v}$ meets $\underline{v}$ in a second point.

In case (ii) we immediately have $d > n+1$. In case (i) we find $(n+1)d \geq n^2 + n + 1$, i.e. $d \geq n+1$. If $w(\underline{v}) = n+1$ then there is a line ℓ of PG(2,n) which meets $\underline{v}$ in at least 3 points. If there is a point of ℓ not on $\underline{v}$, then every line $\neq \ell$ through this point meets $\underline{v}$ by (i). This would yield $d \geq n+3$. □

Definition 5.1. An s-arc in PG(2,n) is a set of s points no three of which are collinear.

Theorem 5.4. The vectors of weight n+2 in C are precisely the (n+2)-arcs of PG(2,n).

Proof. (i) Let $\underline{v} \in C$ and $w(\underline{v}) = n+2$. Every line meets $\underline{v}$ in an even number of points. Let ℓ be a line and suppose $\underline{v}$ and ℓ have 2a points in common. Each of the n lines $\neq \ell$ through one of these 2a points meets $\underline{v}$ at least once more. Therefore $2a+n \leq n+2$, i.e. $a = 0$ or $a = 1$.

(ii) Let $\underline{v}$ be an (n+2)-arc. Let S be the set of $\frac{1}{2}(n+1)(n+2)$ distinct lines of PG(2,n) through the pairs of points of $\underline{v}$. Each line of S contains n-1 points not in $\underline{v}$. In this way we count $\frac{1}{2}(n+2)(n^2-1)$ points. There are n^2-1 points not in $\underline{v}$ and each of these is on at least $\frac{1}{2}(n+2)$ lines of S. Therefore each of these is on exactly $\frac{1}{2}(n+2)$ lines of S.

Each point of $\underline{v}$ is on n+1 lines of S. Therefore $\underline{v}$ is the sum of the lines of S, i.e. $\underline{v} \in C$. (Also see Assmus and Mattson [10].) □

Remark. We leave it as an interesting exercise for the reader to check that Theorem 5.4 also holds for the code generated by PG(2,4).

In fact this code is even more interesting from a geometrical point of view. It is easy to check that the code has

(i) 21 words of weight 5, the lines of PG(2,4) ,

(ii) 210 " " " 8, pairs of lines of PG(2,4) ,

(iii) 280 " " " 9, triples of nonconcurrent lines in PG(2,4) ,

(iv) 360 " " " 7, all the subplanes PG(2,2) contained in PG(2,4) ,

(v) 168 " " " 6, the 6-arcs of the plane ,

(vi) 1008 " " " 10, each a subplane + a line meeting it in one point ,

(vii) the complements of these .

Using a little group theory (cf. Lüneburg [11]) one can show that the 6-arcs and subplanes can be split into 3 equivalence classes in such a way that the following construction works: Take 3 new points p, q, r. Make new blocks as follows :

(a) to a line add p,q,r

(b) to a pair of lines add nothing

(c) to a 6-arc in "class r" add p,q (cyclic)

(d) to a subplane in class r add r ,

(cf. Cameron and Van Lint [3]).

The result is a set of 759 blocks of size 8 which is now a 5-design, namely the Steiner system 5-(24,8,1). Since one can show that this design and the Golay code are both unique it follows that these 8-tuples are exactly the words of weight 8 in the extended binary Golay code! (cf. Example 3.4).

For a self-dual (n,k) code C over GF(q) we find from Theorem 2.1 the following relation for the weight enumerator $A(\xi,\eta)$:

$$A(\xi,\eta) = q^{-k} A(\eta - \xi, \eta + (q-1)\xi) , \tag{5.1}$$

where $k = \frac{1}{2}n$. This means that the polynomial is invariant under the linear transformation with matrix $q^{-\frac{1}{2}}\begin{pmatrix} -1 & q-1 \\ 1 & 1 \end{pmatrix}$. If q = 2, all code words of C have even weight, i.e. $A(\xi,\eta)$ is invariant under the transformation $\xi \to -\xi$. The 2 transformations generate the dihedral group $\mathcal{D}_8$. It was shown by A.M. Gleason [12] that the ring of polynomials in ξ and η which are invariant under this group is the free ring generated by $\xi^2 + \eta^2$ and $\xi^2\eta^2(\xi^2 - \eta^2)^2$.

Let us now consider a possible plane of order 10. From Definition 5.1 and Theorems 5.1 and 5.2 we know that the incidence matrix of this plane generates a code C for which $\bar{C}$ is a (112,56)-self-dual code and that the weight enumerator $A(\xi,\eta)$ of C has coefficients $A_0 = 1$, $A_1 = A_2 = \dots = A_{10} = 0$, $A_{11} = 111$.

Since all the generators of $\bar{C}$ have weight 12 and any two words of $\bar{C}$ have an even number of 1's in common we see that all weights in $\bar{C}$ are divisible by 4. Therefore $A_{13} = A_{14} = 0$. By substituting this in (5.1) or by using Gleason's result one sees that $A(\xi,\eta)$ is uniquely determined if we know A_{12}, A_{15} and A_{16}. Recently F.J. MacWilliams, N.J.A. Sloane and J.G. Thompson [13] investigated the code words of weight 15 in C. It was assumed that the incidence matrix of the plane led to a code for which $A_{15} \neq 0$. Arguments of the same type as the ones we used in proving Theorems 5.3 and 5.4 severely restricted the possibilities. In fact it was found that the plane had to contain a particular configuration of 15 lines. A computer search showed that starting from such a configuration the plane could not be completed. Therefore we now know that if a plane of order 10 exists, then

$$A_{15} = 0 .$$

Another way in which coding theory could help in finding PG(2,10) is to use Theorem 5.2 and 5.3 as follows. Construct a (112,56) self-dual code and then find the words of minimum weight. A very promising approach is to use ideas similar to symmetry codes. We give one example. There is a block design 2-(56,11,2) for which the incidence matrix A is a symmetric matrix of size 56×56. Clearly $(I_{56} \quad A)$ is the generator matrix of a (112,56) self-dual code $\bar{C}$. In the same way as we did in Example 3.5 it is easy to show that $\bar{C}$ has minimum weight 12. That is where our luck ends! The code C has only 48 words of weight 11. It is still possible that another choice for A would yield the required result!

Projective planes are also connected to so called *equidistant codes*.

Definition 5.2. An equidistant (m,k)-code is an m-subset S of $R^{(n)}$ such that

$$\forall_{\underline{x}\in S}\ \forall_{\underline{y}\in S}\ [\underline{x} \neq \underline{y} \Rightarrow d(\underline{x},\underline{y}) = k] \ .$$

If H is a Hadamard matrix of order n then the n rows of $\frac{1}{2}(H+J)$ form an equidistant binary $(n,\frac{1}{2}n)$-code. From now on we take q = 2. With an equidistant (m,2k)-code S we associate the matrix C which has as its rows all the words of S. Each column C of S, interpreted as a binary vector, has a weight. If all these weights are 0, 1, m-1 or m, we call S a trivial equidistant code. E.g. if $C = (I_m I_m \ldots I_m)$, k copies of I_m, then S is trivial with distance 2k.

Let B be the incidence matrix of PG(2,k) and let J be the k^2+k+1 by k-1 matrix of 1's. Then

$$C = \begin{pmatrix} 0 & 0 \ldots 0 & \vdots & 0 \ldots 0 \\ & B & & J \end{pmatrix}$$

represents an equidistant $(k^2+k+2,2k)$-code which is nontrivial. It was shown by M. Deza [14] that a nontrivial equidistant (m,2k)-code has $m \le k^2+k+2$. The case of equality is interesting.

Theorem 5.5. If a nontrivial equidistant $(k^2+k+2,2k)$-code exists, then the projective plane PG(2,k) exists.

For a proof we refer to Van Lint [15].

For the case $k = 6$, where the projective plane does not exist, the theorem states that the maximum number m of words in an equidistant code with $d = 12$, is ≤ 43. Using PG(2,5) one easily constructs an example with 32 words. Recently A.J.E.M. Jansen, A.W.J. Kolen and the author have shown that in fact $m \leq 33$. The final step was made in the week before this course when J.I. Hall and the author showed that $m \leq 32$. Clearly, solving the problem for $k = 10$ is only possible if one can decide first whether PG(2,10) exists or not.

VI. UNIFORMLY PACKED CODES

We shall now consider a class of codes which generalize the idea of perfect codes. These codes are being studied extensively because they lead to t-designs. As an introduction we consider a special case first (cf. Van Lint [16]). Let C be a binary code of length n and minimum distance $d = 2e+1$. We define

$$C_e := \{\underline{x} \in R^{(n)} \mid \rho(\underline{x},C) \geq e\} , \tag{6.1}$$

where $\rho(\underline{x},C)$ is the distance from $\underline{x}$ to the nearest code word. For all $\underline{z} \in C_e$ we define

$$r(\underline{z}) := |C \cap S_{e+1}(\underline{z})| , \tag{6.2}$$

i.e. the number of code words with distance e or $e+1$ from $\underline{z}$.

By the triangle inequality

$$r(\underline{z}) \leq \left\lfloor\frac{n+1}{e+1}\right\rfloor . \tag{6.3}$$

Since

$$\sum_{\underline{z}\in C_e} r(\underline{z}) = |C| \{\binom{n}{e} + \binom{n}{e+1}\}$$

and

$$C_e = 2^n - |C| \sum_{i=0}^{e-1} \binom{n}{i} ,$$

we find that the *average value* r of $r(\underline{z})$ satisfies

$$|C| \left\{\sum_{i=0}^{e-1} \binom{n}{i} + \frac{1}{r}(\binom{n}{e} + \binom{n}{e+1})\right\} = 2^n . \tag{6.4}$$

Observe that $r = \frac{n+1}{e+1}$ in (6.1) would imply that C is perfect.

Definition 6.1. A binary *uniformly packed* code C is a code for which $r(\underline{z}) = r$ for all $\underline{z} \in C_e$.

Example 6.1. Consider the matrix H_{12} of (1.9). We form

$$A := \begin{pmatrix} \frac{1}{2}(H_{12} + J) \\ \\ \frac{1}{2}(-H_{12} + J) \end{pmatrix}$$

and then remove the first column. The result is a list of 24 words in $R^{(11)}$ with all distances ≥ 5. Let this be the code C. Suppose there is a $z \in C_2$ with $r(\underline{z}) = 4$. By suitable multiplications of certain positions by -1 and by permuting symbols this would mean w.l.o.g. that $\underline{z}$ and the four code words $\underline{x}_1,\dots,\underline{x}_4$ at distance 2 or 3 are

$$
\begin{array}{llllll}
\underline{z} & = - - & + + + & + + + & + + + \\
\underline{x}_1 & = + + & + + + & + + + & + + + \\
\underline{x}_2 & = - - & - - - & + + + & + + + \\
\underline{x}_3 & = - - & + + + & - - - & + + + \\
\underline{x}_4 & = - - & + + + & + + + & - - -
\end{array}
$$

W.l.o.g. the removed first coordinate of $\underline{z}_1$ to $\underline{x}_4$ is respectively +,-, -, -. Then $\underline{x}_1 - \underline{x}_2 - \underline{x}_3 - \underline{x}_4 = 4(1,1,1,0,0,\ldots,0)$ and no row of $\pm$ 1's can be orthogonal to this. It follows that for all $\underline{z} \in C_2$ we have $r(\underline{z}) \geq 3$. For r we find form (6.4) the value 3. Hence $r(\underline{z}) = 3$ for all $\underline{z} \in C_e$. Hence C is a uniformly packed 2-error-correcting code. Observe that again the words of minimum weight in the code C form a design, namely a Hadamard 3-design. We shall see later that this is not a coincidence.

Example 6.2. Let C be the Preparata code of length 2n+1, where $n = 2^m - 1$, m odd. Again e = 2. By (6.3) we have $r(\underline{z}) \leq \lfloor \frac{1}{3} 2^{m+1} \rfloor = \frac{2^{m+1} - 1}{3}$. Substituting the known values of $|C|$, e and n in (6.4) we find

$$
2^{2n-2m} \left\{ 1 + (2^{m+1} - 1) + \frac{1}{r} \frac{2^{m+1}(2^{m+1} - 1)(2^{m+1} - 2)}{6} \right\} = 2^{2n+1} ,
$$

i.e. $r = \frac{2^{m+1} - 1}{3}$. Therefore all $r(\underline{z})$ must be equal to the maximum value! Therefore this is a uniformly packed code with equality in (6.3). Such a code is called *nearly perfect* (cf. Goethals and Snover [17]).

We now look at the more general case (alphabet GF(q)) (cf. Goethals and Van Tilborg [18]).

Definition 6.2. The *covering radius* $\rho(C)$ of a code $C \subset R^{(n)}$ is the smallest number ρ such that $R^{(n)} \subset \bigcup_{\underline{x} \in C} S_\rho(\underline{x})$.

Let C be a code with covering radius $\rho(C) = e+1$ and minimum distance $d \geq 2e+1$. We again consider the set C_e of words of $R^{(n)}$ with distance e or $e+1$ to the code.

Definition 6.3. The code C is called *uniformly packed* with parameters λ and μ if

(i) every $\underline{z} \in C_e$ with $\rho(\underline{z},C) = e$ is at distance $e+1$ form exactly λ code words,

and

(ii) every $\underline{z} \in C_e$ with $\rho(\underline{z},C) = e+1$ is at distance $e+1$ from exactly μ code words.

Remarks. a) in Definition 6.1 we had $q = 2$ and $\lambda + 1 = \mu = r$,

b) $\lambda = 0 \Leftrightarrow d = 2e+2$ or $2e+3$,

c) if $\lambda = 0$ and $\mu = 1$ then $d = 2e+3$ and C is a *perfect* (e+1)-error-correcting code!

From the point of view of design theory the interesting thing about these codes is that the words of fixed weight form a design. We shall only prove part of this.

Theorem 6.1. Let C be a q-ary code with $\rho(C) = e+1$, $d = 2e+1$ and let C be uniformly packed with parameters λ and μ. Assume $\underline{0} \in C$. Then the words of weight $2e+1$ in C form a q-ary e-$(n,2e+1,\lambda)$.

Proof. Let $\underline{u}$ be any word of weight e in $R^{(n)}$. Since $d(\underline{u},\underline{0}) = e$ and C has minimum distance $2e+1$, we have $d(\underline{u},\underline{c}) \geq e+1$ for all nonzero $\underline{c} \in C$. By Definition 6.3 (i) there are exactly λ code words $\underline{c}_1,\ldots,\underline{c}_\lambda$ such that $d(\underline{u},\underline{c}_i) = e+1$. For such a code word

$$w(\underline{c}_i) \leq w(\underline{u}) + d(\underline{u},\underline{c}_i) = 2e+1 ,$$

with equality only if $\underline{u}$ is covered by $\underline{c}_i$. However, equality must occur because C has minimum distance $2e+1$ and $\underline{0} \in C$. Therefore $\underline{u}$ is covered by the λ code words $\underline{c}_i$ of weight $2e+1$. On the other hand, if $\underline{u}$ is covered by a code word $\underline{c}$ of weight $2e+1$, then $d(\underline{u},\underline{c}) = e+1$, i.e. $\underline{c}$ is one of the $\underline{c}_i$. □

The methods which are used to treat uniformly packed codes involve quite a lot of abstract algebra. The results are deep and provide us among others with a very strong necessary condition for existence. Very recently H.C.A. van Tilborg [19] used this condition to show that (except for known perfect codes) there is *no* code satisfying Definition 6.1 with $e > 2$.

We mention one interesting result obtained by using the algebraic methods and by applying Theorem 2.1.

Theorem 6.2. A *linear* single-error-correcting code C is uniformly packed (with certain parameters) iff $C^\perp$ is a two-weight code.

Example 6.3. Consider the quadric Q in AG(2m,2) described in (1.6). Let the $n := 2^{2m-1} + 2^{m-1} - 1$ non-zero points of Q be coordinate places for a code space $R^{(n)}$. As in the description of RM codes consider the 2^m characteristic functions $\underline{a}_i$ of the hyperplanes $\{\underline{x} \in AG(2m,2) \mid x_i = 1\}$, but only on the points of Q, i.e. we intersect the hyperplanes with Q. A relatively simple counting argument shows that any hyperplane $\{\underline{x} \in AG(2m,2) \mid \sum_{i=1}^{2m} \alpha_i x_i = 1\}$ intersects $Q\backslash\{\underline{0}\}$ in w_1 or w_2 points. In other words: the 2m vectors $\underline{a}_i$ are the basis vectors of a linear code $C^{\perp}$ with word length $2^{2m-1} + 2^{m-1} - 1$ which has w_1 and w_2 as its only weights. By Theorem 6.2 this implies that the dual code C is uniformly packed. Therefore by Theorem 6.1 the words of weight 3 in C form a 1-design. This is not too interesting but a simple extension of Theorem 6.1 shows that the words of weight 4 in $\bar{C}$ form a 2-design. The reader should check that this also follows from Theorem 3.1.

As an exercise we invite the reader to show that the codes of Example 3.7 are uniformly packed, thus providing a second explanation for the occurrence of 3-designs in their extended codes.

REFERENCES

1. Berlekamp, E.R., *Algebraic Coding Theory*, McGraw Hill, New York, 1968.
2. Lint, J.H. van, *Coding Theory*, Lecture Notes in Math. 201, Springer Verlag, Berlin, 1971.

3. Cameron, P.J. and Lint, J.H. van, *Graph Theory, Coding and Block Designs*, London Math. Soc. Lecture Notes Series 19, Cambridge Univ. Press, 1975.

4. Hall, M., *Combinatorial Theory*, Blaisdell, Waltham, Mass. 1967.

5. Goethals, J.M., Generalized t-designs and majority decoding of linear codes, Report R282, M.B.L.E. Research Lab., Brussels 1975.

6. Hughes, D.R. and Piper, F.C., *Projective Planes*, Springer Verlag, New York, 1973.

7. Goethals, J.M. and Seidel, J.J., Orthogonal matrices with zero diagonal, *Canad. J. Math.* 19, 1001, 1967.

8. Assmus, E.F. and Mattson, H.F., New 5-designs, *J. Comb. Theory* 6, 122, 1969.

9. Pless, V., Symmetry codes over GF(3) and new 5-designs, *J. Comb. Theory* 12, 119, 1972.

10. Assmus, E.F. and Mattson, H.F., Algebraic Theory of Codes, Report AFCRL-0013, Appl. Research Lab. of Sylvania Electronic Systems, Bedford, Mass. 1971.

11. Lüneburg, H., Über die Gruppen von Mathieu, *Journal of Algebra* 10, 194, 1968.

12. Gleason, A.M., Weight polynomials of self-dual codes and the MacWilliams identities, in *Actes Congrès Intern. Math.* 1970, vol. 3, 211.

13. Mac Williams, F.J., Sloane, N.J.A., and Thompson, J.G., On the existence of a projective plane of order 10, *J. Comb. Theory*, 14, 66, 1973.

14. Deza, M., Une propriété extremal des plans projectifs finis dans une classe de codes equidistants, *Discrete Math.* 6, 343, 1973.

15. Lint, J.H. van, A theorem on equidistant codes, *Discrete Math.* 6, 353, 1973.

16. Lint, J.H. van, Recent results on perfect codes and related topics, in *Combinatorics* I (Hall, M. and Lint, J.H. van, Eds.) Mathematical Centre Tracts 55, 158, 1974.

17. Goethals, J.M. and Snover, S.L. Nearly perfect binary codes, *Discrete Math.* 2, 65, 1972.

18. Goethals, J.M. and Tilborg, H.C.A. van, Uniformly packed codes, Philips Res. Repts. 30, 9, 1975.

19. Tilborg, H.C.A. van, All binary (n,e,r) uniformly packed codes are known, Memorandum 1975-08, T.H. Eindhoven.

SYMMETRIES OF THE STATE DIAGRAM OF THE SYNDROME FORMER OF A BINARY RATE-½ CONVOLUTIONAL CODE

J.P.M. Schalkwijk
Department of Electrical Engineering
Eindhoven University of Technology
Eindhoven, The Netherlands

I. INTRODUCTION

We extend and generalize some earlier results [1] on syndrome decoding of binary rate-½ convolutional codes. Figure 1 represents a familiar example of such a code. The additions in Figure 1 are modulo-2 and all binary sequences $\ldots, b_{-1}, b_0, b_1, \ldots$ are represented as power series $b(\alpha) = \ldots + b_{-1}\alpha^{-1} + b_0 + b_1\alpha + \ldots$. The encoder has connection polynomials $C_1(\alpha) = 1 + \alpha^2$ and $C_2(\alpha) = 1 + \alpha + \alpha^2$. In general, the encoder outputs are $C_1(\alpha)\ x\ (\alpha)$ and $C_2(\alpha)\ x\ (\alpha)$. The syndrome $z(\alpha)$ only depends on $n_1(\alpha)$ and $n_2(\alpha)$, i.e., not on the data sequence $x(\alpha)$, for

$$\begin{aligned} z(\alpha) &= C_2(\alpha)[C_1(\alpha)x(\alpha)+n_1(\alpha)] + C_1(\alpha)[C_2(\alpha)x(\alpha)+n_2(\alpha)] \\ &= C_2(\alpha)n_1(\alpha) + C_1(\alpha)n_2(\alpha). \qquad (1) \end{aligned}$$

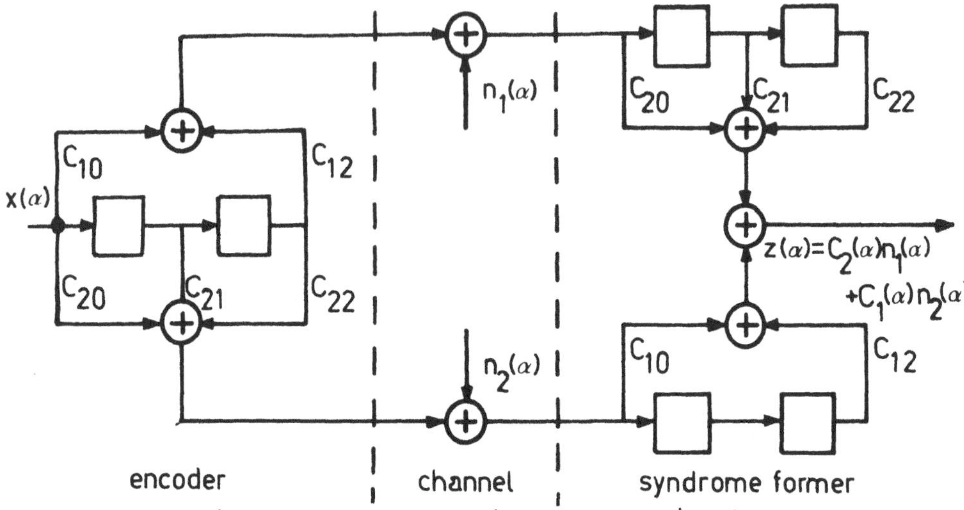

Figure 1. Encoding and syndrome forming for a R = ½ code.

Having formed the syndrome $z(\alpha)$, section III describes a recursive algorithm like Viterbi's [2] to determine from the syndrome $z(\alpha)$ the noise sequence pair $[\hat{n}_1(\alpha), \hat{n}_2(\alpha)]$ of minimum Hamming weight that can be a possible cause of this syndrome.

Given the estimate $[\hat{n}_1(\alpha), \hat{n}_2(\alpha)]$ of the noise sequence pair, one derives an estimate $\hat{x}(\alpha)$ of the original data sequence $x(\alpha)$ as follows. For a noncatastrophic code, $C_1(\alpha)$ and $C_2(\alpha)$ are relatively prime. Hence, by Euclid's algorithm [3] there exist polynomials $D_1(\alpha)$ and $D_2(\alpha)$ such that $D_1(\alpha)C_1(\alpha) + D_2(\alpha)C_2(\alpha) = 1$. For the example of Figure 1, we have $D_1(\alpha) = 1 + \alpha$, $D_2(\alpha) = \alpha$. We receive the sequence pair

$$y_i(\alpha) = C_i(\alpha)\, x(\alpha) + n_i(\alpha), \quad i = 1,2, \tag{2}$$

and form the estimate

$$\hat{x}(\alpha) = D_1(\alpha)[y_1(\alpha) + \hat{n}_1(\alpha)] + D_2(\alpha)[y_2(\alpha) + \hat{n}_2(\alpha)] \tag{3}$$

Note that if the noise sequence estimate $[\hat{n}_1(\alpha), \hat{n}_2(\alpha)]$ is correct we have

$$y_i(\alpha) + \hat{n}_i(\alpha) = C_i(\alpha)\ x\ (\alpha) + n_i(\alpha) + \hat{n}_i(\alpha)$$

$$= C_i(\alpha)\ x\ (\alpha), \qquad i = 1,2,$$

and, hence,

$$\hat{x}(\alpha) = D_1(\alpha)C_1(\alpha)\ x\ (\alpha) + D_2(\alpha)C_2(\alpha)\ x\ (\alpha) = x(\alpha).$$

Note that (3) for the estimate $\hat{x}(\alpha)$ of the data sequence $x(\alpha)$ can be rewritten as

$$\hat{x}(\alpha) = [D_1(\alpha)Y_1(\alpha) + D_2(\alpha)Y_2(\alpha)] + \hat{\omega}(\alpha), \tag{4}$$

where

$$\omega(\alpha) = D_1(\alpha)n_1(\alpha) + D_2(\alpha)n_2(\alpha), \tag{5}$$

and $\hat{\omega}(\alpha)$ equals the RHS of (5) with $\hat{n}_i(\alpha)$ substituted for $n_i(\alpha), i = 1,2$. The term in quare brackets in (4) can be computed directly from the received data using very simple circuitry. As there is no need to distinguish between paire $[\hat{n}_1(\alpha), \hat{n}_2(\alpha)]$ and $[\hat{n}_1(\alpha), \hat{n}_2(\alpha)]'$ that lead to the same value for $\hat{\omega}(\alpha)$ in (4), the algorithm to be discussed in section III computes $\hat{\omega}(\alpha)$ directly.

II. STATE DIAGRAM

In Figure 2 we have redrawn the syndrome former of our example. As, according to (1), the syndrome $z(\alpha)$ only depends on the noise pair $[n_1(\alpha), n_2(\alpha)]$ all other binary sequences have been omitted from Figure 2. For minimum distance decoding we are now presented with the following problem. Given the syndrome $z(\alpha)$, determine the noise pair $[\hat{n}_1(\alpha), \hat{n}_2(\alpha)]$ of minimum Hamming weight that can be a cause of this syndrome. Before tackling this problem in section III, it will be necessary to first derive some general properties of the state diagram of a syndrome former for a binary rate-½ convolutional code.

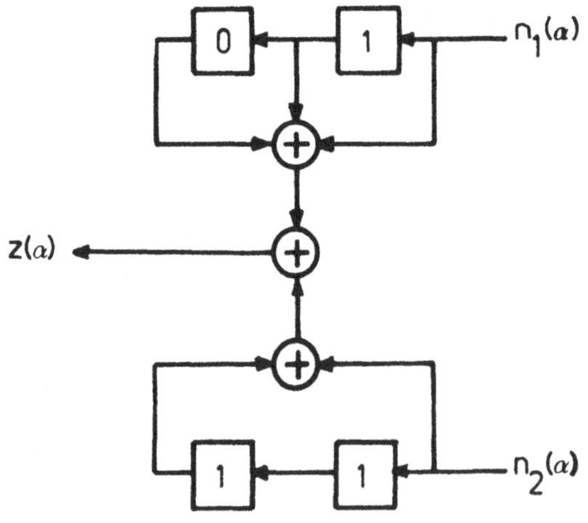

Figure 2. The syndrome former in its base state.

Let ν be the number of memory stages of the encoder, i.e. $\nu = 2$ for the encoder of Figure 1. The corresponding syndrome former of Figure 2 has $2^{2\nu} = 16$ "physical states", where a physical state is defined as the contents $S = [s_1(\alpha), s_2(\alpha)]$, where

$$s_i(\alpha) = s_{i,-\nu}\alpha^{-\nu} + s_{i,-\nu+1}\alpha^{-\nu+1} + \dots + s_{i,-1}\alpha^{-1}, \quad i = 1.2 \ ,$$

of the $2\nu = 4$ memory cells of the syndrome former. Thus, at first sight the state diagram of the syndrome former appears more complicated than the state diagram used to implement the classical Viterbi decoder [2], that has only $2^{\nu} = 4$ states. However, on closer inspection, it turns out that the $2^{2\nu} = 16$ physical states of the syndrome former can be devided into $2^{\nu} = 4$ equivalence classes or "abstract states", where any two physical states in the same equivalence class give the same output $z(\alpha)$ irrespective of the input pair $[n_1(\alpha), n_2(\alpha)]$. In general, to prove the existence of the 2^{ν}, $\nu = 1,2,\dots$, abstract states defined above, we need the following definitions. As the syndrome former is a time invariant circuit we assume without loss of generality that the state S is present at time $t = 0$.

<u>Definition 1</u>: A "zero-equivalent" state is a physical state with the property that if the syndrome former is in such a state, an all zero input $[n_1(\alpha), n_2(\alpha)]_0^{\infty}$ gives rise to an all zero output $[z(\alpha)]_0^{\infty}$, where $[b(\alpha)]_{k_1}^{k_2}$ indicates that part of the power series $b(\alpha)$ for which

$k_1 \leq \exp \alpha \leq k_2$.

<u>Definition 2</u>: A "base" state $S^b = [\alpha^{-1}, s_2^b(\alpha)]$ is a zero-equivalent state with a single "1" in the rightmost position of the top register of the syndrome former, see Figure 2.

A base state can be constructed as follows. Start with the top and bottom registers of the syndrome former, Figure 2, all zero. Put a 1 in the leftmost position of the top register. Assuming that $C_1(\alpha)$ and $C_2(\alpha)$ both have a nonzero term of degree ν we now have to put a 1 in the leftmost position of the bottom register, as otherwise the corresponsing digit of the syndrome $z(\alpha)$ would differ from zero.

Subsequently, shift the contents of the top- and bottom register one place to the right, feeding 0's into both leftmost positions, respectively. If the corresponding digit of the syndrome $z(\alpha)$ differs from zero set the leftmost position of the bottom register equal to 1 thus complementing the corresponding syndrome digit, etc. This process continues until the single 1 in the top register is in the rightmost position. The bottom register now contains $s_2^b(\alpha)$. It is clear that the above construction leads to a unique result. This base state S^b is indicated in the example of Figure 2. However, there might conceivably be another construction leading to a different base state. The following theorem shows that this is not the case.

Theorem 1: The base state $S^b = [\alpha^{-1}, s_2^b(\alpha)]$ is unique.
Proof: Suppose there are two base states S_1^b and S_2^b. These base states are zero-equivalent states, hence, so is their sum $S = S_1^b + S_2^b$. But as the sum of two base states the physical state S has all zeros in the top register of the syndrome former. As $C_1(\alpha)$ has a nonzero term of degree ν the only zero equivalent state with the top register contents all zero, is the all zero state. Hence, S is the all zero state and the physical states S_1^b and S_2^b are equal. Q.E.D.

We will now show that there are 2^ν equivalence classes of physical states and that each class has a unique representative physical state for which the contents of the top register of the syndrome former, Figure 2, is all zero. It is these representative states $S = [0, s_2(\alpha)]$, to be referred to as "the states", that will be used in the remainder of the paper.

Theorem 2: The $2^{2\nu}$, $\nu = 1,2,\ldots$, physical states of the syndrome former, corresponding to a binary rate-½ encoder with ν memory cells, can be divided into 2^ν equivalence classes or abstract states. Each equivalence class has a unique representative physical state $S = [0, s_2(\alpha)]$ for which the top register, see Figure 2, of the syndrome former is all zero.
Proof: Two physical states were related if they resulted in the same output $z(\alpha)$ irrespective of the input pair $[n_1(\alpha), n_2(\alpha)]$.

To prove that this relation is an equivalence relation we have to show that it is reflexive, symmetric, and transitive. Reflexivity and symmetry are obvious. To show transitivity let S_1 be related to S_2 and S_2 be related to S_3. Since S_1 and S_2 produce the same output $z(\alpha)$, their sum $S_1 + S_2$ is a zero equivalent state, as is $S_2 + S_3$. But $S_1 + S_3 = (S_1 + S_2) + (S_2 + S_3)$. Hence, $S_1 + S_3$ is the sum of two zero equivalent states and thus also zero equivalent. In other words, the physical states S_1 and $S_1 + (S_1 + S_3) = S_3$ produce the same output $z(\alpha)$ and thus the relation defined above is transitive. This completes the first part of the proof. The relation defined above is an equivalence relation and, hence, divides the set of physical states into equivalence classes or abstract states. As the sum of zero-equivalent states is again zero equivalent, left shifts of the base state S^b can be added to the all zero state to obtain a zero equivalent state for which the top register has any desired contents. Two zero-equivalent states S_1 and S_2 that have the same top register contents are identical, for their sum $S = S_1 + S_2$ is a zero-equivalent state with top register contents all zero. Hence, as shown in the proof of Theorem 1, S is the all zero state and thus $S_1 = S_2$. In other words, there are 2^ν zero-equivalent states and, in fact, all equivalence classes have 2^ν members, giving $2^{2\nu}/2^\nu = 2^\nu$ abstract states. As we can add left shifts of the base state S^b to any particular physical state without leaving its equivalence class, each equivalence class has a representative member, called the state $S = [0, s_2(\alpha)]$, that has the contents of the top register, Figure 2, of the syndrome former all zero. To prove uniqueness of the representative state within an equivalence class assume two representative states S_1 and S_2. The sum $S_1 + S_2$ of two representative states S_1 and S_2 within the same equivalence class is a zero-equivalent state with top register contents all zero. This sum state again must be the all zero state. Hence, $S_1 + S_2 = 0$ or $S_1 = S_2$ proving that the representative state of an equivalence class is unique. Q.E.D.

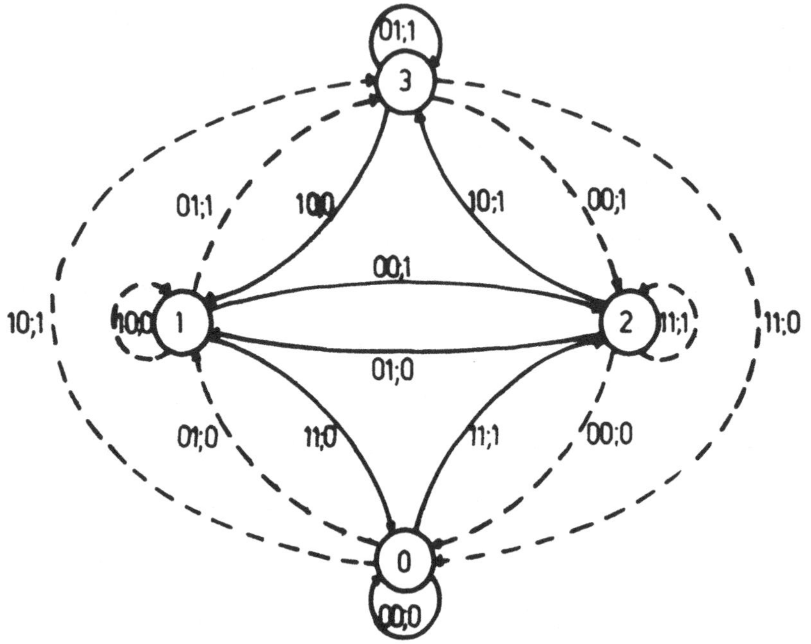

Figure 3. State diagram of syndrome former.

We are now ready, as an example, to construct the state diagram, see Figure 3, of the syndrome former of Figure 2. The states $S_0 = [0,0]$, $S_1 = [0,\alpha^{-1}]$, $S_2 = [0,\alpha^{-2}]$, and $S_3 = [0,\alpha^{-2} + \alpha^{-1}]$ are representative states with the contents of the bottom register, Figure 2, of the syndrome equal to 00,01,10 and 11, respectively. An input $[n_1(\alpha), n_2(\alpha)]_0^0 = [0,1]$ brings us from state S_0 to state S_1. An input $[n_1(\alpha), n_2(\alpha)]_0^0 = [1,0]$ brings us from state S_0 to state $S' = [\alpha^{-1}, 0]$, which is not a representative physical state. The representative state in the equivalence class of S' can be found through addition of the base state $S^b = [\alpha^{-1}, s_2^b(\alpha)]$, where $s_2^b(\alpha) = \alpha^{-2} + \alpha^{-1}$ from Figure 2. Hence, $S' + S^b = [0, \alpha^{-2} + \alpha^{-1}]$, i.e. an input $[n_1(\alpha), n_2(\alpha)]_0^0 = [1,0]$ brings from state S_0 to state $S_3 = S' + S^b$.

In the same fashion $[n_1(\alpha), n_2(\alpha)]_0^0 = [1,1]$ brings us from state S_0 to state S_2. All states in the state diagram of Figure 3 have now been identified and we leave it to the reader to fill in the remaining edges. A solid edge in Figure 3 indicates that the syndrome digit corresponding to the particular transition is 0, a dashed edge corresponds to a syndrome digit 1. The numbers next to the edges are the values $n_1, n_2; \omega$. As has been explained in section I, it is the coefficients $\ldots, \omega_{-1}, \omega_0, \omega_1, \ldots$ of the power series $\omega(\alpha)$ of (5) that one is really interested in. It requires some explanation that the generic value ω of these coefficients can also be indicated next to the edges in Figure 3.

Theorem 3: The value of the coefficient ω_k of the power series $\omega(\alpha) = \ldots + \omega_{-1}\alpha^{-1} + \omega_0 + \omega_1\alpha + \ldots$ defined by (5) is uniquely determined by the state $S(k)$ of the syndrome former at time $t = k$ and by the value of its input $[n_{1k}, n_{2k}]$, $k = \ldots, -1, 0, +1, \ldots$.

Proof: As the syndrome former is a time invariant circuit all one has to prove is that ω_0 is uniquely determined by $S(0)$ and $[n_{10}, n_{20}]$. Eq. (5) can be rewritten as

$$\omega_0 = [D_1'(\alpha)n_1(\alpha) + D_2'(\alpha)n_2(\alpha)]_0^0 + (D_{10}n_{10} + D_{20}n_{20}), \tag{6}$$

where the prime on $D_i'(\alpha)$, $i = 1,2$, indicates that a possible constant term D_{i0} has been omitted. The second term $(D_{10}n_{10} + D_{20}n_{20})$ on the RHS of (6) is completely determined by the input $[n_{10}, n_{20}]$ to the syndrome former at time $t = 0$. Now if the state $S(0)$ of the syndrome former at time $t = 0$ determines $[n_1(\alpha), n_2(\alpha)]_{-\nu}^{-1}$ and if $\deg D_1'(\alpha) \leq \nu$ and $\deg D_2'(\alpha) \leq \nu$ then $S(0)$ determines the value of the first term $[D_1'(\alpha)n_1(\alpha) + D_2'(\alpha)n_2(\alpha)]_0^0$ on the RHS of (6) and we are done.

Now from Berlekamp [3, p. 27] we know that there exist polynomials $D_1(\alpha)$ and $D_2(\alpha)$ satisfying $D_1(\alpha)C_1(\alpha) + D_2(\alpha)C_2(\alpha) = 1$ and thus that $\deg D_1(\alpha) < \deg C_2(\alpha)$ and $\deg D_2(\alpha) < \deg C_1(\alpha)$. Hence, the degrees of both $D_1'(\alpha)$ and $D_2'(\alpha)$ are less than the common degree ν of $C_1(\alpha)$ and $C_2(\alpha)$. However, the state $S(0)$ determines $[n_1(\alpha), n_2(\alpha)]_{-\nu}^{-1}$ only to within an equivalence class.

It thus remains to be shown that addition of a zero-equivalent state $S = [s_1(\alpha), s_2(\alpha)]$ does not affect the value of $[D_1'(\alpha)n_1(\alpha) + D_2'(\alpha)n_2(\alpha)]_0^0$. For a zero-equivalent state we have by definition

$$[C_2(\alpha)s_1(\alpha) + C_1(\alpha)s_2(\alpha)]_0^\infty = 0 \tag{7}$$

From $D_1(\alpha)C_1(\alpha) + D_2(\alpha)C_2(\alpha) = 1$ it follows that $D_1'(\alpha)C_1(\alpha) + D_2'(\alpha)C_2(\alpha) = 0$. Thus we can define the polynomial $P(\alpha)$ by

$$P(\alpha) = D_1'(\alpha)C_1(\alpha) = D_2'(\alpha)C_2(\alpha) \tag{8}$$

It now follows that

$$P(\alpha)[D_1'(\alpha)s_1(\alpha) + D_2'(\alpha)s_2(\alpha)] = D_1'(\alpha)D_2'(\alpha)[C_2(\alpha)s_1(\alpha)+C_1(\alpha)s_2(\alpha)] \tag{9}$$

As deg $C_1(\alpha)$ > deg $D_2'(\alpha)$ we have deg $P(\alpha)$ > deg $D_1'(\alpha)D_2'(\alpha)$. Thus, if $[D_1'(\alpha)s_1(\alpha) + D_2'(\alpha)s_2(\alpha)]$ had a nonzero term of degree 0, then $[C_2(\alpha)s_1(\alpha) + C_1(\alpha)s_2(\alpha)]$ would have a nonzero term of degree larger than 0. As, according to (7), this cannot be the case it follows that $[D_1'(\alpha)s_1(\alpha) + D_2'(\alpha)s_2(\alpha)]_0^0 = 0$. Q.E.D.

In fact, we even have the stronger result that all edges leading to the same state $S(k + 1)$, $k = \ldots, -1,0,+1,\ldots$, have the same value of ω_k associated with them.

<u>Corollary</u>: The value of ω_k, $k = \ldots, -1,0,+1,\ldots$, is uniquely determined by the value of $S(k + 1)$.

Proof: As the syndrome former is a time invariant circuit all one has to prove is that ω_0 is uniquely determined by the state $S(1)$ of the syndrome former at time $t = 1$. According to (6) the value of ω_0 is uniquely determined by $[n_1(\alpha), n_2(\alpha)]_{-\nu+1}^0$ as the degree of both $D_1(\alpha)$ and $D_2(\alpha)$ is less than the common degree ν of $C_1(\alpha)$ and $C_2(\alpha)$. In fact, we only need to know $[n_1(\alpha), n_2(\alpha)]_{-\nu+1}^0$ to within an equivalence class. The proof is identical to the proof of Theorem 3, except that we redefine $P(\alpha)$ of (8), as

$$Q(\alpha) = D_1(\alpha)C_1'(\alpha) + D_2(\alpha)C_2'(\alpha) \tag{10}$$

As S(1), in fact, defines $[n_1(\alpha), n_2(\alpha)]_{-\nu+1}^{0}$ to within such an equivalence class, S(1) uniquely determines ω_0. Q.E.D.

III. ALGORITHM

As the recursive algorithm to be described in this section is similar to Viterbi's [2] we can be very brief. For reasons of clarity the decoding algorithm will be explained using the code generated by the encoder of Figure 1 as an example. Figure 4 represents the k-th section, k = ..., -1,0,+1,... , of the trellis diagram corresponding to the state diagram of Figure 3.

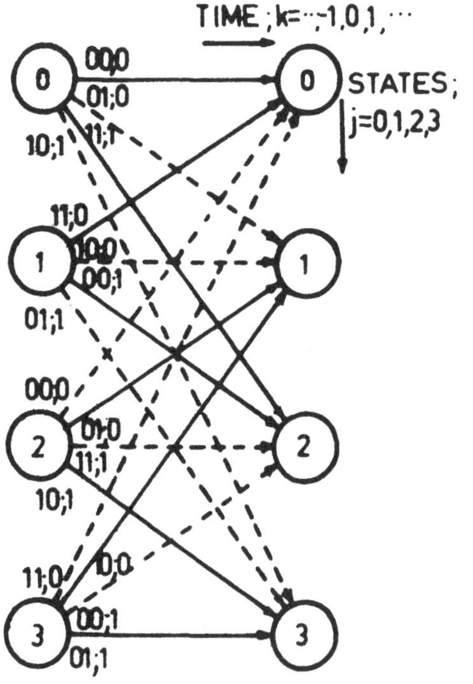

Figure 4. The k-th section of the trellis diagram, k = ...,-1,0,+1,...

The decoding algorithm is to find the coefficients ω_k of the power series $\omega(\alpha) = \ldots + \omega_{-1}\alpha^{-1} + \omega_0 + \omega_1\alpha + \ldots$ associated with the path of minimum weight through the trellis diagram. The pertinent weight is the Hamming weight of the pair $[\hat{n}_1(\alpha), \hat{n}_2(\alpha)]$ associated with the particular path. As in the Viterbi algorithm [2] to find the minimum weight path we associate a metric with each possible state. The metrics at time $t = k$ can be computed recursively given the metrics at time $t = k-1$. For the trellis diagram of Figure 4 the recursion is given by

$$M_0(k+1) = \bar{z}_k \min [M_0(k), M_1(k) + 2] + z_k \min [M_2(k), M_3(k) + 2] \quad (11a)$$

$$M_1(k+1) = \bar{z}_k \min [M_2(k) + 1, M_3(k) + 1] + z_k \min [M_0(k) + 1, M_1(k) + 1] \quad (11b)$$

$$M_2(k+1) = \bar{z}_k \min [M_0(k) + 2, M_1(k)] + z_k \min [M_2(k) + 2, M_3(k)] \quad (11c)$$

$$M_3(k+1) = \bar{z}_k \min [M_2(k) + 1, M_3(k) + 1] + z_k \min [M_0(k) + 1, M_1(k) + 1], \quad (11d)$$

where $\bar{z}_k$ is the modulo-2 complement of z_k, $k = \ldots, -1, 0, +1, \ldots$. Note that for each value $z_k = 0$ or $z_k = 1$ two arrows impinge on each $(k+1)$-state. The arrow associated with the minimum within the relevant pair of square brackets in (11) is called the "survivor". If both arrows have this property flip a coin to determine the survivor. In the classical Viterbi [2] implementation of the algorithm each state S_j, $j = 0,1,2,3$, has a metric register MR_j and a path register PR_j associated with it. The metric register is used to store the current metric value $M_j(k+1)$ at time $t = k$, $k = \ldots, -1, 0, +1, \ldots$, associated with state S_j, $j = 0,1,2,3$. The path register $PR_j[0:D-1]$ stores the ω-values associated with the current sequence of the D most recent survivors leading up to state S_j at time $t = k$. The pertinent output is

$$\hat{\omega}_{k-D} = \text{CONTENTS } PR_{j(k)}[D-1:D-1], \quad (12a)$$

where $j(k)$ minimizes $M_j(k+1)$, i.e.

$$M_{j(k)}(k+1) = \min_j M_j(k+1) \quad (12b)$$

If more than one j satisfies (12b), select j(k) arbitrarily among the candidates. As the algorithm returns $\hat{\omega}_{k-D}$ at time t = k, k = ...,-1,0,+1,... , the path register length D is also referred to as the coding delay. The resulting bit error probability P_b decreases as the coding delay D increases. Increasing D beyond $5(\nu + 1)$ does not lead to appreciable further decrease in the value of P_b.

IV. SYMMETRIES

Comparing (11b) and (11d) for the code of Figure 1 one observes that S_1 and S_3 have the same metric value. Moreover, selecting the identical surviver in case of a tie, S_1 and S_3 also have the same path register contents. As far as metric and path register contents are concerned the states S_1 and S_3 are not distinct. The metric register and the path register of either state S_1 or state S_3 can be eliminated. We will prove that, in general, for codes with $C_{1,0} = C_{2,0} = C_{1,\nu} = C_{2,\nu} = 1$ one can eliminate the metric and path registers of half the odd numbered states, where the state number of a representative state $S = [0,s_2(\alpha)]$ is the value of the contents of the bottom register of the syndrome former interpreted as a binary number, i.e. odd states have $s_{2,-1} = 1$.

Theorem 4: The odd numbered (representative) states $S(1) = [0,s_2(\alpha)]$ and $S'(1) = [0,s_2'(\alpha)]$, where $s_2'(\alpha) = s_2(\alpha) + s_2^b(\alpha) + \alpha^{-1}$ have identical metric equations, compare (11b) and (11d), iff $C_{1,0} = C_{2,0} = C_{1,\nu} = C_{2,\nu} = 1$.

Proof: An odd numbered state $S(1) = [0,s_2(\alpha)]$ has $s_{2,-1} = 1$. If both connection polynomials $C_1(\alpha)$ and $C_2(\alpha)$ have a nonzero term of degree ν it follows from the construction of the base state S^b that $s^b_{2,-1} = 1$. Hence, $s_2'(\alpha) = s_2(\alpha) + s_2^b(\alpha) + \alpha^{-1}$ has $s'_{2,-1} = 1$, and the requirement that both $S(1)$ and $S'(1)$ are odd numbered states is consistent. Consider the following parent states

$$S_a(0) = [0,\alpha s_2(\alpha)]_{-\nu}^{-1}$$

$$S_b(0) = [0,\alpha^{-\nu} + \alpha s_2(\alpha)]_{-\nu}^{-1}$$

$$S_c(0) = [0,\alpha s_2'(\alpha)]_{-\nu}^{-1}$$

$$S_d(0) = [0,\alpha^{-\nu} + \alpha s_2'(\alpha)]_{-\nu}^{-1}$$

As both $C_1(\alpha)$ and $C_2(\alpha)$ have a nonzero term of degree ν, $S_a(0)$ and $S_b(0)$ give rise to complementary syndrome digits, and so do $S_c(0)$ and $S_d(0)$. For an input $[n_{10}, n_{20}] = [0,1]$ the parent states $S_a(0)$ and $S_b(0)$ go into S(1) and the parent states $S_c(0)$ and $S_d(0)$ go into S'(1), and vise versa for an input $[n_{10}, n_{20}] = [1,0]$. Assuming that $C_1(\alpha)$ and $C_2(\alpha)$ both have a nonzero constant term and that $[n_{10}, n_{20}]$ is either [0,1] or [1,0], the syndrome value only depends on the parent state S(0). Hence, S(1) and S'(1) have identical metric equations. Q.E.D.

Now consider the class $\Gamma_{\nu,\ell}$ of binary rate-½ convolutional codes of constraint length ν with $C_{1,0} = C_{2,0} = C_{1,\nu} = C_{2,\nu} = 1$, and $C_{1,j} = C_{2,j}$, $C_{1,\nu-j} = C_{2,\nu-j}$, $1 \leq j \leq \ell-1$, where ℓ is a positive integer $\leq \nu/2$. Let k represent the largest integer smaller than or equal to $\nu/2$. Then note that $\Gamma_{\nu,1} \supset \Gamma_{\nu,2} \supset \ldots \supset \Gamma_{\nu,k}$. Theorem 4 concerned the class $\Gamma_{\nu,1}$. It can be generalized as follows.

<u>Theorem 5</u>: Let $S = [0,s_2(\alpha)]$ and $S' = [0,s_2'(\alpha)]$ be two (representative) states of a code in $\Gamma_{\nu,\ell}$, $1 \leq \ell \leq \nu/2$. Then S and S' have an identical metric value if $s'_{2,-j} = s_{2,-j}$ for $1 \leq j \leq \ell$, and

$s_2'(\alpha) = s_2(\alpha) + \sum_{j\in I} [\alpha^{-j+1}x(\alpha)]_{-\nu}^{-1}$, where I is a subset of

$J_S = \{j{:}1 \leq j \leq \ell,\ s_{2,-j} = 1\}$, and $x(\alpha) = s_2^b(\alpha) + \alpha^{-1}$.

We will first discuss the consequences of Theorem 5. Fix the set J_S. Let its cardinality be $j = |J_S|$, $0 \leq j \leq \ell$. This set J_S determines a state suffix $[s_2(\alpha)]_{-\ell}^{-1}$. There are $2^{\nu-\ell}$ states with the given state suffix $[s_2(\alpha)]_{-\ell}^{-1}$. According to Theorem 5 these $2^{\nu-\ell}$ states can be divided into $2^{\nu-\ell}/2^j$ equivalence classes of states, such that states in the same equivalence class have identical metric values. Hence, a set J_S of cardinality j, $0 \leq j \leq \ell$, gives rise to $(2^{\nu-\ell}/2^j)(2^j-1)$ redundant states. The total number of redundant states is thus equal to

$$\sum_{j=0}^{\ell} \binom{\ell}{j} (2^{\nu-\ell}/2^j)(2^j-1) = 2^{\nu-2\ell}(4^\ell - 3^\ell), \quad 1 \leq \ell \leq \nu/2, \tag{13}$$

as claimed in the abstract. We now turn to the proof of Theorem 5. The key to this proof is contained in the following Lemma.

<u>Lemma 6</u>: For codes in $T_{\nu,\ell}$ the polynomial $x(\alpha) = s_2^b(\alpha) + \alpha^{-1}$ satisfies the following properties.

1. $[x(\alpha)]_{-\ell}^{-1} = 0$
2. $[\alpha^{-j+1}x(\alpha)]_{-\nu}^{-1}$, $1 \leq j \leq \ell-1$, does not contribute to the value of the syndrome digit.

Proof: Property 1 follows directly from the construction of the base state $S^b = [\alpha^{-1}, s_2^b(\alpha)]$ and the fact $C_{1,\nu} = C_{2,\nu} = 1$, and $C_{1,\nu-j} = C_{2,\nu-j}$, $1 \leq j \leq \ell-1$. Property 2 follows from the fact that $[0, x(\alpha)] = S^b + [\alpha^{-1}, \alpha^{-1}]$. The base state and its left shifts $[\alpha^{-1-j}, \alpha^{-j}s_2^b(\alpha)]_{-\nu}^{-1}$, $0 \leq j \leq \nu-1$, do not contribute to the value of the syndrome digit. Likewise, $[\alpha^{-1}, \alpha^{-1}]$ and its left shifts $[\alpha^{-j}, \alpha^{-j}]$, $2 \leq j \leq \ell-1$, do not contribute to the value of the syndrome digit as $C_{1,j} = C_{2,j}$, $1 \leq j \leq \ell-1$. Q.E.D.

We are now ready for the proof of Theorem 5.

Proof: This proof proceeds by induction on ℓ. Theorem 4 proves our result for $\ell = 1$, i.e. for codes in $\Gamma_{\nu,1}$. The parent 4-tuples of equivalent states in the sense of $\Gamma_{\nu,\ell}$ are element wise equivalent in the sense of $T_{\nu,\ell-1}$ as $[x(\alpha)]_{-\ell}^{-1} = 0$ according to property 1 of Lemma 6. As parent states that are equivalent is the sense of $\Gamma_{\nu,\ell-1}$ differ by $\sum_{j\in I} [\alpha^{-j+1}x(\alpha)]_{-\nu}^{-1}$, $I\subset\{1,2,\ldots,\ell-1\}$, these parent states result in the same syndrome digit according to property 2 of Lemma 6. Hence, like in the proof of Theorem 4 it follows from the metric equation that if states equivalent in the sense of $\Gamma_{\nu,\ell-1}$ have identical metric values, so do states equivalent in the sense of $\Gamma_{\nu,\ell}$. Q.E.D.

V. CONCLUSIONS

This paper considers the syndrome decoding of binary rate-½ convolutional codes. It is shown that symmetries in the state diagram of the syndrome former allow for an exponential saving in the decoder hardware.

The idea of syndrome decoding can be extended to rate -k/n convolutional codes. Forney [4,5] describes the mathematical tools necessary to find the general syndrome former equations and the equations of the inverse encoder. It appears that syndrome decoding offers the largest hardware savings in the case of rate-½ codes, considered in this paper.

ACKNOWLEDGEMENT

The author wants to thank A.J. Vinck and K.A. Post for many stimulating discussions on the subject matter of the present manuscript. He also wants to thank Mrs C.J.M. Keijzer for the accurate typing.

REFERENCES

1. Schalkwijk, J.P.M., and Vinck, A.J., Syndrome decoding of convolutional codes, *IEEE Trans. Communications*, 23, 789, 1975.
2. Viterbi, A.J., Convolutional codes and their performance in communication systems, *IEEE Trans. Communication Technology*, 19, 751, 1971.
3. Berlekamp, E.R., *Algebraic Coding Theory*, McGraw Hill, New York, 1968.
4. Forney Jr., G.D., Convolutional codes I: Algebraic structure, *IEEE Trans. Inform. Theory*, 16, 720, 1970; correction appears in 17, 360, 1971.
5. Forney Jr., G.D., Structural analysis of convolutional codes via dual codes, *IEEE Trans. Inform. Theory*, 19, 512, 1973.

NOTES ON CYCLIC CONVOLUTIONAL CODES

Ph. Piret
MBLE Research Laboratory
2 av. Van Becelaere
1170-Brussels BELGIUM

INTRODUCTION

Let F_q be the finite field of order q. We then denote by $F_q[D]$ the set of polynomials in D with coefficients in F_q, and by $F_q(D)$ the set of sequences on F_q :

$$F_q(D) = \{a(D) = \sum_{i=\lambda}^{\infty} a_i D^i \; ; \; a_i \in F_q, \quad \lambda \in Z\}$$

Hereabove Z denotes the set of the integers. The set $F_q[D]$ is a ring and the set $F_q(D)$ is a field. For each set A, the set of ordered n-tuples on A is denoted by A^n. Using this notation, we shall for example denote by $F_q^n[D]$ the set of polynomials whose coefficients are n-tuples over F_q ; this set can also be seen as the set of n-tuples of polynomials over F_q.

Definitions : A convolutional code is the row space on $F_q(D)$ generated by a k×n basis G(D), all rows of which are elements of $F_q^n[D]$. A convolutional code that has at least one k×n basis with all its rows in F_q^n is a block code.

From the above definitions it follows that block codes can also have a basis (or generator matrix) with some rows in $F_q^n[D]$. The following generator matrix is an example of this situation (q=2) :

$$G_1(D) = \begin{bmatrix} 1+D & D+D^2 & 1+D^2 \\ D & 1+D^2 & 1+D+D^2 \end{bmatrix}$$

Indeed by choosing the matrix A(D) as follows

$$A(D) = \begin{bmatrix} 1+D & D \\ D/(1+D) & 1 \end{bmatrix}$$

we check that the following equality holds :

$$A(D)G_1(D) = \begin{bmatrix} 1 & 0 & 1 \\ 0 & 1 & 1 \end{bmatrix}$$

This last matrix denoted by G_2, generates the same code as $G_1(D)$ since A(D) is a nonsingular matrix. (Forney[1]). This code is thus a block code and any word in a sequence of this code can be chosen independently of all its predecessors. This is not true for general convolutional codes, that are not equivalent to a block code. In this case the relative dependence between successive words of a sequence is measured by the parameter μ, that is defined as follows. We first choose for the (n,k) considered code C, a polynomial k×n generator matrix G(D), and we define $\mu[G(D)]$ as being the maximum degree of the $k \times k$ determinants of $G(D)$ minus the degree of the g.c.d. of these determinants. It can then be shown that for all $k \times n$ polynomial matrices $G(D)$ that generate the same code C, the corresponding value of $\mu[G(D)]$ is a constant (Forney[1]). If this constant is equal to zero, the code C is a block code, even if it is generated by a strictly polynomial matrix. In the above example, it is sufficient to check that $\mu[G_1(D)]$ is equal to zero, to be sure that the matrix $G_1(D)$ can be transformed in a matrix G_2, all elements of which are in F_2.

Remark : In the following, only binary codes will be considered.

A. DO THERE EXIST CYCLIC CONVOLUTIONAL CODES?

What could be a cyclic convolutional code of odd block length n? To answer this question we shall represent the words of any sequence by polynomials of formal degree equal to (n-1). Any sequence, denoted by v(X,D) can be written as follows :

$$v(X,D) = \sum_i v_i(X)\, D^i \qquad (1)$$

but it can also be represented as

$$v(X,D) = \sum_{j=0}^{n-1} g_j(D)\, X^j. \qquad (2)$$

It is well known that a cyclic block code can be defined by the fact that if v(X) is a code word, then Xv(X) is also a code word. (We always suppose that the multiplication of polynomials is performed modulo X^n-1). We could then define a cyclic convolutional code C by the fact that if v(X,D) is a code sequence, then Xv(X,D) is also a code sequence :

$$v(X,D) \in C \Rightarrow Xv(X,D) \in C \qquad (3)$$

However, as we now prove it this definition is somewhat disappointing.

Theorem 1. Any code C, of odd block length n, for which (3) holds, is a block code.

Proof. Suppose that C is a code for which (3) holds. We then represent any sequence such as (2) by an n-tuple V of elements of $F_2(D)$.

$$V = [g_0(D), \ldots, g_j(D), \ldots, g_{n-1}(D)] \qquad (4)$$

Let now K(D) be the n×n circulant matrix whose first row is V :

$$K(D) = \sum_j K_j D^j \qquad (5)$$

All the rows of K(D) are code sequences since (3) is true by hypothesis, and all K_j are circulant matrices on F.

Now let T be the square matrix whose element $t_{i,j}$ $(0 \leq i, j \leq n-1)$ is $\alpha^{i(j+1)}$, with α, a primitive n^{th} root of unity that is in $GF(2^m)$, an appropriate extension of GF(2).

It is well known (Marcus and Minc[2]) that T diagonalizes, by similitude all circulant n×n matrices on GF(2) and, in particular, all matrices K_j of (5). K(D) can thus be written as follows

$$K(D) = T\, H(D)\, T^{-1} \qquad (6)$$

where H(D) is a diagonal matrix whose nonzero components $h_{r,r}(D)$ are in $F_{2^m}(D)$.

Denote now by R the set of indices r such that $h_{r,r}(D)$ is nonzero, by t_r the rth row of T^{-1} and by $\tau(R)$ the submatrix of T^{-1} that contains the rows t_r with $r \in R$. Finally denote by $\tau_2(R)$ a generator matrix for the largest binary subfield subcode of the block code generated by $\tau(R)$. Then from (6) it is easy to see that the row spaces of K(D) and $\tau(R)$ are identical as vector spaces on $F_{2^m}(D)$, and that the row spaces of K(D) and $\tau_2(R)$ are also identical as vector spaces on $F_2(D)$. Since $\tau_2(R)$ is a matrix on F_2, (not on $F_2(D)$), the code generated by K(D) is a block code. Since the same reasoning can be applied to any sequence of C, the theorem is proved ***.

Since the preceding definition was not useful, we modify it as follows. The multiplication of v(X,D) by X is now denoted by X * v(X,D) and it is interpreted as follows :

$$X * v(X,D) = \sum_i X^{e(i)} v_i(X) D^i \qquad (7)$$

where e(i) is a mapping from Z, the set of the integers, into Z_n the integers modulo n.

We shall now investigate what are these mappings e(i) for which interesting codes can be obtained.

We remark that it is natural to extend (7) as follows :

$$u(X,D) * v(X,D) = \sum_{i,j} u_j(X^{e(i)}) v_i(X) D^{i+j} \qquad (8)$$

Since block codes can be defined as ideals in the algebra of polynomials modulo (X^n-1), we try to generalize this situation. More precisely we investigate to which conditions the set of sequences v(X,D) is an algebra, i.e. (roughly) a vector space with an associative multiplication and a multiplicative unity.

Cyclic convolutional codes will then be defined as ideals in this algebra.

<u>Theorem 2</u> The set of sequences v(X,D) with the multiplication defined by

(8) is an associative linear algebra if and only if $e(i) \equiv \Pi^i$ modulo n, with $(n,\Pi) = 1$.

Sketch of the proof : We see that 1 is the left unity :

$$1 * v(X,D) = v(X,D)$$

It follows that it must also be the right unity. Since one has

$$v(X,D) * 1 = v(X^{e(0)},D)$$

it is necessary that e(0) be congruent to 1 modulo n.

The multiplication is associative if

$$X*(D^jX*D^kX) = (X*D^jX)*D^kX$$

or equivalently if

$$X^{e(j+k)+e(k)+1} = X^{e(j)e(k)+e(k)+1}$$

so that the following must hold

$$e(j+k) \equiv e(j)e(k) \mod n. \tag{9}$$

The solution of (9) when e(0)=1 is given by

$$e(i) \equiv \Pi^i \mod n \quad (n,\Pi) = 1 \tag{10}$$

The sufficiency of these conditions is obtained by straightforward verification ***

In the following we always suppose that equation (10) is satisfied. The corresponding algebra will be denoted by B(D) and the "block algebra", i.e. the algebra of polynomials modulo (X^n-1), will be denoted by B.

B. CONSTRUCTION OF CYCLIC CONVOLUTIONAL CODES

Definitions : The span of the sequence $v(X,D) = \sum_{j=a}^{b} v_j(X)D^j$, where $v_a(X)$ and $v_b(X)$ are nonzero polynomials is defined to be b-a.

A short sequence of an ideal of B(D) is a nonzero sequence of this ideal that has the smallest possible span.

We now give a theorem that is useful to construct codes. The proof is omitted but it can be found elsewhere. (Piret[3])

Theorem 3. Any short sequence v(X,D) of a minimal ideal of B(D) has the following form :

$$v(X,D) = D^r \sum_{i=0}^{m} [a(X^{e(i)})]^{f(i)} \varepsilon(X^{e(i)})D^i$$

where $\varepsilon(X)$ is the idempotent polynomial of a minimal ideal of B, whose irreducible parity check polynomial is denoted by h(X). Then a(X) is a primitive element for the field of polynomials mod h(X). By convention, $f(i) = \infty$ if the coefficient of D^{i+r} is zero.

As an illustration (Piret[4]) we shall now obtain codes of length 7 and dimension 3 that are minimal ideals in the algebra B(D) defined by $e(i)=(-1)^i$. By theorem 3, short sequences can be written as follows :

$$v(X,D) = D^r \sum_{i=0}^{m} X^{(-1)^i f(i)} \varepsilon(X^{(-1)^i})\, D^i \qquad (11)$$

and one has

$$\varepsilon(X) = 1 + X + X^2 + X^4$$

$$h(X) = 1 + X + X^3$$

Codes are then ideals generated by (11), (where r=0). For this class of codes, the free distance d_f is upperbounded (Layland and Mc Eliece[5]) as follows

$$d_f \leq 4(m+1) \qquad (12)$$

Moreover we can obtain (Piret[4]) the following results in this case :

a) If f(i) is replaced by b+f(i) for even i and by c+f(i) for odd i, the new obtained code has the same free distance as the original one, for any integer value of b and c.

b) If f(i) is replaced by 2f(i) the free distance is not modified.

c) If f(i) is replaced by f(m-i) the free distance is not modified.

These properties strongly restrict the number of codes to be investigated so that we can determine for $m \leq 5$, all codes that achieve (12) with equality and are not equivalent by the three preceding propositions.

For each of these optimal codes we give now its (m+1)-tuple [f(0),...,f(s),...,f(m)] .

m	d_f	[f(0),..., f(s), ..., f(m)]
1	8	[0,0]
2	12	[0,0,0] ,[0,0,1]
3	16	[0,0,1,3] ,[0,0,3,1] ,[0,0,1,2]
4	20	[0,0,3,2,2] ,[0,0,1,1,4] ,[0,0,1,4,5]
5	24	[0,0,1,1,3,4]

References

1. Forney G. D., Convolutional codes I : Algebraic structure, IEEE Trans. on Inf. Theory, vol. IT-16, 720, 1970.

2. Marcus M. and Minc H., A survey of matrix theory and matrix inequalities, Allyn and Bacon, Boston 1964.

3. Piret Ph., Structure and construction of cyclic convolutional codes. To appear in IEEE Trans. on Inf. Theory, vol. IT-22, 1976.

4. Piret Ph., On a class of alternating cyclic convolutional codes, IEEE Trans. on Inf. Theory, vol. IT-21, 64, 1975.

5. Layland J. and Mc Eliece R., An upper bound on the free distance of a tree code, J. P. L. Cal. Tech. Pasadena Space Program Summary 37-62, vol. 3, 63-64, April 1970.

GLOBAL QUADRATIC ABELIAN CODES

P. Camion

C.N.R.S. - Paris

1. Introduction

Let L be an algebraic number field. We call Global Code a module C_∞ over the ring A of integers of L, consisting of all the points with integral components in a linear L-subspace of L^n.

Let I be a prime ideal in A, factor of (p), where p is a rational prime. For every ideal J of A, the homomorphism $J/I \cap J - A/I$ is surjective or zero according to whether J is not contained or is contained in I, since I is a maximal ideal of A. Then the image of C_∞ modulo I may be defined in an obvious way, and it is a code in F_q^n, i.e. a linear subspace of F_q^n, where F_q is the finite field with $q = p^m$ elements, that is the field of integers in L modulo I.

More specifically, given a prime n, Assmus and Mattson consider the unique subfield L of $K = Q(\zeta)$ of degree two over Q, where ζ is a primitive nt-h root of unity.

Throughout the paper we shall be dealing with two distinct primes namely n and characteristic p of the finite field over which a code has to be constructed.

Let us denote by B the ring of integers of K. The way in which a rational prime p can be factored into prime ideals of B is known (Henri B. Mann [3]).

For p distinct from n, we write

$$\sum_{0 \leq i \leq n-1} X^i \equiv \prod_{1 \leq j \leq r} f_j(X) \quad (\mathrm{mod}\ p), \tag{1.1}$$

where the $f_j(X)$ are pairwise distinct and all have degree $s = (p-1)/r$, degree which is the order of p in F_n.

Then, since index $(\zeta) = 1 \not\equiv 0 \pmod p$,

$$(p) = \prod_{1 \leq j \leq r} (p, f_j(\zeta)), \tag{1.2}$$

where each factor has degree s.

Let us see how to use this for performing the passage from the global code to the finite code. We know that $1, \zeta, \ldots, \zeta^{n-2}$ form a basis over Z (the ring of rational integers) of B and a basis over F_p of $B/(p)$ as well. Let us first consider the representation of an element in B mod $(p, f_j(\zeta))$. If $\bar{\zeta}$ is the class of $\zeta \bmod (p, f_j(\zeta))$, every element in $B/(p, f_j(\zeta))$ has a representative $h(\bar{\zeta})$, where $h(X)$ is a polynomial with coefficients in F_p and degree less than s. But this representation by such a polynomial is unique, since $(p, f_j(\zeta))$ has degree s.

Now, we have to consider the actual elements of A modulo I, where I is any prime ideal containing (p). A/I is isomorphic to F_{p^2} or to F_p according to whether p is not or is a quadratic residue mod n. Here is an argument for this well-known fact. Let us put

$$\eta = T_{K/L}(\zeta) = \sum_{i \in R} \zeta^i , \tag{1.3}$$

where R denotes the group of quadratic residues of F_n , that is the Galois group K over L . $1, \eta$ form a basis over Z of A and a basis over F_p of $A/(p)$. The minimum polynomial of η is known to be

$$X^2 + X + (1 \pm n)/4 , \tag{1.4}$$

where the sign is chosen to make $(1 \pm n)/4$ an integer. Hence, by the theorem already used for (1.2), if I is a prime ideal of A containing (p), I has degree 2 or 1 according to whether (1.4) is or is not irreducible over F_p , or equivalently: p is not or is a quadratic residue mod n (quadratic reciprocity law for odd p , or from the formula $\left(\frac{2}{n}\right) = (-1)^{\frac{n^2-1}{8}}$ for $p = 2$).

Now, let us first remark that I has necessarily the form $(p, f_j(\zeta)) \cap A$ for some j . Indeed, I B contains (p) in B and consequently, according to (1.2) factors into prime ideals of the form $(p, f_j(\zeta))$. One has

$$I \subset IB \cap A \subset (p, f_j(\zeta)) \cap A , \tag{1.5}$$

and since I is a maximal ideal, $I = (p, f_j(\zeta)) \cap A$.

The homomorphism $A/(p, f_j(\zeta)) \cap A \to B/(p, f_j(\zeta))$ is injective, which shows that A/I is the subfield of F_{p^1} of degree 2 or 1, as seen above, formed by the classes of $B/(p, f_j(\zeta))$ met by A . Their representatives as polynomials of degree ≤ 1 in ξ will be easily computed once the representative of $\sum_{i \in R} \zeta^i$ in $B/(p, f_j(\zeta))$ as such a polynomial is determined.

2. The Fourier Transform

In the first section, n was a prime. For the generalization that we have in view, n becomes the power of an odd prime: $n = e^r$. Let F_n be the finite field whose additive group is the elementary Abelian group with exponent e, denoted by G. Let R_0 be the cyclic subgroup of order $(n-1)/2$ of F_n^*, i.e. the subgroup of squares in F_n^*. The set $F_n^* \setminus R_0$ is denoted by R_1.

Let χ be a non-trivial character of G in the group of the e-th roots of unity. One of these roots is denoted by $\zeta \neq 1$. We put $K = Q(\zeta)$ and follow the notations of section 1, only the prime n is replaced by the prime e. It is known that addition, defined on the set G^* of characters of G in the cyclic group $[\zeta]$ by

$$\forall\, g \in G: \quad (\chi + \chi')(g) = \chi(g) \cdot \chi'(g), \tag{2.1}$$

makes G^* an Abelian group isomorphic to G.

As in H. Mann [4],

$$x = \sum_{g \in G} x_g X^g \tag{2.2}$$

denotes an element of the algebra LG. Conventionally $X^g . X^h = X^{g+h}$, and, with x_g in L for all g, we have

$$xy = \Big(\sum_{g \in G} x_g X^g\Big)\Big(\sum_{h \in G} y_h X^h\Big) = \sum_{h \in G}\Big(\sum_{g+h=k} x_g y_h\Big) X^h \tag{2.3}$$

for the product of x and y in the convolution algebra LG.

A character may be extended linearly to LG or to KG yielding a homomorphism of algebra into K. The image under χ of x is denoted by $\hat{x}_\chi$. The mapping $x \rightsquigarrow \hat{x} = (\hat{x}_\chi)_{\chi \in G^*}$ is defined, which is an isomorphism of LG (resp. KG) into the Cauchy algebra K^{G^*} (resp. <u>onto</u> K^{G^*}). (In the Cauchy algebra the product is defined componentwise.) The mapping $KG \xrightarrow{\wedge} K^{G^*}$ is a Fourier transform. Such a transformation of an algebra of a finite Abelian group has been studied in detail in P. Camion [2] .

When G is cyclic, (2.2) is an ordinary polynomial and the image of x under a character χ may be obtained by replacing X by ζ in the polynomial (2.2). Then the character χ_i is defined by (2.2) where X is replaced by ζ^i, where $i \in F_e$. Then $\chi_i(g) = \zeta^{ig}$ and from (2.1) it is seen that $i \rightsquigarrow \chi_i$ is an isomorphism of G onto G^* which identifies G with G^* and with the additive group of F_e . This identification is valuable for studying quadratic-residue codes. We will see how to obtain the corresponding identification when G becomes an Abelian group.

Proposition 1. Let G be the subjacent Abelian group of any finite ring. G is supposed to have exponent e and let G^* denote the group of characters of G into the cyclic group $[\zeta]$ as above. Let $\alpha \in G$ and denote by χ_α the character obtained by composition of the endomorphism $g \rightsquigarrow \alpha g$ of G (αg is a product in the ring) with the non trivial character χ . Then the mapping $\alpha \rightsquigarrow \chi_\alpha$ is an isomorphism of G onto G^* iff $\operatorname{Ker} \chi$ does not contain any nonzero right ideal.

The described mapping is a homomorphism; indeed

$$\chi_{\alpha+\beta}(g) = \chi(\alpha+\beta)g = \chi(\alpha g)\chi(\beta g) = \chi_\alpha(g)\chi_\beta(g) = (\chi_\alpha + \chi_\beta)(g). \quad (2.4)$$

It is known, on the other hand, that G and G^* are isomorphic groups, hence equipotent sets. Thus all we have to prove is that $\alpha \rightsquigarrow \chi_\alpha$ is injective, i.e. that $\operatorname{Ker}\chi \neq \{0\}$. Assume $\alpha \in \operatorname{Ker}\chi$. This means $\chi(\alpha g) = 1$ for all $g \in G$, in other words the right ideal αG is contained in $\operatorname{Ker}\chi$.

Example 1. The ring of integers modulo q is denoted by Z_q , q being any integer. Let $G = Z_q^n$. If every element $x \in G$ is identified with the polynomial $\sum_{i<n} x_i Y^i$, representative of a class in the ring $Z_q[Y]$ modulo the

ideal (Y^n-1), then G makes up a cyclic algebra. The non-trivial character χ is chosen as follows

$$\chi : x \rightsquigarrow \chi(x) = \zeta^{x_0},$$

where ζ is a primitive q-th root of unity.

Example 2. Let G be the additive group of the finite field F_{e^r}. Then as χ any non-trivial character of G may be chosen.

In the sequel we shall use Example 2 for Proposition 1.

3. Isometric Automorphism of KG.

3.1 A Group of Isometric Automorphisms Associated with the Squares of $G = F_{e^r}$.

The convolution algebra KG has been defined in the section 2. If we introduce the Hamming distance d, KG becomes a metric space. The Hamming distance is defined as follows:

$$\forall x,y \in KG : \ d(x,y) = w(x-y) = \text{Card}\left\{g \mid g \in G, x_g - y_g \neq 0\right\}.$$

The Hamming metric is invariant under any permutation of G, which yields the following obvious statement.

Proposition 2. Every automorphism $g \rightsquigarrow g^G$ of the group G extends into an isometric automorphism of the convolution algebra KG.

In Proposition 2 K may be replaced by any ring, in particular by the field L.

We have in view the study of the ideals of AG (A the ring of integers in L). But it is more convenient to study the ideals of LG , which is easily done with the Fourier transform whose inverse exibits the denominator Card $G = n$. (The Fourier transform maps LG into K^{G^*}). Anyway the submodulo of integral points in an ideal of LG is invariant under all the isometries $x \leadsto xX^G$ and consequently is an ideal of AG . The image of such an ideal in its turn is an ideal of $(A/I)G$, which is an ordinary code over a finite field.

Clearly an invariance of an ideal of LG (in the sense of coding theory, cf. E. F. Assmus & H. F. Mattson [1] , p. 129) is an invariance of the corresponding ideal in AG and of the corresponding ideal of $(A/I)G$ as well.

From now on, we will confine ourselves to the ideals of LG which are invariant under the transformation

$$\Sigma\, x_g X^g \leadsto \Sigma\, x_g\, X^{\alpha g} \tag{3.1}$$

for any square α in $F_n = F_{\ell^r} = G$ (the multiplication αg is to be understood in the field F_n), which, by Proposition 2, permutes the set of ideals of LG . These transformations form a group, isomorphic with the group R_0 of squares in F_n .

3.2 Remarkable Fixed Points

Three remarkable fixed points of that group of transformations are: the unit of LG , and the elements $u = \sum_{g \in R_0} X^g$ and $v = \sum_{g \in R_1} X^g$, where R_1 is the set of non-squares in F_n^* . (R_0 has index 2 in F_n^* .)

Let us consider the Fourier image $\hat{u}$ of u .

Example 2 for Proposition 1 of Section 2 allows the identification of G

with G^*; we write:

$$\hat{u} = (\hat{u}_\alpha)_{\alpha \in G},$$

where

$$\hat{u}_\alpha = \chi_\alpha(u) = \sum_{g \in R_0} \chi(\alpha g) \in K. \tag{3.2}$$

$\hat{u}_\alpha$ is seen to have only three possible distinct values: $(n-1)/2$ for $\alpha = 0$ and π_0 and π_1, say, for $\alpha \in R_0$ and for $\alpha \in R_1$, respectively.

The inverse formula for the Fourier transform gives

$$n u_g = (n-1)/2 + \pi_0 \sum_{\alpha \in R_0} \chi_\alpha(-g) + \pi_1 \sum_{\beta \in R_1} \chi_\beta(-g); \tag{3.3}$$

whence, by letting $g = 0$ in (3.3),

$$\pi_0 + \pi_1 = -1. \tag{3.4}$$

Case $n \equiv 3$ (mod 4)

Letting g be a square in (3.3),

$$n = (n-1)/2 + \pi_0 \pi_1 + \pi_1 \pi_0. \tag{3.5}$$

Case $n \equiv 1$ (mod 4)

Letting g be a non-square in (3.3), we get:

$$0 = (n-1)/2 + \pi_0 \pi_1 + \pi_1 \pi_0, \tag{3.6}$$

whence

$$\pi_0^2 + \pi_0 + \varepsilon(n+\varepsilon)/4 = 0, \tag{3.7}$$

where $\varepsilon \in \{1,-1\}$ is chosen to make $(n+\varepsilon)/4$ an integer. In (3.7) π_0 may be replaced by π_1 and from (3.4) it is seen that π_0 and π_1 are the roots of the first member of (3.7). For a suitable choice of χ one gets

$$\pi_0 = \left(-1+\sqrt{-\varepsilon n}\right)/2\ ,\quad \pi_1 = \left(-1-\sqrt{-\varepsilon n}\right)/2 . \tag{3.8}$$

Remarks. For α in the ground field F_e, $\alpha \neq 0$,

$$\sum_{g\in R_0} \chi(\alpha g) = \sum_{g\in R_0} \chi^{\alpha}(g) = \Big(\sum_{g\in R_0} \chi(g)\Big)^{\alpha},$$

since exponentiation by α is an automorphism of K.

Thus $\pi_0^p = \sum_{g\in R_0} \chi(pg)$ equals either π_0 or π_1 according to whether p is a square or is not a square in F_n. Anyway π_0 is in L. Mapping L modulo $(p, f_j(\zeta)) \cap L$ as in section 1, the image of π_0 belongs to F_p or to F_{p^2} and not to F_p according to whether (3.7) is or is not reducible mod (p). If $\pi_0^p = \pi_0$, $\pi_0 \in F_p$ and (3.7) is reducible. Then, for p odd, by (3.8) $-\varepsilon n$ is a square mod $(p, f_j(\zeta))$, that is a square in F_p (see section 1 for the unique representability of the integer $-\varepsilon n$ mod $(p, f_j(\zeta))$). If $\pi_0^p = \pi_1$, $-\varepsilon n$ is not a square in F_p. The quadratic reciprocity law replying the question of knowing if p is a square in F_n follows for odd p. The formula for $p=2$ comes directly through (3.7).

As it will appear clearly in the following, here is a property that generalizes the known conditions for the existence of a quadratic binary cyclic code.

Property I $\pi_0\pi_1 \equiv 0$ mod $(p, f_j(\zeta))$ iff (p is a square in F_n and) $n \equiv \pm 1$ (mod $4p$).

This follows directly from (3.7) and the sentence " p is a square in F_n " is in brackets because, from the above remark, this is always true when $n \equiv \pm 1$ (mod $4p$).

3.3 The Invariant Ideals

As above, the prime subfield of F_n is F_e ; $R_0 \cap F_e$ will be denoted by R and $R_1 \cap F_e$ will be denoted by R^1 .

It is known that any ideal of an algebra of an Abelian group G, over a domain whose characteristic does not divide the exponent of G , is characterized thoroughly by the support of its Fourier image. This support is the smallest subset of G^* containing the indices of the nonzero components of the Fourier image $\hat{x}$ of every nonzero x in the ideal.

On the other hand,

$$x \in LG \text{ iff } \forall r \in R, \ \hat{x}_\alpha^r = \hat{x}_{r\alpha} ; \tag{3.9}$$

indeed $x_g^r = x_g$ for all $r \in R$ iff $x_g \in L$

$$x = \sum_{g \in G} x_g X^g \in LG \Rightarrow \Big(\sum_{g \in G} x_g \chi_\alpha(g)\Big)^r = \sum x_g \chi_\alpha^r(g) =$$

$$= \sum_{g \in G} x_g \chi_{r\alpha}(g) = \hat{x}_{r\alpha} , \tag{3.10}$$

for any character χ_α , and denoting by P'' a set of representatives of F_n^*/R , from the inverse formula we obtain

$$n x_g = \hat{x}_0 + \sum_{\alpha \in P''} T_{K/L} \hat{x}_\alpha \chi_\alpha(-g) \in L , \tag{3.11}$$

where the trace from K to L is denoted by $T_{K/L}$.

From (3.9) it follows that every ideal in LG is preserved by the sub-group R of R_0 . Further, the support of the Fourier image of any ideal in LG preserved by the whole R_0 is necessarily $\{0\}$, R_0 , R_1 , or the union of some of these sets. Since the dimension of an ideal is the cardinality of the support of its Fourier image, we have the following theorem.

Theorem 1 The non-trivial ideals of LG preserved by the group R_0 of automorphisms of LG are the following:

Case $n \equiv -1 \pmod 4$

A , generated as an ideal by $(n-1)/2 + \pi_1 u + \pi_0 v$; $\dim A = (n-1)/2$.

A^+ , generated as an ideal by $(n+1)/2 - \pi_0 u - \pi_1 v$; $\dim A^+ = (n+1)/2$.

Case $n \equiv 1 \pmod 4$

A , generated as an ideal by $(n-1)/2 + \pi_0 u + \pi_1 v$; $\dim A = (n-1)/2$.

A^+ , generated as an ideal by $(n+1)/2 - \pi_1 u - \pi_0 v$; $\dim A^+ = (n+1)/2$.

B and B^+ , with dimension $(n-1)/2$ and $(n+1)/2$, respectively, are obtained by interchanging π_0 and π_1 in each generator expression for A and A^+.

The supports of $\hat{A}, \hat{A}^+, \hat{B}, \hat{B}^+$ are $R_0, \{0\} \cup R_0, R_1, \{0\} \cup R_1$, respectively.

To prove the theorem it is sufficient to verify that the supports of the Fourier images of the indicated generators are precisely the given sets. This verification is performed by means of (3.4) and (3.7) and taking the definitions of π_0 and π_1 into account.

3.4 Orthogonality Relationships

Proposition 3 The following equalities hold:

Case $n \equiv -1 \pmod 4$	Case $n \equiv +1 \pmod 4$	
$A^\perp = A^+$	$A^\perp = B^+$	(3.12)
$B^\perp = B^+$	$B^\perp = A^+$	

Lemma. If $xy = 0$ for the convolution product in an Abelian group algebra, then

$$\sum_{h \in G} x_{-h} y_h = 0. \tag{3.13}$$

Let us consider the matrix representation of the group algebra in the canonical basis G . The image under multiplication by x of an element x^h of the basis is

$$x X^h = \sum_{g \in G} x_g X^{g+h} = \sum_{g \in G} x_{g-h} X^g . \qquad (3.14)$$

This means that the matrix $(m_{g,h})$ representing x is (x_{g-h}) . This proves the lemma.

<u>Case $n \equiv -1 \pmod 4$</u>

The zero ideal of A is B^+ since the support of the Fourier image of B^+ and the one of A are complementary sets in G^*. But the mapping

$$x = \sum_{g \in G} x_g X^g \rightsquigarrow x' = \sum_{g \in G} x_g X^{-g} \qquad (3.15)$$

maps B^+ onto A^+, whence the statement follows. In the same way, it is seen that $B^{\perp} = B^+$.

<u>Case $n \equiv 1 \pmod 4$</u>

The argument is identical. Here the mapping (3.15) preserves both B^+ and A^+, whence the thesis follows.

At this point, the present paper can be linked with [1] . For the sake of clarity, some extra explanations are given referring to the general case of an Abelian group G . The reader, however, is referred to [1] to convince himself that the arguments given there are perfectly adequate for the more general setup considered here.

4. An Extended Global Quadratic Code is Invariant under a Projective Unimodular Group

4.1 The Coordinate Functions

Let P denote a set of representatives of the classes of R_0/R ; similarly, let P' denote a set of representatives of all classes of non squares of F_n^*/R .

From Theorem 1 of Section 3 and from (3.11), the coordinate functions of the code A^+ are seen to be linear forms $f_g : L \times K^{(n-1)/(e-1)} \to L$ defined by

$$(c_0, c_p) f_g = c_0 + \sum_{\alpha \in P} T_{K/L}\, c_\alpha \chi_\alpha(g), \tag{4.1}$$

where the element $(c_\alpha)_{\alpha \in P} \in K^{(n-1)/(e-1)}$ is denoted by c_p for brevity and where $T_{K/L}$ denotes the trace from K to L . (It is thus L-linear and $T_{K/L}\zeta = \sum_{r \in R} \zeta^r$.)

From the last assertion of Theorem 1, A is the subcode of A^+given by the restrictions of the f_g to $\{0\} \times K^{(n-1)/(e-1)}$, i.e., it is the code obtained from (4.1) by setting $c_0 = 0$.

B^+ is obtained replacing P by P' in (4.1); further, B is defined by setting $c_0 = 0$.

4.2 Embeddings

Since A is a subcode of A^+ , it is convenient to define the notion of a code embedded in the code A^+ . To this end a new coordinate function is introduced

$$F_\infty = \gamma \sum_{g\in G} F_g , \tag{4.2}$$

where γ is to be chosen in such a way that the new code, denoted by A_∞ or B_∞, verify

$$A_\infty^{\perp} = \begin{cases} A_\infty , & n \equiv -1 \pmod 4 \\ B_\infty , & n \equiv +1 \pmod 4 \end{cases} \tag{4.3}$$

To be more precise, whenever we deal with B instead of A in (4.1) and (4.2) each F is replaced by F' and γ becomes $-\gamma$.

F_∞ has a simple expression. Indeed, fixing an α in P or in P' and an r in R, one gets:

$$\sum_{g\in G} c_\alpha^r \chi_\alpha^r(g) = c_\alpha^r \sum_{g\in G} \chi(rg) = c_\alpha^r \sum_{g\in G} \chi(g) = 0 \tag{4.4}$$

$$\begin{cases} (c_0 , c_p)\, F_\infty = \gamma n c_0 \\ (c_0 , c_{p'})\, F'_\infty = -\gamma n c_0 \end{cases} \tag{4.5}$$

From (4.5) the kernel of F_∞ (resp. F'_∞) is seen to be $\{0\} \times K^{(n-1)/(e-1)}$. Thus, according to section 4.1, A (resp. B) is the subcode of A_∞ (resp. B_∞) with "infinite" coordinate equal to 0. Hence, from the last assertion of theorem 1:

$$\begin{aligned} (n+1)/2 &= \dim A_+ = 1 + \dim A = \dim A_\infty \\ (n+1)/2 &= \dim B_+ = 1 + \dim A = \dim B_\infty . \end{aligned} \tag{4.6}$$

Let $<c_0 , c_p>$ denote the word of the code A corresponding to (c_0 , c_p). As we have just seen,

$$A_\infty = A \oplus <1,0> L \ ; \quad B_\infty = B \oplus <1,0>' L . \tag{4.7}$$

From (4.1) and (4.2)

$$<1,0> = (1,\ldots,1;n\gamma)\ ; \quad <1,0>' = (1,\ldots,1;-n\gamma). \tag{4.8}$$

On the other hand, $\{0\}$ is contained both in the support of $\hat{A}^+$ and in that of $\hat{B}^+$. This means

$$\sum_{g\in G} X^g \in A^+ \cap B^+. \tag{4.9}$$

Then, from (3.12), $<1,0>$ is orthogonal to the embedded A and to the embedded B in both cases (mod 4).

Consequently, if (4.3) is to be verified, according to (4.7) and (3.12), it is necessary that $<1,0>$ be orthogonal to itself for $n \equiv -1$ (mod 4) or to the corresponding vector $<1,0>'$ in B_∞ for $n \equiv 1$ (mod 4). Namely:

$$\begin{cases} 1+n\gamma^2 = 0\ , & n \equiv -1 \pmod 4 \\ 1-n\gamma^2 = 0\ , & n \equiv +1 \pmod 4 . \end{cases} \tag{4.10}$$

Thus γ is determined up to the sign as $1/\sqrt{\pm n}$, which is in L as it should be.

5. Invariance of A_∞ and B_∞ Under the Projective Unimodular Group $PSL_2(n)$.

The projective unimodular group $PSL_2(n)$ is the group of all 2×2 matrices over $F_n = F_{\ell^r}$ with determinant 1 modulo the center $\pm\begin{pmatrix}1&0\\0&1\end{pmatrix}$. It operates on the set of columns

$$\left\{\begin{pmatrix}\alpha\\1\end{pmatrix}\right\}_{\alpha\in F_n} \cup \left\{\begin{pmatrix}1\\0\end{pmatrix}\right\}. \tag{5.1}$$

The first term in (5.1) is identified in a natural way with $G = F_n$ and $\binom{1}{0}$ is the infinite point. The subgroup fixing the infinite point happens to be generated by the translations in G and the group of multiplications of elements in G by the squares in F_n . So the invariance of A_∞ and B_∞ under that subgroup follows in a straighforward way from the definition of A^+ and B^+ given in section 3.3.

We refer the reader to [1] for the proofs of the statements given in the sequel. We only point out the small changes in the notation. In this paper ℓ has been replaced by n all over; ε_i by ε_g , $g \in F_n^*$, where ε_g is the image of g under the surjective morphism $F_n^* \to \{1,-1\}$. Moreover in [1] , p. 131, last line, $\sum_{g \in F_n^*} \varepsilon_g = 0$ is correct; and it has to be verified that $<1,0> \sigma \perp <0, c_p>$ for any $c_p \in K^{(n-1)/(e-1)}$ ([1] , p. 132). That is

$$\varepsilon n \gamma \sum_{\alpha \in P} T_{K/L} c_\alpha + \sum_{g \in R_0} \sum_{\alpha \in P} T_{K/L} c_\alpha \chi_\alpha(g) - \sum_{h \in R_1} \sum_{\alpha \in P} T_{K/L} c_\alpha \chi_\alpha(h) \qquad (5.2)$$

cancels.

For a given α , it is seen that

$$\sum_{g \in R_0} T_{K/L} c_\alpha \chi_\alpha(g) = T_{K/L} \sum_{g \in R_0} c_\alpha \chi_\alpha(g) = T_{K/L} c_\alpha \sum_{h \in R_0} \chi(h) = T_{K/L} c_\alpha \pi_0 ,$$

where π_0 belongs to L and is given in (3.8).

It is finally found out that

$$\varepsilon n \gamma \sum_{\alpha \in P} T_{K/L} c_\alpha + (\pi_0 - \pi_1) \sum_{\alpha \in P} T_{K/L} c_\alpha$$

should cancel for any α . As seen from (4.10) and (3.8), this is true if $\varepsilon = 1$.

All conclusions of [1] are valid for the more general situation considered in this paper.

Final Remark

The survey of some material from Algebraic Number Theory contained in the introduction enabled us to show how to pass from a word in a global code to a word over a finite field having a characteristic prime to the length of the words.

If the problem, however, is to directly define a finite code over a field F_p or F_{p^2} (according to whether $n \equiv \pm 1 \pmod{4p}$ or not, cf. (3.2), Property 1), then we can compute π_0 directly from (3.8), or from (3.7) if it has to be found in the extension F_{p^2} ; then π_1 can be computed from (3.4) and the generator of the code from Theorem 1, section 3.3.

References

[1] E. F. Assmus, Jr. and H. F. Mattson, Jr., New 5-Designs, J. Combinatorial Theory 6, (1969), 122-151.

[2] P. Camion, Abelian Codes, MRC Technical Summary Report 1059 (1971).

[3] Henry B. Mann, Introduction to Algebraic Number Theory, The Ohio State University, Columbus (1955).

[4] Henry B. Mann, Addition Theorems, Wiley & Sons (1965).

[5] Pierre Samuel, Théorie algébrique des nombres, Hermann, Paris (1967).

Preparata Codes and Goethals' Generalization:

The Dual of a Nonlinear Code

A. Huberman and A. Chouchan
Université Paris VII
Département de Mathématiques
2, Place Jussieu, PARIS V°

Introduction

There are great many non linear codes and we can hope to find some of them that fill the space much more than linear codes do. The Preparata codes, for example, contain twice as many codewords as the double-error-correcting BCH code of the same length: they are optimal codes, i.e. they have the largest possible number of codewords for given length and distance.

It is possible to generalize the Mac William identities to the nonlinear codes and define the dual code.

J.M. Goethals has found a generalization of Preparata codes for correcting three errors: in fact, he has found two dual families of nonlinear codes.

Preparata codes: A class of optimum nonlinear double-error-correcting codes.

Interest in this class of codes is motivated by the following facts:

1) These codes are optimal;

2) They are systematic and encoding can be accomplished by shift registers;

3) For decoding a syndrome-like quantity can be used and the complexity is approximately that of the corresponding BCH code.

Description:

We construct a linear code C_n, called the kernel, with minimum distance five, and we complete this code with some of its cosets. The union of C_n and of a subset of its cosets is the nonlinear code K_n (the Preparata code of length n) and the minimum distance is still five. This construction gives a "flower code".

We consider polynomials belonging to the algebra A_{n-1} of polynomials over GF(2) modulo $(x^{m-1}+1)$ with $m=2^{n-1}$ and $n \geq 4$.

Let $a(x) \in A_{n-1}$ denote the row vector $(a_{m-2}, a_{m-3}, \dots, a_0)$, where $a(x) = \sum a_j x^j$, and let $\{m(x)\}$ be a single-error-correcting BCH code of length $m-1$, generated by $g_1(x)$, a primitive polynomial of degree $(n-1)$; that is, if α denotes a primitive element of $GF(m)$, $g_1(\alpha) = 0$. Also, let $\{s(x)\}$ be the code whose generator polynomial has roots $1, \alpha, \alpha^3$. This code is a BCH of minimum weight six and $\{s(x)\} \subset \{m(x)\}$.

Let $u(x)$ be the polynomial $x^{m-1}+1/x+1$; let $m(x) \in \{m(x)\}$, $s(x) \in \{s(x)\}$, and let i be an arbitrary binary parameter.

The linear code C_n is formed by the vectors V having the following form:

$$V = [m(x), i, m(x) + (m(1)+i)u(x) + s(x)] .$$

The number of information bits of C_n is $2^n - 3n + 1$. C_n is a $(2^{n-1}, 2^n - 3n + 1)$ linear code of minimum distance five.

We now consider the polynomial $\varphi(x) = x^{m+1}+1/g_1(x)$, a minimum-degree maximum-length sequence of length $(m-1)$.

We find an $s, 0 \le s \le m-2$, such that $(x^s\varphi(x))^2 = x^s\varphi(x)$ and put $f(x) = x^s\varphi(x)$. The polynomial $q(x) = ax^j$ $(a = 0$ or 1; $j = 0,1,\dots,m-2)$ is a minimum weight coset leader of $\{m(x)\}$ for $a = 1$. We can now construct the code K_n, which is formed by the $2n-1$ component vector W having the following form:

$$W = \left[m(x)q(x), i, m(x) + q(x)f(x) + (m(1)+i)u(x) + s(x)\right],$$

where $m(x), q(x), i, s(x)$ are independent. The number of information bits is $2^n - 2n$. The code K_n is a $(2^n-1, 2^n-2n)$ nonlinear code of minimum distance five.

The generic vector W can be decomposed as follows: $W = V + U$, where $V \in C_n$ and U is a vector of the form:

$$U = \left[q(x), 0, q(x)f(x)\right].$$

Every non-zero vector U is identified with a coset of C_n, since $q(x) \neq 0$ is identified with a coset of $\{m(x)\}$. K_n can be viewed as the union of C_n and of a subset of its cosets. The cardinality is $2^{n-1} - 1$. These codes are optimal, because they meet the Johnson bound $A(N,d)$ for $N = 2^n - 1$ (n even) and $d = 5$. $A(N,d)$ is the maximum number of rows in a binary matrix with N columns with minimum row distance at least d.

The Preparata code is nearly perfect. The Preparata and Kerdock codes are "dual", in the sense that their weight distributions satisfy the Mac Williams identities.

<u>The Dual of a Nonlinear Code</u>

We begin with the following definition: two codes C and D are "weakly dual" if their distance enumerators satisfy the Mac Williams identity:

$$A_D(z) = \frac{1}{|C|}\left(1+(q-1)z\right)^n A_C\left(\frac{1-z}{1+(q-1)z}\right).$$

The distance enumerator of a code C is defined as $A_C(z) = \sum_{i=0} A(i)z^i$; $A(i)|C|$ is the number of codewords at distance i in C.

For a linear code, the distance enumerator coincides with the weight enumerator. If two codes of length n over $GF(q)$, C and D, are weakly dual, then $|C||D| = q^n$.

Now we give another definition. Write $F = GF(q)$; let G be an additive group of F^n, $\mathbb{C}G$ the group algebra of G over $\mathbb{C}$:

$$\mathbb{C}G = \left\{ \sum_{v \in G} a(v)x^v ;\ a(v) \in \mathbb{C} \right\}.$$

For a code $C \subset F^n$ we define:

$$\bar{C} = \sum_{v \in C} x^v \in \mathbb{C}G,\quad \bar{C}^* = \sum_{v \in C} x^{-v} \in \mathbb{C}G,\quad \frac{1}{|C|}\bar{C}\bar{C}^* = \sum_{u \in G} (u)x^u$$

this gives: $|C|\mathscr{A}(u) = \left|\{(v,v') \in C \times C / u = v - v'\}\right|$.

If u, $v \in F^n$, $<u,v>$ denotes their inner product. Let $\mathscr{X}$ be a non-principal character of the additive group of F, $\mathscr{X} : F \longrightarrow \mathbb{C}$: Then for all $u, v \in F^n$, we define

$$\mathscr{X}_u(v) = \mathscr{X}_v(u) = \mathscr{X}(<u,v>).$$

Then for all $u \in G = F^n$, $\mathscr{X}_u$ is a character of G, and this character can be extended linearly to the algebra $\mathbb{C}G$ by

$$\mathcal{X}_u\Big(\sum_v a(v)\,x^v\Big) = \sum_v a(v)\,\mathcal{X}_u(v)$$

$\forall \mathcal{A}\,\mathcal{B} \in \mathbf{C}G$ we have $\mathcal{X}_u(\mathcal{A},\mathcal{B}) = \mathcal{X}_u(\mathcal{A})\,\mathcal{X}_u(\mathcal{B})$.

We define the Fourier transform of $\mathcal{A} \in \mathbf{C}G$ by

$$\hat{\mathcal{A}} = \sum_{u\in G} \mathcal{X}_u(\mathcal{A})\,x^u.$$

The map $f : \mathbf{C}G \to \mathbf{C}G$ which yields $f(\mathcal{A}) = \hat{\mathcal{A}}$ from $\mathcal{A} \in \mathbf{C}G$ is bijective and $f^{-1} = \frac{1}{q^n} f$, since $f(\hat{\mathcal{A}}) = q^n$.

For any element $\mathcal{A} \in \mathbf{C}G$, we define its weight enumerator:

$$W_{\mathcal{A}}(z) = \sum_{v\in G} \mathcal{A}(v)\,z^{W(v)};$$

we have $W_{\mathcal{A}}(z) = \sum_{i=0} A(i)z^i$, where $\sum_{W(v)=i} \mathcal{A}(v) = A(i)$.

In particular, if $\mathcal{A}$ is the element defined by

$$\frac{1}{|C|}\,\bar{C}\,\bar{C}^* = \sum_{u\in G} \mathcal{A}(u)\,x^u = \mathcal{A},$$

then its weight enumerator coincides with the distance enumerator of the code C.

Theorem: The weight enumerators of $\mathcal{A}$ and $\hat{\mathcal{A}}$ are related by the Mac Williams identity

$$W_{\hat{\mathcal{A}}}(z) = \big(1+(q-1)z\big)^n\,W_{\mathcal{A}}\left(\frac{1-z}{1+(q-1)z}\right).$$

If C is a linear code, its dual is $C^{\perp}$, and we have:

$$\frac{1}{|C|}\,\bar{C}\,\bar{C}^* = \bar{C} = \bar{C}^* \text{ and } \hat{\bar{C}} = \bar{C}^{\perp} q^k.$$

Definition: Two q-codes C and D are dual if $\mathcal{A}$ and $\mathcal{B}$ are defined by $\mathscr{A} = \frac{1}{|C|}\bar{C}\,\bar{C}^*$ and $\mathscr{B} = \frac{1}{|D|}\bar{D}\,\bar{D}^*$; then $\mathscr{B} = \frac{1}{|C|}\hat{\mathscr{A}}$ and $\mathscr{A} = \frac{1}{|D|}\hat{\mathscr{B}}$.

The distance enumerators of two dual codes C and D are related by the Mac Williams identities and $|C||D| = q^n$.

Two Dual Families of Nonlinear Binary Codes Found by J.M. Goethals

We use the same method as for Preparata codes: we construct a linear code and we take some of its cosets; these codes that correct three errors are also "flower codes".

We define two nonlinear dual codes, C and C', for all blocks of length $n = 2^{2t+2}$, $t \geq 2$. They are formed by the union of 2^{2t+1} cosets of a linear code, called kernel, and are described by a pair of vectors in extended cyclic codes of length $m+1 = 2^{2t+1}$.

More precisely, any vector $u \in C$ or C' is described as follows:

$$u = \left[a(x),\ a(1),\ b(x),\ b(1)\right] \qquad [1]$$

i.e. by a pair of polynomials $a(x), b(x) \in F[x]/(x^m-1)$ together with their overall parity checks $a(1), b(1) \in F$.

Let ω be a primitive element in $GF(c), c = 2^{2t+1}$, $\Theta_i(x)$ the minimal polynomial of ω^{-i}, $\varepsilon_i(x)$ the unique idempotent of the irreductible ideal generated by $(x^m-1)/\Theta_i(x)$, that is the unique polynomial satisfying:

$$\varepsilon_i(\omega^{-i2k}) = 1$$

$$\varepsilon_i(\omega^j) = 0 \qquad \forall j \neq -i\,2^k \bmod (m), 0 \leq k \leq 2t.$$

Note that $\varepsilon_i(x)$ and $\varepsilon_i(x)+1$ are generating idempotents for the ideals generated by $x^m-1/\Theta_i(x)$ and $\Theta_i(x)$, respectively.

The Code C :

The kernel, that we denote by ker C , consists of the vectors of the form [1] with $a(x)$ belonging to the cyclic code generated by $\Theta_1(x)$ and $c(x) = a(x) + b(x)$ belonging to the cyclic code generated by $\Theta(x) = \Theta_1(x)\Theta_u(x)\Theta_s(x)$, where $u = 1+2^{t-1}$ and $s = 1+2^t$.

Hence, ker C is a linear code of length 2^{2t+2} and dimension $2^{2t+2} - 4(2t+1) - 2$.

The coset leaders are $v_0 = 0$ and the $2^{2t+1} - 1$ vectors v_j of the form:

$$v_j = \left[x^j, 1, x^j \varepsilon_1(x), 0\right], \quad 1 \leq j \leq m.$$

Thus, the code C can be expressed as $C = \bigcup_{j=0}^{m} \{\ker C + v_j\}$. This code contains 2^k vectors, where $k = 2^{2t+2} - 6t + 5$. The minimum distance of C is eight, hence this code contains four times as many codewords as the corresponding BCH code.

The Dual Code C' :

The kernel of C', ker C', consists of all vectors of the form [1] with

$$a(x) = a_0 \varepsilon_0(x) + a_1 x^{i_1} \varepsilon_1(x) + a_3 x^{i_3} \varepsilon_3(x)$$

$$b(x) = b_0 \varepsilon_0(x) + a_1 x^{i_1} \varepsilon_1(x) + a_3 x^{i_3} \varepsilon_3(x),$$

where $a_i, b_i \in F$; $i_1, i_3 \in \{0,1,\ldots,m-1\}$.

It is a linear code of dim $4t+4$. The coset leaders are $u_0 = 0$ and the $2^{2t+1} - 1$ vectors u_j of the form:

$$u_j = \left[x^j \, \varepsilon(x), 0, \, x^j \left(\varepsilon(x) + \varepsilon_1(x) \right), 0 \right], \qquad 1 \leq j \leq m$$

where $\varepsilon(x) = \sum_{k=1}^{t} \varepsilon_{1+2^k}(x)$.

Hence, the code C' can be expressed as $C' = \sum_{j=0} \{\ker C' + u_j\}$ and contains 2^{6t+5} vectors. This code has only six distincts nonzero values for the distances between codewords.

Acknowledgement

The authors gratefully acknowledge the benefit of correspondence and discussions with J.M. Goethals, who gave the definition of the dual of a nonlinear code.

References

Goethals J.M.: "Two dual families of nonlinear binary codes" Electronics Letters, 10, 471 (1974).

Goethals J.M. and Snover S.L.: "Nearly perfect binary codes" Discrete Mathematics, 3, 65 (1972).

Mac Williams J., Sloane N., and Goethals J.M.: "The Mac Williams identities for nonlinear codes" Bell System Tech. J., 51, 803 (1972).

Preparata F.: "A class of optimum nonlinear double error correcting codes" Information and Control, 13, 378 (1968).

PROPERTIES OF WEIGHT ENUMERATOR POLYNOMIALS.

G. COHEN and S. HARARI
Université PARIS VI - CETHEDEC
26 Bld Victor - 75996-PARIS FRANCE

The weight enumerator polynomial (noted w.e.p. in the sequel) is a helpful way of characterising a code. The minimum weight provides us with the minimum distance and hence with the error correction capacity. The McWilliams identities give us relations with the weight enumerator of the dual code. Also some other relations use the w.e.p. to compute various decoding probabilities. Finally the properties of the coefficients allow the deduction of some existence and non-existence theorems for linear codes. In this short paper we will first list some definitions and classical properties of w.e.p. and then give a few others.

Let us recall that (1), in every cyclic binary code C of odd length n , there exists a unique polynomial having the following properties

(i) $c(x) = c^2(x) \bmod (x^n - 1)$

(ii) $c(x)$ is a unit for C, i.e. $\forall v(x) \in C \quad c(x)v(x) = v(x) \bmod (x^n - 1)$

(iii) $c(x)$ generates C.

Let $C_1, C_2, \ldots, C_t$ be the cycles of the permutation $\pi_2 : i \to 2i \bmod n$ of the integers $1,2,\ldots,n$. It follows from (i) that $c(x)$ is of the form $c(x) = \Sigma_i x^{c_i}$ (I) where the exponents c_i form a union of cycles.

Classically let $w(z) = \sum_{i=0}^{n} w_i z^i$ be the w.e.p. of C. We have the following properties for an (n,k) linear code.

1) $\sum_{i=0}^{n} w_i = 2^k$

2) $\sum_{i=0}^{n} i\, w_i = n\, 2^{k-1}$

3) if the all-one vector belongs to the code then

$w_i = w_{n-i}$ for all i

4) for a cyclic code which is invariant under a doubly transitive group we have

$w_{i+1} = \frac{n-i}{i+1} w_i$ for odd i

5) the sphere-packing condition provides us with the following upper bound, which becomes an equality if the code is perfect :

$w_{2i+1} \leq \binom{n}{i+1} / \binom{2i+1}{i}$

Properties 1),2),3) are elementary. For 4),5) see ([1]). We have :

Proposition 1 : Let $\mathcal{C}$ be a (n,k) cyclic code, $C_1,C_2,\dots,C_t$ the cycles of π_2 as defined above. If for each ℓ , and each ℓ-tuple of integers not greater than t , $j_1,j_2,\dots,j_\ell$, $\sum_{k=1}^{\ell} |C_{j_k}| \neq i$, then there is no idempotent of weight i .

Proof : obvious by formula (I)

Proposition 2 : For each (n,k) binary cyclic code C , of w.e.p. W(z) we have :

$$i\, w_i \neq 0 \text{ implies } n \text{ divides } i\, w_i \ .$$

Remark : If n is a prime n divides w_i .

Proof : Suppose that a(x) belongs to C , with $w(a(x)) = i$ and $per\,(a(x)) = m$, where $m|n$.

We have $a(x)(x^m - 1) = (x^n - 1)\, p(x)$ for some polynomial p(x) of degree not greater than m . Hence $a(x) = (x^{n-m} + x^{n-2m} + \dots + 1)\, p(x)$. The fact that degree $p(x) \leq m$ implies that no term cancels out in the right-hand side multiplication, so $i = (n/m)\, w(p(x))$ and $n|m_i$. Doing this for all the possible periods of the codewords of weight i , we get the result.

Remark : Blake and Mullin in ([2]) stated the proposition for codes which are invariant under a simply transitive group of permutations (which is equivalent to prop. 2). $n|i\,A_i$ can be written as

$\frac{n-i}{n} \times A_i \in \mathbb{N}$, and generalised : if a code is invariant under a p-transitive permutation group, then $\frac{(n-i)(n-i-1)\dots(n-i-p+1)}{n(n-1)\dots(n-p+1)} \times A_i \in \mathbb{N}$. (II)

Proposition 3 : Let p be the order of 2 mod n , and e be the exponent of a codeword $a(x)$, i.e. the smallest integer such as $a(x)^{2^e} = a(x) \pmod{x^n - 1}$. We know that e divides p . We have

$$\mathrm{per}(a(x)) = \mathrm{per}(a(x)^2) = \dots = \mathrm{per}(a(x)^{2^{e-1}}) .$$

Proof : Per $(a(x)) = m$ implies that $a(x)(x^m - 1) = 0 \bmod (x^n - 1)$. Hence $a^2(x)(x^m - 1) = 0 \bmod (x^n - 1)$.

So we get

$$\mathrm{per}\ (a(x)) \geqq \mathrm{per}\ (a^2(x)) \geqq \dots \geqq \mathrm{per}\ (a^{2^e}(x)) .$$

From $a^{2^e}(x) = a(x)$ follows the result.

We now construct the following array A starting from a nonzero codeword $a(x)$ of period m and exponent e .

$$\begin{array}{l} a(x)\ ,\ x\,a(x),\ \dots,\ x^{m-1}\,a(x) \\ a^2(x),\ x\,a^2(x), \dots,\ x^{m-1}\,a^2(x) \\ \\ a^{2^{e-1}}(x),\ x\,a^{2^{e-1}}(x), \dots,\ x^{m-1}\,a^{2^{e-1}}(x) . \end{array}$$

Set-theoretically, the rows of A are pairwise disjoint or identical.

Proposition 4 : Let r denote the number of distinct rows of A, then r divides e .

Proof : Let i be the smallest integer such that the i-th row of A is identical to the first one modulo a cyclic shift. This can be written as

$$a(x) = a(x)^{2^i} x^j \mod (x^n - 1) \quad \text{for some integer } j .$$

Squaring the congruence we get

$$a^2(x) = a^{2^{i+1}} . x^{2j} \mod (x^n - 1)$$ where the exponents are taken mod n .

This equality shows that the second and (i+1)-th rows are identical. Iterating this, we get a partition of the e rows into subsets of cardinality $i-1$. We have $r = i-1$ and this shows that $r|e$.

Proposition 5 : The array is reduced to one row if and only if this row contains an idempotent.

Proof : $r = 1$ is equivalent to the existence of an integer i such that

$$a^2(x) = x^i \, a(x) \mod (x^n - 1)$$ which leads to

$$a^2(x) \, x^{n-2i} = x^{n-i} \, a(x) \mod (x^n - 1)$$

So we have that $x^{n-i} \, a(x)$ is an idempotent.

Application : Consider the (23,12) binary Golay. Its distance is 7, 23 is a prime,hence 23 divides w_7 . Let $a(x)$ be a codeword of weight 7. We know that there is no idempotent of weight 7, so $r \neq 1$. r divides the order of 2 mod 23, so $r = 11$.

Hence the array gives us $11.23 = 253$ codewords of weight 7 . In fact $w_7 = 253$ because of bound 5). One can apply formula (II) with $p = 5$ for the (24,12) self-dual extended Golay code, which has 759 words of weight 16 . We get that

$$\frac{8.\ 7.\ 6.\ 5.\ 4}{24.23.22.21.20} \cdot 759 \text{ is an integer.}$$

As another application, consider the (89,11) binary B.C.H. code. Its minimum distance is 40 , and we get that 89×11 divides w_{40} . This number is very large compared to the total number of codewords. Keeping this in mind, and using properties 1), 2), 3) one can compute the complete w.e.p.

$$B(z) = 1 + 979\, z^{40} + 979\, z^{48} + 89\, z^{56}\ .$$

BIBLIOGRAPHY

(1) Van Lint, J.H., Coding theory, L.N.M. N.201, Springer Verlag, 1971.

(2) Blake, J.F., and Mullin, R.C., Mathematical theory of Coding, Academic Press, 1975.

RESIDUAL ERROR RATE OF BINARY LINEAR BLOCK CODES

G. D. COHEN AND P.J. GODLEWSKI
Laboratoire des Communications,
Ecole Nationale Supérieure des Télécommunications
46 rue Barrault, 75013 PARIS, FRANCE.

1. Introduction

We consider two decoders: an incomplete decoder, D_i, as defined in [1], which corrects up to t errors, and a complete one, D, derived from D_i (see section 4). In section 2 the decoding probability corresponding to D_i, P_d, is expanded in series up to the two first orders. We then compute an exact expression for the residual error rate R_{re} for both D_i and D, and derive a straightforward upper bound for R_{re} of D. Series expansions of these quantities are given, based on the results of section 2. Basically, a classical result on the decoding probability due to J. Mac Williams [1] is used.

All the computations are performed referring to a binary symmetric channel with transition probability p. Put $q = 1 - p$, and let $w(.)$ be the Hamming weight, $S(x,r)$ the sphere of radius r and centre x. Let e be the (1,n) error vector. Consider a binary linear block code C of length n,
channel with transition probability p. Put $q=1-p$, and let $w(.)$ be the Hamming weight, $S(x,r)$ the sphere of radius r and centre x. Let e be the (1,n) error vector. Consider a binary linear block code C of length n, minimum

distance d, which is characterized by its weight enumerator A(z) :

$$A(z) = \sum_{i=o}^{n} A_i z^i .$$

Let us recall that the correct decoding probability is

$$P_{cd} = \sum_{i=o}^{t} \binom{n}{i} p^i q^{n-i} \sim 1 - \binom{n}{t+1} p^{t+1} + \binom{n}{t+1} \frac{(n-t-1)(t+1)}{(t+2)} p^{t+2} \quad (1)$$

2. Series expansions of the decoding probability (P_d).

The computation of P_d, due to Mac Williams, is done in[1]and[2]:

$$P_d = \sum_{i=o}^{t} f^{(i)}(0) / (i!) \quad (2.1)$$

where $f(x) = (px+q)^n A(\frac{qx+p}{px+q})$. (2.2)

We are only concerned with a series expansion of P_d up to the order p^{t+2} :

$$f(x) = (1-p+px)^n + A_d (x-px+p)^d (1-p+px)^{n-d}$$

$$+ A_{d+1} (x-px+p)^{d+1} (1-p+px)^{n-d-1} + \ldots$$

the non written terms of f(x) are useless, for their t-th derivatives at zero have degrees in p greater than d+1-t. For the computation, we set :

$$a(x) = (1-p+xp)^n$$

$$b(x) = A_d\ (x-px+p)^d\ (1-p+xp)^{n-d}$$

$$c(x) = A_{d+1}(x-px+p)^{d+1}\ (1-p+xp)^{n-d-1}\ ;$$

then :

$$\sum_{i=o}^{t} a^{(i)}(0)\ /\ (i\,!) = \sum_{i=o}^{t} \binom{n}{i} p^i\ (1-p)^{n-i} = P_{cd}. \qquad (2.3)$$

In b(x), the t-th derivative of $(x-xp+p)^d$ at zero will provide terms of order (d-t+1) and (d-t), the (t-1)-th derivative at zero terms of order (d-t+1). These terms are the only ones of sufficiently low degree.

$$b^{(t-1)}(0)\ /\ (t-1)! = \binom{d}{t} A_d\ p^{d-t+1} + \varepsilon(p^{d-t+1}) \qquad (2.4)$$

$$b^{(t)}(0)\ /\ (t\,!) = A_d\ \binom{d}{t}\ p^{d-t}\left[1-p(n-d+t)\right] + \varepsilon(p^{d-t+1}). \qquad (2.5)$$

In c(x) we have just to consider the t-th derivative :

$$c^{(t)}(0)\ /\ (t!) = \binom{d+1}{t} A_{d+1}\ p^{d-t+1} + \varepsilon(p^{d-t+1}). \qquad (2.6)$$

We call P_{ed} the erroneous decoding probability : $P_{ed} = P_d - P_{cd}$;

summing (2.4), (2.5), (2.6) and reordering :

$$P_{ed} = A_d \binom{d}{t} p^{d-t} \tag{2.7}$$

$$+ \binom{d}{t} \left[A_{d+1} \frac{(d+1)}{(d-t+1)} - A_d \left(n-d+t - \frac{t}{(d-t+1)}\right) \right] p^{d-t+1} + \varepsilon(p^{d-t+1}).$$

For d=2t+1, we have

$$P_d = P_{ed} + P_{cd} = 1 - p^{t+1} \left[\binom{n}{t+1} - A_{2t+1} \binom{2t+1}{t} \right] +$$

$$+ p^{t+2} \left\{ \binom{n}{t+1}(n-t+1) \frac{(t+1)}{(t+2)} + \binom{2t+1}{t} \left[A_{2t+2} \frac{(2t+2)}{(t+2)} - A_{2t+1} \left(n-t-1-\frac{t}{(t+2)}\right) \right] \right\}$$

$$+ \varepsilon(p^{t+2}). \tag{2.8}$$

Important special case : If the extended code is invariant under a transitive permutation group (which is the case for example with the primitive BCH codes)([2], p. 70) : $A_{2t+1} = 2(A_{2t+1}+A_{2t+2})(t+1)/(n+1)$. Computing A_{2t+2}, and letting $(n-t-1)(t+1)/(t+2) = m$, formula (2.8) can be written in a simpler way :

$$P_{ed} \sim A_{2t+1} \binom{2t+1}{t} p^{t+1} (1-mp) \tag{2.9}$$

$$P_d \sim 1 - \left[\binom{n}{t+1} - A_{2t+1} \binom{2t+1}{t} \right] p^{t+1} (1-mp). \tag{2.10}$$

3. Residual error rate with the incomplete decoder D_i.

3.a. We still consider D_i ; the received word v=u+e is decoded if is at a distance at most t of a code word c. We set $\hat{u}$=c, $\hat{u}$ is an estimation of u,the transmitted word. When v is decodable, we intend to calculate the expected value N_e of the number of errors occuring, i.e. of the weight of $\hat{u}$-u.

$$N_e = \sum_{k=o}^{n} \sum_{i=o}^{n} \quad i \quad \mu_k^{(i)} \tag{3.1}$$

where $\mu_k^{(i)}$ is the probability of the conditional event :

$$\left\{\left[\{w(e)=k\} \text{ and } \{e \in S(c,t) \text{ with } c \in C \text{ and } w(c)=i\}\right] \text{ knowing v is decodable}\right\}$$

By arguments similar to those leading to (2.1), and using Berlekamp's notation ($W_{j,k}^{(i,n-i)}$, see [1]), it can be established that :

$$N_e = \sum_{k=o}^{n} \sum_{i=o}^{n} \sum_{j=o}^{t} \quad i \; A_i \quad W_{j,k}^{(i,n-i)} \quad p^k \, q^{n-k} \; / \; P_d. \tag{3.2}$$

Let us define :

$$g(x) = \sum_{k=o}^{n} \sum_{i=o}^{n} \sum_{j=o}^{n} \quad i \; A_i \quad W_{j,k}^{(i,n-i)} \quad p^k \, q^{n-k} \quad x^j \; ; \tag{3.3}$$

it can be shown that :

$$g(x) = (px+q)^{n-1} \; (qx+p) \quad A'\left(\frac{qx+p}{px+q}\right). \tag{3.4}$$

To obtain (3.2) from (3.3) we may, for example, expand g(x) in a Taylor series, then :

$$P_d\, N_e = \sum_{j=o}^{t} g^{(j)}(0) \,/\, (j!). \tag{3.5}$$

If the code is systematic and if we suppose (hypothesis H) the residual errors equally distributed between information and check digits, then the residual error rate with D_i equals N_e/n.

3.b. Series expansions of $P_d\, N_e$. The computations are the same as in section 2. One has just to change in the formula giving P_d (or $P_{ed}=P_d - A_0 P_{cd}$) A_i into iA_i. Thus, by (2.7)

$$P_d\, N_e = d\, P_{ed} + \binom{d+1}{t} A_{d+1}\, p^{d-t+1} + \varepsilon(p^{d-t+1}). \tag{3.6}$$

4. Residual error rate (R_{re}) with the complete decoder D.

4.a. R_{re} is the average number of errors per information bit after decoding. The code is supposed to be systematic, and d=2t+1. For the complete decoder drawn in Fig. 1, we now determine R_{re}. Gate G1 is in "a" when D_i is successful(event of probability P_d), then under the H hypothesis R_{re} equals N_e/n. When D_i fails (event of probability $1-P_d$), G1 comes in position "b" and R_{re} equals N'_e/n (N'_e is defined and computed in the appendix). It follows that :

$$R_{re} = P_d\ (N_e/n) + (1-P_d)\ (N'_e/n).$$

We consider P_d and $P_d\ N_e$ as applications of ($\mathbb{Z}[z]\times\mathbb{N}$) into $\mathbb{Z}[p]$ (by means of the truncated series expansions of f(x) and g(x) ; observe (2.1), (2.2), (3.4) and (3.5)) : $(A,n) \longrightarrow P_d\ (A,n)$,

$(A, n) \longrightarrow P_dN_e(A,n) = P_d(B,n)$, where $B_i = iA_i$. Then from (A.4) :

$$n\ R_{re} = P_dN_e(A,n) + np - n\left[P_d(A,n)-qP_d(A,n-1)\right]$$

$$+ P_dN_e(A,n)-qP_dN_e(A,n-1) - pP_d(A',n-1). \qquad (4.1)$$

We now give another estimation of R_{re}, less tigth but simpler, since it does not need the code weight enumerator. We still consider the complete decoder D. If $w(e) \leq t$ the errors are corrected, if $w(e) > t$, we suppose that the worst case happens : e belongs to a sphere S(.,t) the center of which is a code word of weight w(e)+t. Under the H hypothesis R_{re} is then overbounded by

$$R_{re} < (1/n) \sum_{i=t+1}^{n} (i+t)\ \binom{n}{i}\ p^i\ (1-p)^{n-i}. \qquad (4.2)$$

4.b. Let us expand (4.1) and (4.2), only keeping the terms in p^{t+1}. With (3.6), (2.7) and (A.5), (4.1) becomes

$$R_{re} \sim (p^{t+1}/n) \left[\ A_{2t+1}\binom{2t+1}{t}\ t + \binom{n}{t+1}\ (t+1)\right] . \qquad (4.3)$$

The expansion of (4.2) is straightforward

$$R_{re} < (p^{t+1}/n) \binom{n}{t+1} (2t+1) . \tag{4.4}$$

The second expression being less tight than the first one, $A_{2t+1} \leqslant \binom{n}{t+1} / \binom{2t+1}{t}$, which then proves in a "probabilistic" way a classic result, obvious in (2.8), based upon the sphere packing condition ([2], p.94).

Example : We consider the (31,21) BCH code : $d=2t+1 = 5$, $A_5 = 186$;

(2.9) : $P_{ed} \sim 1860\, p^3 (1-21p)$

(2.10) : $P_d \sim 1 - 2635p^3\, (1-21p)$

(3.6) : $N_e/n \sim 300p^3 (1-19.7p)$

(4.3) : $R_{re} \sim 555p^3 = R$

(4.4) : $R_{re} < 725p^3 \sim 1.3\, R.$

APPENDIX : Computation of N'_e

A.a. Formal computation.

N'_e is the average weight of the error vector e, knowing that D_i fails. The number of words of weight k, not decodable by D_i, i.e. located at distance greater than t from any code word, is :

$$\binom{n}{k} - \sum_{j=o}^{t} \sum_{i=o}^{n} A_i \; W_{j,k}^{(i,n-i)} , \text{ hence}$$

$$N'_e\,(1 - P_d) = \sum_{k=o}^{n} \left(\binom{n}{k} - \sum_{j=o}^{t} \sum_{i=o}^{n} A_i\, W_{j,k}^{(i,n-i)} \right) k\, p^k\, q^{n-k}$$

$$= n\,p - \sum_{j=o}^{t} h^{(j)}(0) \,/\, (j!), \tag{A.1}$$

$$\text{where } h(x) = \sum_{i=o}^{n} \sum_{j=o}^{n} \sum_{k=o}^{n} A_i\, W_{j,k}^{(i,n-i)}\, k\, p^k\, q^{n-k}\, x^j. \tag{A.2}$$

If we consider the expression of f(x) given by (2.2) as a function of x and y = p/q :

$$f(x,y) = q^n\,(xy+1)^n\, A\left(\frac{x+y}{xy+1}\right) = q^n \sum_{j=o}^{n} \sum_{i=o}^{n} \sum_{k=o}^{n} A_i\, W_{j,k}^{(i,n-i)} y^k\, x^j,$$

then from (A.2) $h(x) = y\, f'_y(x,y)$. Denoting $\frac{qx+p}{px+q}$ by Z, h(x) may be rewritten

$$h(x) = n\,p\,x\,(px+q)^{n-1}\, A(Z) + p\,q\,(1-x^2)\,(px+q)^{n-2}\, A'\,(Z). \tag{A.3}$$

Noticing that px = (px+q)-q and $p\,q\,(1-x^2) = -(px+q)(qx+p) + q\,(qx+p) + p\,(px+q)$, (A,3) becomes

$$h(x) = n\left[(px+q)^n A(Z) - q\,(px+q)^{n-1} A(Z)\right] - (px+q)^{n-1}\,(qx+p)\,A'(Z) +$$

$$+ q\,(px+q)^{n-2}\,(qx+p)\,A'(Z) + p\,(px+q)^{n-1}\,A'(Z)\,;$$

then, with the notations of section 4

$$np - \sum_{j=o}^{t} \frac{h^{(j)}(0)}{j!} = n\,p - n\left[P_d(A,n) - qP_d(A,\,n-1)\right] + P_d Ne(A,n)$$

$$- qP_d N_e(A,n-1) - pP_d(A',\,n-1). \tag{A.4}$$

A.b. First order series expansion of $N'_e\,(1 - P_d)$.

Using (2.8) :

$$n\left[P_d(A,n) - q\,P_d(A,n-1)\right] \sim n\left\{p - p^{t+1}\left[\binom{n}{t+1} - \binom{n-1}{t+1}\right]\right\}$$

$$\sim np - p^{t+1}\,(t+1)\binom{n}{t+1}.$$

From (2.7) :

$$p\,P_d(A',\,n-1) \sim p\,A'_\delta\,\binom{\delta}{t}\,p^{\delta-t},\ \text{with } \delta = d-1 \text{ and } A'_\delta = d\,A_d$$

$$\sim (2t+1)\,A_{2t+1}\,\binom{2t}{t}\,p^{t+1}\ ,\ \text{for } d = 2t+1.$$

These are the only terms of order $\leqslant p+1$ occuring. Finally :

$$N'_e\,(1-P_d) \sim p^{t+1}\,(t+1)\left[\binom{n}{t+1} - A_{2t+1}\,\binom{2t+1}{t}\right]. \tag{A.5}$$

$N'_e\,(1-P_d) \sim (t+1)\,(1-P_d)$: This result can be obtained by more direct considerations.

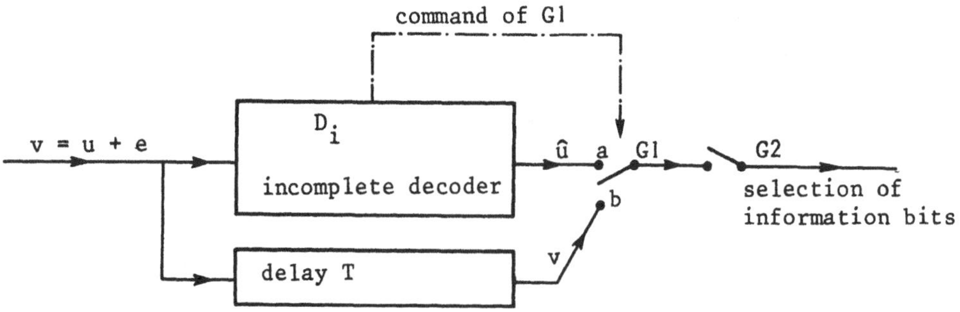

Fig. 1. Complete decoder D.

REFERENCES

[1] Berlekamp, E.R., Algebraic Coding Theory. New York : Mc Graw-Hill, 1968, pp. 397-399.

LIST OF CONTRIBUTORS

CAMION, Paul : 3, rue François Couperin, Domaine de la Bataille, 78370 PLAISIR (France)

CHOUCHAN, Alain : Université de Paris VII – Département de Mathématiques – Tour 45-55. 2, place Jussieu, 75005 PARIS V (France)

COHEN, Gérard : Université de Paris VI – Cethedec – 26, Bld. Victor, 75996 PARIS (France)

DELLA RICCIA, Giacomo : Department of Mathematics – Ben Gurion University of the Negev – BEER- SHEVA (Israel)

EVANS, Frank : Department of Electrical and Electronics Engineering – Queen Mary College (University of London) – Mile End Road, LONDON E1 4NS (Great Britain)

GODLEWSKI, P.J. : Laboratoire des Communications – Ecole Nationale Supérieure des Télécommunications – 46, rue Barrault, 75013 PARIS (France)

GOTTINGER, Hans W. : Institute of Mathematical Economics – University of Bielefeld – 48 BIELEFELD P.O. Box 8640 (F.R. of Germany)

HARARI, Sami : Université de Paris VI – Cethedec – 26, Bld. Victor, 75996 PARIS (France)

HUBERMAN, Alain : Université de Paris VII – Département de Mathématiques – Tour 45-55. 2, Place Jussieu, 75230 PARIS 75005 (France)

KÖRNER, János : Mathematical Institute of the Hungarian Academy of Sciences – V. Reáltanoda u. 13-15. BUDAPEST V (Hungary)

LINT, Jacobus H. van : Department of Mathematics – University of Technology –

P.O. Box 513, EINDHOVEN (the Netherlands)

LONGO, Giuseppe : Istituto di Elettronica – Università di Trieste – 34100 TRIESTE (Italy)

PIRET, Philippe : MBLE Research [illegible] oratory – 2, av. van Becelaere B – 1170 BRUSSELS (Belgium)

SCHALKWIJK, Johan Pieter Marius : Department of Mathematics – University of Technology – P.O. Box 513, EINDHOVEN (the Netherlands)

WOLF, Jack Keil : Department of Electrical and Computer Engineering – University of Massachusetts – AMHERST, (Massachusetts) 01002 (USA)

ZAKAI, Moshe : Department of Electrical Engineering, Technion – Israel Institute of Technology – HAIFA (Israel)

ZIV, Jacob : Department of Electrical Engineering, Technion – Israel Institute of Technology – HAIFA (Israel)

CISM SUMMER SCHOOL ON

"New Trends and Open Problems in Information Theory"

Udine, September 3-12, 1975

LIST OF PARTICIPANTS

AHLSWEDE, Rudolph : Lotzestr. 13, 34 GÖTTINGEN (West Germany)

BEREZINSKI, Miroslaw : Institute for Control and Management Science – KRN 55 – 00-818 WARSZAWA (Poland)

BERGAN, Kjell W. : H.Q. Def. Com. Nor. – Oslo Mil/Akershus – OSLO 1 (Norway)

BERGER, Erich R. : Eschenallee 31, D-1 BERLIN 19 (West Germany)

BRAVAR, Diego : Via del Pratello 11, 34100 TRIESTE (Italy)

CONTE, Ernesto : Istituto Elettrotecnico – Università di Napoli – Via Claudio 21, 80125 NAPOLI (Italy)

ELIA, Michele : Istituto Matematico – Politecnico di Torino – Corso Duca degli Abruzzi 24, 10129 TORINO (Italy)

LONGO, Maurizio : Istituto di Elettrotecnica – Università di Napoli – Via Claudio 21, 80125 NAPOLI (Italy)

MARTON, Katalin : Mathematical Institute of the Hung. Academy of Sciences – Reáltanoda u. 13-15 – H-1053 BUDAPEST (Hungary)

MATUSZEWSKI, Andrzej : Al. I Armii W.P. 16m. 18 – 00-982 WARSZAWA (Poland)

MIERZEJEWSKI, Henryk : Instytut Organizacji i Kierowania PAN – KRN 55 – 00-818 WARSZAWA (Poland)

PATTERSON, Nicholas James : S.S.O at G.C.H.Q., 27 Overbrook Drive, CHELTENHAM (Great Britain)

PINKAS, Wolfgang : Keplerstr. 36 A, A-8020 GRAZ (Austria)

SGARRO, Andrea : Via S. Francesco 34, 34133 TRIESTE (Italy)

SIMIONESCU, Claudia-Lidia : Facultatea de Stünte ale Naturii – Dept. of Mathematics – University of Brasov, BRASOV (Romania)

STUDZINSKI, Jan : Instytut Organizacji i Kierowania PAN – KRN 55 – 00-818 WARSZAWA (Poland)

WONG, Eugene : Dept. of Electrical Engineering and Computer Science – University of California at Berkeley – BERKELEY, California 94720 (USA)

Printed in the United States
By Bookmasters